"When you come to a
fork in the road . . .
take it."
–Yogi Berra (attrib.)

WAYFINDING

People, Signs, and Architecture

Paul Arthur and Romedi Passini

McGraw-Hill Book Company

New York St. Louis San Francisco
Auckland Bogotá Caracas Lisbon
London Madrid Mexico Milan
Montreal New Delhi Paris San Juan
Singapore Sydney Tokyo Toronto

WAYFINDING
People, Signs, and Architecture

First published in the United States of America by
McGraw-Hill, Inc.
11 West 19th Street
New York, N.Y.   10011
U.S.A.

Acquisitions Editor: Denise Schon
Sponsoring Editor: Glen Ellis
Substantive and Supervising Editor: Andrea Gallagher Ellis

Book, jacket, and text design: Paul Arthur VisuCom Limited.

The freehand drawings and cartoons in this book are by Romedi Passini. The electronic drawings and diagrams are by Paul Arthur.

1234567890 D 1098765432

ISBN 0-07-551016-2

Printed and bound in Canada.

Who will help me find my way?

The term "wayfaring" has been in the English language since the 16th century. "Way-finding" was first used by the American architect Kevin Lynch in his influential book, *The Image of the City* (1960).[1]

Although early in his book Lynch used the term "way-finding devices" to describe maps, street numbers, route signs, and so on, his work is based on the concept of "spatial orientation" and its prerequisite, the cognitive map or, as he calls it, the image.

We must credit him as the first person to recognize the importance of "imaging" to people finding their way. An environmental image, he wrote, is the generalized mental representation of the external physical world that every individual tries to form. It is the product of immediate sensation *plus* the memory of past experience, both of which combine to interpret information and guide action.

Perhaps the best known and certainly most quoted part of Lynch's book is his analysis of the city in terms of its elements. These he called paths, edges, landmarks, nodes, and districts. These are terms that continue to be used in wayfinding design and theory today.

Lynch had a major influence on research during the 60s which abounded in investigations into city images. Unfortunately, they had no immediate influence on "signage and graphics" and very little on architecture. It was in the early 70s that an important conceptual shift occurred. Cognitivists, such as Steven Kaplan,[2] Roger Downs, and David Stea,[3] argued that in order to understand what people do and how they find their way, one has to understand the underlying process. The relevant concept was, therefore, no longer "spatial orientation" but a new notion incorporating all the perceptual, cognitive, and decision-making processes necessary to find one's way. This new concept was baptized "wayfinding."

Over twenty years separate Lynch's book from the publication of *Wayfinding in Architecture* in 1984 by my co-author, Romedi Passini.[4] He presented the design profession with the first global conceptualization of wayfinding based on empirical data, and he identified major difficulties people had with architecture and signage when finding their way in complex urban settings.

He also showed that spatial orientation and wayfinding have fascinated people through the ages and that this fascination has found expression in art and folklore. Most important however, he showed that wayfinding was a key design issue and could no longer be ignored.

It is fair to say that while the notion of wayfinding is now accepted by many people, it has not yet made its full impact on the design profession. This book is an attempt to bring this about.

The *Shorter Oxford English Dictionary (SOED)* has the following definitions for analogous words:

Make one's way, To travel or proceed in an intended direction or to a certain place.

Wayfarer (1440), A traveller by road, especially one who travels on foot.

Wayfaring (1836), Travelling or journeying by road, usually *a wayfaring man*, a traveller by road (Isa. 35:8).

The roles that are currently fulfilled by architects and graphic designers are still hostages to the status quo – to that outworn but still prevailing notion that architects design buildings, while graphic designers come along at the end of the building process and install some signs, and that the public is somehow helped by this. It is admittedly difficult to break out of this straitjacket, but it is important that we do so.

Society no longer tolerates the idea that people's inability to find their way around in the built environment is either trivial or unimportant. Moreover, there is ample evidence that society is now prepared to satisfy the demands of the disabled by making public and commercial facilities more accessible to them.

There is, therefore, an urgent need for us to escape from the tyranny of the status quo and to explore new approaches to coping with these very real but, until recently, largely unacknowledged problems.

It is the authors' fervent wish that the example of this book will create the matrix through which a new profession, Wayfinding Design, can begin to emerge – one that will indeed extend the boundaries of professional practice in both the architectural and the design professions.

PAUL ARTHUR

Acknowledgements

Wayfinding and wayfinding design are activities that are made possible only through collaborative effort. This fact has been consistently stressed throughout the course of this book.

In expressing our gratitude to those who have helped make this book possible, we have special pleasure in identifying at the very top of the list the person who brought us together as collaborators in the first place.

Donald Henning is an architect on the staff of Public Works Canada with a special interest in accessibility in public buildings. Some years ago, he invited us to work together on one of his projects and from this collaboration emerged several documents which are listed in the Bibliography. Eventually, it also resulted in the development of this book on wayfinding as a new kind of profession within the architecture and design disciplines.

We take this opportunity to express our thanks to the following persons who have kindly provided us with advice and permission to reproduce works in the book: Ruth Bellan, Winnipeg, for advice on reading problems; John Branigan, New York City, of Edwin Schlossberg Inc., for the Siteguide™ information and illustration on page 203; Marc Caloren, Ottawa, for the Canada Post Corporation sign on page 190; Danny Cushing, Toronto, for the George Brown College signs and maps on pages 146, 187, 196, and 199; E. R. Gosse, Toronto, for the SunLife leasing sign on page 145; VisuCom Limited for its selected glyphs and pictographs from its copyrighted Picto'graficSystems (©1991) and for the use of other VisuCom systems throughout the book; and Don Watt and Loblaws Limited, Toronto, for illustrations of the packaging designs on page 164.

Those who have contributed their skills in the main activities involved in making this book include: Sally Kert, Toronto, for her endless patience and dedication to this project over the past many years as well as for her administrative support and guidance; Cathy Ferris, Ottawa, for her help with the electronic illustrations; Cathy Arthur, and B J Weckerle, both of Toronto, for assistance in typesetting and making up the pages of the book; the graduate students at the School of Architecture, the University of Montreal, in particular François Lagacé and Sylvain Thériault; and finally, but only in the chronological sense, Andrea Gallagher Ellis, Toronto, the best of editors, for her meticulous and unrelenting scrutiny of every word, phrase, sentence, paragraph, and page in the MS, and for the extent to which she has improved upon it.

Contents

**Part Three:
Principles of
wayfinding design**

**Part Six:
Audible and tactile
components of
wayfinding design**

Part One:
The issue

The nature of wayfinding difficulties

The emergence of wayfinding difficulties, one may think, is a recent phenomenon brought on by the complexity of contemporary buildings and cities. Nobody can deny that these difficulties are exacerbated in today's urban settings, but a little bit of digging shows clearly that difficulties with knowing where one is, where to go, and how to get there, all go back a very long way. An anthropological view of the labyrinth – which is both the artifact and the symbol of being disoriented and lost – brings to light a preoccupation with this subject which is as old as humankind.

In this chapter we introduce the nature of contemporary wayfinding difficulties. There are so many of them that even making a representative choice is difficult.

1.1 A potpourri of wayfinding difficulties

You, the reader, may just scan through this chapter to get an overall picture of what the difficulties are. Each issue will be looked at in detail later on in the book.

Put yourself in a travel mood – you are going for an imaginary journey. In fact, you are already in a foreign city, and you have to catch a train. You are in a bit of a hurry.

Is this the railway station?

You look at a building and wonder whether it is a railway station or a supermarket or the head office of an insurance company. You have ten minutes before the train leaves.

Where is the entrance?

You have to search for the entrance to the parking lot, and then you have to search for the entrance of the building.
You have seven minutes left.

The layout appears to be a labyrinth.

Once inside, you cannot figure out the layout. You don't understand how the spaces relate to each other, nor can you identify any underlying organizational principle. The circulation system remains a mystery to you.

You cannot locate yourself in the station.

You know you are somewhere in it, but where? Everything around you tends to look similar. For all you know, you may even have been at that same spot just a minute ago.

Where are the elevators?

You try one corridor, then another.
Now you have five minutes left.

You may have missed a sign.

You wonder if there was a sign or a map which could have been of help but which you, in your hurry, just overlooked.

Then you see a sign or a directory, but it is hard to read.

The lettering is too small, the contrast with the background poor. It is not well illuminated and the little light there is, comes bouncing back at you as if it had hit a mirror.

There is too much information on the sign. It is chunked together or scattered so that you can't read it. You see an electronic, changeable-message sign but it moves too rapidly.
Three minutes left.

You see a map but it is illegible.

Looking at the map display, you get confused. It shows too many things and not what you think you need. It somehow does not seem to represent the space you are in. It seems that it is not aligned with the setting.
You have lost another valuable minute.

Chapter 1
The nature of wayfinding difficulties
1.1 A potpourri of wayfinding difficulties

You see a sign and can read it, but what does it mean?
The wording appears to you unclear, ambiguous, meaningless.
You just don't understand the message, or you do understand some
of it, but you don't know if, and how, it applies to your situation.
You feel you will interpret the message wrongly, and be misled.
One minute left.

The information is contradictory.
You discover a contradiction between what the sign tells you to do
and what the architecture tells you to do. Which one do you believe?

You also have trouble concentrating.
You have the feeling that there is so much useless information
around you that you cannot see or hear anything coherent.

There is an announcement, but you cannot hear it properly.
The public address system is delivering its messages in a frequency range for which your ears do not seem to be attuned.
By now, you think you may have missed the train
altogether.

If you are a wheelchair user . . .
You may have to take an alternative route, and then you will have
no chance to catch that train.
  You may find the accessible route to be much longer, or to
require more decisions to be taken and to have even less relevant
wayfinding information than the pedestrian route.

Or if you are hearing impaired or deaf . . .
You may not hear the receptionist because of static noise in your
hearing aid caused by some features in the setting. You will not
hear what is said because of strong background noises. You may
not be able to use your lip-reading skills because the lighting is
poor or because the receptionist has her hand over her mouth.

If you are visually impaired or blind . . .
As a visually-impaired person with some sight, you may be totally
blind for a few minutes after the impact of strong lighting contrasts.
  As a blind person, the difficulties will seem insurmountable –
although you know that you *could* cope if only...

Or if you are illiterate . . .
You will be painfully aware of how much people rely on written
messages.

Or if you are an elderly person . . .
You will find that your eyes are not as good as they used to be, that
you don't understand as well anymore, that you are not as agile
and are easily tired, that sometimes your concentration is failing
and you are easily confused.

And what if the unthinkable should happen?
If there were a fire or some other emergency that required you to escape, you might only have seconds left in which to do it.

How would you do it?

1.2 Who is inept at wayfinding?

Well, to start off, in many settings users do not pay enough attention to the information available. Often they may be looking at information without actually seeing it, and not very much can be done about that. On the other hand, they tend also to be forgetful. If, for example, they are given a description of how to reach a destination, they may not retain it for very long. People tend not to understand, or to mix up, the meaning of the most rudimentary pictographs, and many find that maps are quite useless to them. Many fail to understand architectural layouts.

While all this is true, it is also true that these are the reasons given to excuse what is nothing more than poor design. Pictographs are not necessarily confusing and maps not necessarily useless. There is such a thing as architectural space that people can understand.

The bottom line is, and has to be, the user, and not a super-user either, but a representative of the population at large. Architects and designers have to plan for the real world.

If it appears that users don't pay enough attention to the information provided, it may be an indication that the information is badly placed. If they look at information without seeing it, the graphic presentation may well be at fault. Messages may not be retained because they are too long or are poorly structured.

Pictographs may be misread because they are not self-explanatory or because they have not been around for a sufficient length of time to be learned. Maps may be too complex; sometimes they may not even be aligned with the surrounding setting.

Architectural layouts may not be understood because they are amorphous or because the architectural language is garbled.

The only way to approach wayfinding issues intelligently is for architects and designers to pay attention to how people perceive and understand the environment, how they situate themselves in space, and how they use information in the decision-making and decision-executing processes.

But then, of course, to do this intelligently, architects and designers must first know what wayfinding is.

Chapter 2

The impact of wayfinding difficulties

From a discussion of the causes of our wayfinding difficulties, we turn now to the effect that they have on contemporary life, particularly in terms of exposing us to unnecessary frustration and stress, to making things work less well than they should, and to safety in public spaces.

2.1 Frustration and stress

The frustrations and stresses we are subjected to in just getting around the built environment are bad enough in themselves without having to put up with getting lost in it as well.

We don't build "understandable" cities and, as a result, being lost in them (particularly in places with which we are unfamiliar) is just something we feel we have to put up with – like being stuck in traffic jams, breathing noxious emissions, sharing the roads with drunks and the sidewalks with muggers.

But, because all of these latter conditions can actually result in bodily harm or death, whereas it is unlikely that a person will actually die from the stress of getting lost, we have tended to downgrade this problem as being relatively unimportant.

Most efforts to cope with the issue of people's getting lost, and to prevent them from getting lost, have relied on putting up signs.

It was well known and fairly universally acknowledged that putting up signs was one of those efforts that somehow had to be complied with, but the rewards for which could, on occasion, be doubtful. People could often be as lost with the signs as they were without them and for a variety of reasons:

- The signs were there, but people could not see them because they were too small.
- The sign was big enough for its message to be seen, but it made no sense; people could see it, but not read or understand it.
- Because the signs were poorly located, people could not find them.
- Because people expected the signs to be unreliable (even if, in fact, they were no such thing), they ignored them, preferring to ask questions instead.

On the other hand, from the viewpoint of the people who paid for and installed these signs in their buildings, the feeling often was that the public actually enjoyed getting lost, or that the public was being deliberately perverse or stupid.

We are now at a point where we might well wonder – as we are doing in this book – whether all those difficulties that people have with signs indicate that signs alone are not the answer, whether there is not a better way.

They are obviously not the answer to people's getting lost if they are illegible or unreadable or unreliably placed. But even if the signs in a building had none of these failings, the burden of helping people find their way to their destinations is shared by architects in the way they plan and design spaces and in the way they provide for the use of such spaces.

An architect friend of mine, Bill Lacy, contributed (several decades ago) to my early education in environmental communication by telling me about a visit with his wife to a department store in Knoxville, Tennessee, to purchase some cotton thread. Not knowing where this particular store kept this item, the Lacys asked a clerk. Her (almost aggrieved) response was instantaneous: "It's where it's always been … over there, under the escalator."

I have remembered this story for twenty years or so because it has always seemed a classic example of a person who is familiar

People have been known to die because ambulance drivers could not find their way to an address in time.

The co-authors will, from time to time, recount wayfinding anecdotes that seem relevant and have stayed with them over the years. These are two by Paul Arthur.

Chapter 2
The impact of wayfinding difficulties
2.1 Frustration and stress

with a particular environment not understanding why everyone else, even strangers, should not be equally knowledgeable about it. The slightly aggressive tone in the clerk's response indicates, of course, her own frustration at being constantly interrupted by the public asking "stupid" questions.

Another occasion I vividly remember is my personal reaction to my inability to find my way to a client's office. He gave the address and told me that he was on the 8th floor in the building. Both of these facts I had carefully noted down.

When my colleague and I arrived on the appointed day at what we thought was the right building, we were distressed to find that his name did not appear on the directory in the lobby. Our immediate conclusion was that I had copied down the address incorrectly. Our second was to assume that maybe the building directory was out of date and that all would still be well once we got to the 8th floor. On arrival there, however, we found that the entire floor was occupied by a single tenant whose name bore no relation whatsoever to that of our client.

At this point we automatically reverted to our initial reaction in the main lobby and were roundly blaming ourselves for getting it all wrong when the receptionist peered up and spoke my name – with, of course a rise in cadence at the end. So, we were at the right place after all!

It turned out that our client rented space from the tenant who had the whole floor and, as so often happens, was prohibited by the owners from having his name as a sub-tenant appear either on the building directory or on the 8th floor.

Our next reaction, instead of relief, was resentment. Having thoroughly blamed ourselves for what turned out to be no reason (we hadn't got it all wrong after all), we greatly resented having been put in such a position, and I know that I entered his office in a decidedly bad mood.

Assuming that people commonly have similar experiences, it is useful to summarize the chain of emotional reactions they are subject to:

- First, you blame yourself.
- Not only do you feel stupid, but you are frustrated because you are lost, and anxious that you might be late or miss your appointment altogether.
- When you discover that you are neither stupid, nor lost, nor late, you feel resentment, possibly anger, that something so seemingly simple and inconsequential should be made so damnably difficult.

2.2 Functional inefficiency

It is probably not enough to make a case for reducing people's wayfinding problems simply on the basis of such unquantifiable aspects of everyday life as frustration and stress. We now turn our attention, therefore, to quantifiable reasons for reducing the chances of people's wandering aimlessly about public and private facilities – and getting lost in the process. The obverse of the getting-lost-and-feeling-helpless coin is anger which manifests itself in a variety of ways including vandalism.

Janet Carpman, well known as co-author of the admirable book *Design That Cares,* has pointed out that the single thing the public most dreads about hospitals and health-care facilities is getting lost in them.[1]

Hospitals rely heavily on the public for their financial support. They must be aware that one of the ways the public expresses its disapproval is to withhold support. (It is for this reason that so many attempts to "improve the signage" in a hospital originate in the public relations department.)

It is well known also that our feelings about a shopping mall or other such commercial facility are colored in large measure by how well or how easily we get around in it. Can we park and unpark with a minimum of hassle? Is there a logic to the layout of the place which makes shopping or parking there a pleasure – or is it something else?

Proprietors of department stores used to design around the concept of actually confusing shoppers on the assumption that if they could keep people on the premises longer, they would buy more merchandise. The fact that there are rarely, if ever, clocks in shopping malls is based on the same assumption. But these ideas are now largely regarded as old fashioned and counter productive. Developers today are discovering that good wayfinding practice is a positive marketing benefit.

There was a time not long ago when the "efficiency" of an office building (and therefore the rents that could be charged for space in it) was measured exclusively in terms of its location, the speed of the elevators, how fast their doors closed or opened, and other functional considerations. In recent years, the concept has dawned on developers that adequate wayfinding provisions are another criterion for evaluating rental costs.

It stands to reason that a building owner has an undeniable edge on his competitors if he can say to prospective tenants that their clients will not have to suffer from lost time in wandering about getting lost, trying to park, or missing their appointments, because he has incorporated the wayfinding component into his building. The prospect of added profits is a wonderful motivator, and references to the "wayfinding component" can be expected to play an increasingly important role in commercial real-estate advertising in the future.

Recent hospital research demonstrated that in a facility of some 800 beds, no less than 8000 hours of professional time are lost in redirecting patients and visitors to their destinations. This is exclusive of the time that the professionals themselves lose in trying to find their way about, particularly when they are new on the job. Nor does it refer to the hidden costs that result from delayed professional interventions which may critically affect patients.

Now, as every administrator knows, 8000 hours of professional time represents at least four person-years – with all that that implies.

2.3 Accessibility

The term "accessibility" has become synonymous with barrier-free design and evokes images of wheelchairs and ramps. Of course there is much more to barrier-free design than ramps. Doors, for example, can be too heavy to be opened by a person in a wheelchair, ramps can be too steep, elevator buttons too high, spaces too narrow to turn around in. One could easily fill a page with architectural barriers encountered by wheelchair users and people with other physical disabilities.

These physical architectural barriers are by now well identified in the literature of architecture and the solutions to overcome them have been translated into design guidelines and supportive legislation. The results are starting to show in our cities and buildings.

The built environment is responsible not only for physical but also for psychological barriers. These also affect accessibility but they are much less known. The fear of being robbed or assaulted can make parts of certain cities virtually inaccessible to large sections of the population. The same applies to buildings. Many people fear underground parking garages to the point where they prefer risking heavy fines by parking illegally in the street.

Quite apart from the fear of getting lost or of being mugged, wayfinding problems posed by certain buildings may be just too much for sections of the population to cope with. For them the problem of wayfinding may be insoluble within acceptable limits of risk and energy investment.

Research and personal observation show that wayfinding difficulties are magnified for the handicapped population. Wheelchair users often have to take tortuous routes and use alternative (and less convenient) accesses. Users with a sensory handicap have difficulties obtaining relevant information. What may be a surmountable wayfinding difficulty for the able-bodied user may become an impossibility for one who is handicapped. A recent survey (Romedi Passini) demonstrated that fully 90 percent of the blind people in Montreal consider public buildings to be inaccessible because of difficulties associated with wayfinding.

All of this, we believe, shows clearly enough that wayfinding problems constitute an important architectural barrier affecting sizable numbers of people.

2.4 Safety

People who get into buildings also have to get out of them – sometimes fast. As settings grow larger and more complex, emergency evacuation becomes a key problem, and wayfinding becomes a matter of life and death.

There is a large body of recent research on how people behave when confronted with the dangers of fire and other emergencies. Two areas link this issue to wayfinding: the design and signage of exit routes and the general quality of wayfinding design of a setting.

The design and signage of exit routes are complex issues. We shall see later on (sections 7.2.3 and 11.2.2) that the notion of a specific emergency exit, used only in situations of danger, should be seriously questioned. Requirements for exit routes are regulated by national fire-codes, but certain aspects of the codes, unfortunately, do not accord with recent research findings.

A setting is safer if it is well understood by the users and if they can easily get around in it. Should an exit be barred by fire or smoke, the users will generally be able to figure out alternative routes in buildings they know. Nonetheless, the literature shows that people have perished in front of congested emergency exits during a fire when, in fact, an alternative exit could have been used.

Increased access to buildings for the handicapped population poses additional questions about safety. How, for example, is a user of a wheelchair evacuated from a high-rise? What is the warning signal of a fire for a deaf person? How does a blind person find his or her way out? These are only some of the issues we shall have to deal with.

To sum up, wayfinding design has a major impact on all users of the built environment:

- It affects their emotional state, including their feelings about the setting and its tenants (as well as about those who own it).
- It has a functional impact which is measurable in terms of efficiency and monetary value.
- It involves accessibility and public safety.

Can anyone still doubt its importance?

Chapter 3

Standing in the way of wayfinding solutions

Having briefly referred to some of the impacts of wayfinding problems in the previous chapter, here we attempt to uncover some of the reasons why wayfinding has been neglected or ignored for so long.

Two of the basic stumbling blocks to a solution are 1) that our society does not yet care enough, and 2) that architects have been too intent on the niceties of architectural design while graphic designers have been too intent on those of typography and on not offending the architects to care either.

But attitudes can change.

3.1 Societal values

3.1.1 Indifference

Indifference is the only thing that will explain why it is that, of all the elements that go into the design and construction of a building complex, the wayfinding component has, in the past, been at the very bottom of the list.

Building standards apparently vary widely throughout the world (as recent earthquakes in places such as Armenia and Mexico have demonstrated). In the so-called developed world, however, and particularly in North America, Europe, and parts of Southeast Asia, they are reasonably consistent. They are consistent in the expectations, for instance, that the building will not fall down and that the plumbing, electrical, and mechanical systems will all function properly. As a result, it is safe to say that it is quite *impossible* for a building to be erected today in which the developer and that small army of consultants who have advised him should "forget" to include washrooms, or lighting, or air conditioning, just to name some of the elements that are regarded as essential.

The various industries that serve the construction business are constantly overhauling, modifying, and improving their products. The equipping of a modern office building complex today is vastly improved in function, in esthetics, and in cost effectiveness over what was installed in a comparable building only a decade or so ago.

This dedication to functional improvement is what makes it all the more difficult to understand why the wayfinding component has been so systematically "forgotten" in the planning of so many of our universities, hospitals, and transportation facilities.

Nor is it as though the persons involved in constructing and financing these facilities are unaware that frequently people have the greatest difficulty trying to make efficient use of them.

Everybody knows, and has known all along, that wayfinding problems exist. Everybody knows it and everybody deplores it. That, however, is not a solution. It is the attitude that counts and this attitude has been that it has always been this way, that we must put up with it, and that nothing really awful ever happened to anyone by merely getting lost on the way to wherever he or she was going.

Indifference, like so many other things, however, is subject to the inevitable erosions of time. Think, for example, of the extraordinarily small time span that separates us today in our relatively smoke-free environments from the days when everybody seemed to be smoking cigarettes – most of the time.

This represents a total turnabout by the public on the one hand (in supporting smoke-free environments), and, on the other, by the owners and operators of these facilities (for providing them).

In other words, what was until recently considered unimportant is now regarded as very important. The penny drops and we all wonder why we put up with such-and-such for so long. One day it will be wayfinding's turn and the same thing will happen. Voices now being raised in protest at the status quo will prevail and society will enthusiastically espouse a cause that only a few years previously was not thought of as having any real importance.

3.1.2 Comparative values

There is an interesting and relevant relationship between the signage component in wayfinding and public art. Both cost about the same. Or should. But whereas the one percent for public art is well established and has been for a long time, the same amount for wayfinding is not and never has been.

Art, of course, serves as a softening and humanizing influence on public opinion. It is highly visible and gets a lot of coverage from the art critics in the Sunday newspapers. Moreover, a perfectly outrageous (or just plain ordinary) building can be rendered publicly more acceptable because of the amount of money spent on public art in or around it. As a result, hardly a commercial building today is without its contribution to public art. And a lot of it can be bought at one percent of, say, 50 to 100 million dollars.

It is a sign of the times that whereas the one percent for public art has *de facto* recognition just about everywhere in Canada and the United States, the same amount (or even less) is considered scandalously extravagant if applied to satisfying the graphic aspect of wayfinding needs.

This is not an argument against exposing the public to art in public spaces. It *is* an argument, however, in support of balance and priorities. It is quite extraordinary, when one stops to think about it, where our priorities lie, and that art should be considered essential when signage is not.

But then the idea that excellence in wayfinding can do a developer just as much good in the public eye as art can, is still in its infancy.

Clouding and confusing the issue, of course, is the fact that "art," through careful manipulation, has become so firmly entrenched in establishment thinking that nothing that is *not* art can be considered seriously. Many architects have cast themselves in the role of artists, while signage designers (with their brass letters on stainless steel faces) are also anxious to be considered as artists. As a result, anything so mundane as helping people find their way about these environments in a practical manner is rarely considered.

Not yet anyway.

3.1.3 Caring enough

The trouble is that we don't care enough about wayfinding (let alone signs) to insist on doing the job properly. This is why planning for wayfinding is all too infrequently anybody's concern when a building complex is in the design stages.

But wayfinding is not only something that takes place inside buildings. First of all we have to find our way to these buildings, and here the situation, in North America at least, is just as bad.

Street names are haphazardly located – if they are located at all. They are mainly illegible. Many buildings have no numbers on them, and when they do, there is no concern for their legibility. In the hours of darkness all this becomes even worse because very few street signs are ever illuminated. The only signs that *are* routinely illuminated in North America are billboards and traffic signals. Signs on major highways may or may not be illuminated.

Nor is there any obvious concern for the quality of signs. They may lean on flimsy posts. They even *look* flimsy, being punched out of thin sheet metal. As a result, they lack either authority or presence – two admittedly rather subjective words which are nevertheless intended to convey the idea that the fact the signs, with their messages, are there in the street is somehow important.

France, in contrast, is a country where the signs one sees in the streets are not leaning at odd angles. They are not stuck onto flimsy poles; they do not look insubstantial (as though they were about to curl). They look as though they had substance and were to be taken seriously.

In this regard, France is probably no better than other European countries, but this is an account of signs in Avignon in Provence. Wayfinding by car or on foot, by day and by night is a pleasure in this 14th-century southern city.

That this should be so is a tribute to urban planners who laid out the streets in those days prior to the rediscovery of the Roman grid which overlies so much of North American cities. While the streets in European cities and towns may seem to meander about, there is at the same time an inevitableness about them in the way they take one to things – such as the central square, or the cathedral, or the market areas. This served effectively as a substitute for the fact that there were no signs in those days.

Today, however, these cities have expanded and developed and now contain motorized traffic. Wayfinding is so easy in Avignon not only because of the layout of the streets, but also because of the signs. The signs are superior because the citizens have been convinced that it is well worth while paying to do the job properly, and because the sign industry, highly sophisticated and well equipped, is capable of performing the work of designing, installing, and maintaining these excellent signs.

In Avignon, signs – those for motorists as well as those for pedestrians – are lighted day and night. As a result, something can be said of Avignon which cannot be said of any North American city we know of – it has actually been designed for pedestrians as much as for motorists. This is impressive. But so is the content of the signs.

In Avignon, the approach to environmental communication is comprehensive. It is more than splendidly designed, fabricated, and illuminated signs for pedestrians and motorists. The system includes good, readable, and interesting electronic *information about* the Avignon environment (cultural information about theaters, museums), tourist information of all kinds (in a number of languages), citizen information (about civic affairs), excellent, well-placed maps, and so on. It includes excellent *directional*

The manufacture of the signs discussed in this section has been undertaken by the private sector and has none of the dull, institutional look that street signs in North America invariably have. The contractor, J. C. Decaux, has made brilliant innovations in this field. All metal signs have a return of approximately 0.6 inches (15 mm). They are porcelainized and not vinyl film. They have a "presence" which is inescapable. Illuminated street-name signs are edge-lit from a fluorescent tube inside the pole to which the sign face is attached. Electronic signs are electromagnetic arrays of seven lines of characters which constantly display variable information on a wide variety of subjects of interest, in several languages.

Typical electronic information sign seen throughout France, J. C. Decaux, Direct Info Municipale, Neuilly, France.

signs for destinations within the city and outside it. It includes reliable, consistently placed *identification of* street names, places of interest, civic and municipal offices, and so on.

The signage in Avignon is complemented by the design of the city streets, by the banning of vehicular traffic from some of them, by the use of handsome bollards, to actually prevent cars from parking, rather than no-parking signs which would litter the streetscape, and by the absence of parking meters, at least in the North American sense.

Instead of parking meters, there is a machine, say every hundred meters, against the wall of a building (streets are narrow, sidewalks even narrower), which dispenses parking tickets. Coins are inserted, a stamped ticket for a given period of time is issued. This is placed, face up, on the motorist's dashboard for inspection by the police. The day will surely come when North American cities care enough to adopt Avignon's alternative to the parking meter.

3.2 Design practice

3.2.1 The architect

Two anecdotes by Romedi Passini.

A few years ago an architect friend, who was working with a large citizen group in Montreal, asked his audience what they considered to be the worst building in the city. He hoped it would not be one of his but rather one of his competitors'. He was lucky, but totally amazed by the response of his audience. Everybody seemed to agree that the worst building in Montreal was a recent commercial center which had been published in respected architectural journals and which was generally held in high esteem by the profession.

This commercial center was architecturally quite appealing. It was constructed in a series of interior terraces with a number of stairs connecting levels at different heights. It had many interesting views and a contemporary architectural look to it. Compared to other commercial centers, it certainly was of superior esthetic quality.

Why was it the worst building, my friend asked in surprise? Because, they said, it is almost impossible to find your way around in it. My friend was stunned. He had never thought about wayfinding when designing *his* buildings either.

This is not the end of the story. The center turned out not to be a commercial success. The shopping turnover never reached the planned levels and many people refused even to enter the building.

In order to save the venture, the management decided to invest in a massive "signage" project. Directional signs were carefully conceived and placed, maps of the settings were produced in various sizes, and even more, supergraphics and color coding were used to identify the floors and the major circulation pattern. No one could quibble about the graphic design.

In addition, the place looked even better. The redesign was followed by a publicity campaign, which had as leitmotiv: "Come visit us, it's so easy to find your way about." Did it work? No, it did not.

16

The various split-levels, the confusing spatial organization, the ambiguous circulation pattern, the repetitive architectural features, the contradictory articulation of the interior and the exterior – none of these factors could be solved by graphics. The problem was clearly architectural. The building was eventually torn down. A press release mentioned that the building was found to be impossible for wayfinding purposes.

Here is another example. During a recent visit to the University of Stuttgart, I was invited to give a lecture on wayfinding to the university's department of planning. I was warned that I would probably not be able to find my way, and took this as one of those jokes I had heard before. But it was not a joke. I had to call for help.

The university is housed in a large, modernist complex with a great number of entrances, all looking about equally important or, what is closer to the truth, equally unimportant, and there is no apparent logic to the layout.

I had been given a complicated code, which described the address of my destination, but although I observed the use of colors on the façades, I still could make no sense of this information. Later, in discussion with my host, I was told a familiar story. After the building was completed, it was discovered that students and staff were having difficulties getting around, so it was decided to improve the signage.

The graphic designer did his best. He tried to impose order with a color code where no architectural order was to be found. His imposed system, however, was far from obvious and it became very complex. Of course, it didn't do much good and he was naturally blamed for the fiasco. The fault, however, lay entirely with the architect.

Architects, one would think, would be very keen to learn about wayfinding. Our experience up to now has been to the contrary. It is still difficult to get practising architects to interest themselves in, or to read about, wayfinding or to attract them to conferences. As we have already noted, it is virtually impossible to get wayfinding courses into the architectural education system.

There must be many reasons for this apathy. Architects may feel, for example, that they already have too much to think about and do not want to be burdened with additional requirements. They may just be badly informed, or the information they have may not be presented in a form suitable for their use. Perhaps, however, it is *we* who are too impatient, perhaps we ought to allow more time for the message to get through.

In this book we try to present not only individual recommendations but a wayfinding design approach. The internal coherence of this approach, we feel, will actually make life easier for architects. We also hope to convince them that wayfinding is a key issue and not a peripheral one, and that wayfinding design is far from being an exclusively graphic design function.

A prime motive for writing this book has been the authors' keen desire to demonstrate that wayfinding, unlike signage, has more to it than graphic design – important as that may be. What used to be regarded, by architects, building owners, and graphic designers, as a purely graphic issue is now gradually coming to be seen as both an architectural and a graphic issue requiring close collaboration by the two disciplines.

We are also beginning to see that this team (architect and graphic designer) will have to have at least a grasp of the fundamentals of environmental perception and cognition and of the principles of wayfinding.

In addition, the team will need to recognize that wayfinding usually involves all of the senses – and not just one.

Where are such people to be found? And, more importantly, who will prepare them for this vocation? Who will do the teaching, and where?

Cover of *The Journal
of the Society of
Typographic Design-
ers,* no. 23, December
1983.

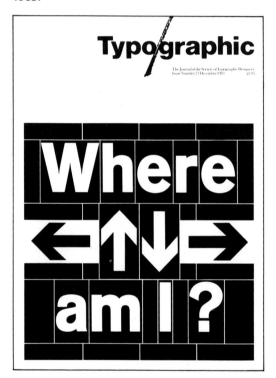

In December 1983, the Society of Typographic Designers in the UK, a founder-member of ICOGRADA (International Council of Graphic Design Associations), published an issue of its journal with the promising title, "Where am I?" in which an article by Richard Dragun with a similar title appeared. There were, of course, arrows pointing up and down, left and right, as is always the case when a publication decides to "do" an article on signs.[1]

Not once in this admittedly very slim issue does the term "wayfinding" occur, nor do any of the contributors really concern themselves at all with how "the graphics" function in terms of helping passengers or pedestrians find their way.

In one of the articles, the well-known industrial designer Sir Misha Black is quoted as saying that in the signage context "the esthetics of transport" should be "robust, assertive and vigorous." There follows what amounts to an apology (in the case of the London Underground) for the fact that its "graphic style is still very much based on the polite typography of Edward Johnston," and is, therefore, neither robust nor assertive nor vigorous.

On the other hand, these "polite" graphics, as every passenger knows, admirably fulfil their wayfinding requirements and help to make the London Underground one of the world's easiest systems to find one's way about in.

The author then goes on to say that most modern transport systems have followed Sir Misha's recommendations and that they have, as a result, emerged as "an almost international look" – a look, he adds, that "most of our transport design clients seem to want" and which, he tells us with pride, he has used in foreign parts such as Hong Kong, Baghdad, and Taipei, as well as in the Middle East.

This attitude towards "the graphics" (that it was enough for them to be robust, assertive, and vigorous and that they should subscribe to an international style or look) is typical of the mindset of many designers in the 20 or so years just past. It was splendidly summed up in a most felicitous phrase of the American environmental graphic designer Boyd Morrison, when he said that most designers "approach solutions to signing and wayfinding problems through the door of visual composition rather than information."

This, of course, is what motivates the graphic designer for print – and has motivated him for the past two decades. "Visual composition" and, in the words of Richard Wurman (author of *Information Anxiety*), "looking good" are what graphic design is *all* about. For 20 years it has had no other function, and because virtually all signage designers (other than architects who have dabbled in the subject) are graphic designers, it follows that they will have transplanted this highly "artistic" and "creative" approach from a one-dimensional medium (print) to a multi-dimensional medium (environmental communication). It is also typical of graphic designers that they assume (as Richard Dragun does in his article) that this international look of "robust" graphics is all that wayfinders will need in order to find their way or make their connections.

But, as anyone who is not a graphic designer knows, the London Underground (despite the "politeness" of its graphics) and the Paris Métro (another excellent wayfinding system, despite the total anonymity of *its* graphics) both rely for their success on more than just typography and graphic design. Just as important, if not more so, are the contributions of the architects and transportation planners who laid out the concourses and other spaces that give access to the mazes of tunnels and corridors, which work so well, so seemingly effortlessly, in getting us to the right platform.

There is no end in sight to the manner in which "visual composition" will continue to enthrall designers for print. Nor, perhaps, should there be, although it would be pleasant, once in a while, to come across one whose professional interest in design extends to an interest in content as well. It should, however, come to an abrupt end when these same designers turn to signage.

Unfortunately too many of us still think that the principles that have worked so well and been acclaimed in the area of print will be equally successful in that of signage. As a result, we are now being increasingly exposed to the robust, assertive, and vigorous use of such things as brass letters on stainless steel backgrounds or of white or charcoal letters on brushed (or satin or, heaven preserve us, mirror-finished) aluminum.

It will require a major change of mindset and of attitude on the part of graphic designers to wean themselves from these admittedly exciting "solutions" and to somehow convince them that true answers to wayfinding problems lie in other directions.

The graphic designer, previously considered as providing a "service" only, emerged in the 80s as "a strong independent force on the printed page, invading it like a virus";[2] "pages of design" are produced rather than "pages of text" and legibility is cheerfully sacrificed on the altar of this new-found independence. Should we be the least bit surprised, then, at the way in which this virus has infected the design of environmental communication devices?

Part Two:
Principles of wayfinding

Chapter 4

What are spatial orientation and wayfinding?

In the literature on spatial behavior, wayfinding is a new-comer. Introduced in the late 70s, it replaced the term "spatial orientation." Wayfinding is not just a new and, we have to admit, now quite fashionable term for an old concept. It reflects a new approach to studying people's movements and their relationship to space. Even more importantly, this new approach opens up new ways to design for people's spatial behavior.[1]

In this chapter we sketch a brief research history and introduce the basic concepts of spatial orientation, cognitive maps, and wayfinding.

4.1 Spatial orientation: the static relationship to space

The oldest mentions of spatial orientation, the forerunner of wayfinding, appeared in neuropsychological literature over a century ago. Neuropsychologists, such as Förster in 1890, Meyer in 1900, and Holmes in 1918, reported case studies of patients who, as victims of brain lesions, were incapable of even the most elementary understanding of where they were and of how to reach given destinations in their everyday environment.[2]

The deficiencies leading to these conditions of disorientation were later identified as topographical or spatial agnosia and topographical or spatial amnesia. The key manifestation of spatial agnosia is an inability to recognize spaces visited on previous occasions, while spatial amnesia leads to an inability to link spaces mentally into an overall representation.[3]

This representation people have of their surrounding environment, also called an image or a cognitive map, is the psychological concept that underlies the notion of spatial orientation. A cognitive map is a mental construct of an environment which cannot be seen from one single vantage point alone. It has to be composed from a series of individual vistas. Cognitive mapping is therefore a mental structuring process that integrates into a whole what has been perceived in parts.

cognitive map: an overall mental image or representation of the spaces and the layout of a setting

cognitive mapping: the mental structuring process leading to the creation of a cognitive map

Brain lesions resulting in spatial or topographical amnesia, can destroy this cognitive mapping ability while leaving intact all other cognitive faculties. This is a fascinating aspect of brain lesion research; it demonstrates the function of a particular ability, such as cognitive mapping, by showing what a person can and cannot do when deprived of that ability.

The effect of spatial amnesia on people's ability to get around is dramatic indeed. At the beginning, amnesic patients are totally incapacitated even if they find themselves in previously familiar environments. After a certain adaptation period, patients can learn to find their way by substituting verbal for the missing spatial information. Rather than relying on a cognitive map of a given route, they will rely on a verbal checklist. A striking illustration is given of a truck driver with spatial amnesia who, after having learned to rely on checklists instead of physical maps, was able to get around sufficiently well to continue working in his profession.[4]

Depending on the spatial characteristics of an environment, cognitive mapping can be very difficult for everyone, and sometimes it is an almost impossible operation. Indeed, one of the main disorienting characteristics of a labyrinth is precisely its inherent difficulty to be understood in spatial terms and to be mentally represented in the form of a cognitive map.

Spatial orientation has been defined in various terms but all refer in one way or another to a person's ability to determine his or her location in a setting.

spatial orientation: the process of devising an adequate cognitive map of a setting along with the ability to situate oneself within that representation

From a cognitive perspective, spatial orientation is based on the ability to form a cognitive map. You are considered spatially oriented if you have an adequate cognitive map of the surrounding setting and are able to situate yourself within that representation.

This conceptualization of spatial orientation has not only

Chapter 4
What are spatial orientation and wayfinding?

4.1 Spatial orientation: the static relationship to space

In *The Image of the City,* Lynch identifies five key environmental components people use to structure a representation of a city. He argues that visual accessibility and the prominence of five elements (paths, landmarks, nodes, edges, and districts) are the design criteria for highly legible and imageable city environments.

generated a great deal of research on cognitive maps, their nature, their composition, their evolution when exploring a new setting, or their evolution through a life span, but it has also proven useful in exploring some of the spatial characteristics that facilitate cognitive mapping. The credit for having made that all-important link between spatial orientation and planning goes without doubt to the pioneering work of Kevin Lynch.[5]

Researchers working in the field of cognitive mapping were confronted by major methodological and conceptual problems. It proved extremely difficult to have people describe and externalize their spatial knowledge and to measure it reliably. Furthermore, it was argued that the term "map" had to be taken in a metaphorical sense: a cognitive map was not really a "map" as we know it from geography or planning. It was maplike only in the sense that it contained the same information as an actual map.[6] The most critical issue concerned the notion of adequacy, which is crucial to the definition of spatial orientation. Researchers asked themselves if the criteria of an adequate cognitive map were its measurement properties, its topological properties, or other geometric characteristics.

The search for an answer was dampened by the observation that in many situations people got around quite well and did not feel disoriented even if they had only a very rudimentary understanding of the setting.[7] Illustrative examples could be found in anthropological literature describing navigation and pathfinding among indigenous populations in homogeneous environments, such as sand deserts, oceans, and snow-covered expanses in the polar regions.

Even wayfinders in contemporary urban settings often cannot rely on any topographical accuracy. Complex underground public transport interchanges, for example, tend to be particularly difficult to map, but people may not consider themselves disoriented as long as they know how to reach certain destinations.[8]

It should be noted that even the most rudimentary cognitive mapping distinguishes itself from spatial amnesia in that the person who is afflicted by the latter is not capable of linking together two spatial experiences, even when one immediately follows the other. The amnesic person can be compared to a reader who is able to read and understand every word but cannot make the link with the previous words of a sentence and therefore cannot understand its meaning.

Even if the terms "spatial orientation" and the underlying concept of "cognitive mapping" are perfectly suited to describe the static relationship of a person to his or her spatial setting, they cannot encompass the dynamic aspects of people's movement (i.e., the process involved in reaching chosen destinations). Moreover, these terms tend to imply disorientation in cases where people not only are able to find their way, but have developed very sophisticated navigational skills, for instance, traditional navigation in Polynesia and Micronesia.[9]

Once this was understood in the late 70s, it became clear that a new concept was needed to account for people's movement in space and their sense of being orientated.

4.2 Wayfinding: the dynamic relationship to space

"Wayfinding" was the term introduced to describe the process of reaching a destination, whether in a familiar or unfamiliar environment. Wayfinding is best defined as spatial problem solving.[10] Within this framework, wayfinding comprises three specific but interrelated processes:

- *Decision making* and the development of a plan of action
- *Decision execution*, which transforms the plan into appropriate behavior at the right place in space
- *Information processing* understood in its generic sense as comprising environmental perception and cognition, which, in turn, are responsible for the information basis of the two decision-related processes

At first, it may seem that the concept of a cognitive map is lost in this definition of wayfinding. But this is not so. Cognitive mapping is part of environmental perception and cognition. The cognitive map is a source of information to make and execute decisions. The relative importance of a cognitive map in the decision-making process depends on the nature of the setting and on the context of wayfinding. In other words, we have not eliminated the cognitive map, we have merely situated it within the much larger process of spatial problem solving.

What about disorientation? We argue that this is a personal, mental, and emotional state. People tend to feel disoriented when they cannot situate themselves within a spatial representation and when, at the same time, they do not have, or cannot develop, a plan to reach their destination.

wayfinding: spatial problem solving comprising the following processes:

- Decision making
- Decision executing
- Information processing

Most settings are laid out in a plan (or "shape") to which people can relate and which allows them to

- determine their location within the setting,
- determine that their destination is within the setting, and
- form a plan of action that will take them from their location to their destination.

When they are denied the ability to do any of these, they cannot form cognitive maps. They are effectively prevented from forming an efficient action plan. This, in turn, means that they must rely on other information sources until they can, in fact, develop an appropriate plan. The undesirable alternative is to let them wander about until, quite by chance, they stumble onto their objective.

Chapter 5

How the wayfinding process works

Having introduced the general idea, we are now ready to study the clockwork of wayfinding, that is, to study what is involved when people attempt to reach spatial destinations.

In this chapter, first we outline how spatial problem solving can be conceptualized, and then we describe in more detail the key characteristics of decision making, decision executing, and information processing. Wayfinding design is based on a good understanding of the wayfinding process.

5.1 Wayfinding as spatial problem solving

Wayfinding is problem solving. Making a journey and reaching a destination are wayfinding goals. Attaining these goals requires action and behavior, some quite obvious and some less so.

Those that are not obvious may require several steps:

- Taking into account previous experiences
- Reading and evaluating the environmental context
- Trying to understand the spatial characteristics of the setting
- Taking in the information displayed on signs, maps, and indicators
- Assessing different options
- Considering the time factor, the interest, or the security that goes with taking a given route

If a journey is taken for the first time and if the destination is unfamiliar, you are confronted with a problem for which you must find a solution. The solution is a plan of action.

Planning a holiday trip may involve comparing a number of possible destinations (where to go), checking on various airlines (how to go), and checking schedules (when to go). Planning to visit a friend who has recently moved may involve identifying the new address, consulting a route map, and checking your diary to decide the three major questions: where, how, and when to go. Planning, in the final analysis, is decision making based on available information.

If the sum total of behavior is the physical solution to a wayfinding problem, the net result of decisions is the mental or cognitive solution to the problem. Each behavior can be formulated in terms of its underlying decision.

We are now ready for a little bit of theory. All the decisions necessary for solving a wayfinding problem are not just lying in our minds like so many potatoes in a sack. Decisions are related to each other; they are ordered.

To open a can of mushrooms, for example, you will need to make some very specific decisions: get the can, get the can opener, apply the can opener, and activate the cutting device. Not only must you make these four decisions, you have to execute them in a certain order. First you have to get the can and the opener, then you have to apply the tool, and only then can you start opening the can.

A decision plan (or plan of action) not only contains the relevant decisions but it reflects the logic that links the decisions to the problem. The same logic links wayfinding decisions.

Wayfinding is also continuous problem solving.
The problem of reaching an unfamiliar destination can normally not be solved in all its details before engaging on the journey. Even with the best of intentions, the wayfinder cannot, *a priori*, develop a detailed decision plan simply because all the required information is not necessarily available. It is only when a person

Decisions are not just lying in our minds like potatoes in a sack.

Chapter 5
How the wayfinding process works
5.1 Wayfinding as spatial problem solving

Animals *do* find their way. Are they problem solving? What about the homing instinct? Most open-minded people who spend a lot of time with animals discover that animals are much smarter than we generally think. Bird and fish migrations are truly puzzling. "Homing instinct" does not explain migration routes. Problem solving, as defined here, can.

Isn't it just our insistence on superiority that hinders us from seeing the obvious? Animals find their way remarkably well and are able to solve spatial problems even if on other accounts they may surprise us with their limitations. Bees, for example, are not only great wayfinders, travelling up to ten miles when collecting, they can also communicate the location of destinations to other bees in the hive. On the other hand, they can be seen to bang against a closed window until they die even if an open door is close by. Windows, it must be admitted, are not part of bee environments.

is provided with all the information in the actual setting that the decision plan can be completely formulated.

If the context and the wayfinding tasks are more or less familiar, a person may well start off with a general and relatively vague plan which, during the journey, becomes more precise.[1] If, however, the context and the task itself are more demanding, a greater planning effort is required. Blind travellers, for example, develop much more detailed decision plans for a prospective trip than do their sighted counterparts.[2]

Wayfinding is problem solving under uncertainty
Adequate information is not always available, and what information there is, is often unclear and ambiguous. Wayfinding must cope with uncertainty by keeping problem solving flexible, by finding new alternatives if a path leads, for example, to a dead end.

Wayfinding is spatial problem solving
The information used to make wayfinding decisions is, at least in part, of a spatial nature. It involves a certain understanding and manipulation of space. It involves, as we have already seen, a certain ability to cognitively map spaces that cannot be perceived from one vantage point alone.

Although we have described wayfinding in terms of spatial problem solving for unfamiliar journeys and destinations, a question poses itself at this point in the discussion: Does it make sense to talk about wayfinding for familiar journeys as well, and should we still be thinking in terms of problem solving?

A familiar journey can be seen as an ensemble of actions or behavior leading from a point of origin to a destination. The mental or cognitive equivalent of this behavioral ensemble is the plan of action described above. To take a familiar route is nothing other than the execution of an already recorded decision plan and is therefore also a part of wayfinding and problem solving. The only difference is that the emphasis has shifted from decision making to decision execution.[3]

5.2 Decision making and decision executing

5.2.1 How decisions are made

The original decision, whether and where to go, and the choice of the means of travel, may involve a variety of practical and motivational considerations. Such decisions can be highly idiosyncratic, depending on circumstances and the value system of the person concerned.

Decision theory proposes two models to describe decision making in such circumstances:

1. The optimizing model, in which the person considers all options in the light of all subjectively relevant criteria and chooses an optimal solution

2. The *satisficing* model, in which an acceptable solution is retained without seeking the optimum[4]

The *satisficing* model tends to be more popular for complex decision making. Different strategies may be used to identify an acceptable solution among available options:

- The rejection of all alternative options because of some unacceptable aspects (you may chose to travel by car because all other options take too much time)
- The choice of an option because some aspects are very desirable (you may choose to walk because you feel like some fresh air)
- The more nuanced comparison of aspects of different options until one aspect clearly dominates and leads to the choice (or the rejection) of an option[5]

For wayfinding design, we are really interested only in decisions that have to be taken to reach a certain destination once the original decision to go is made. For these wayfinding decisions, you'd not normally have to choose between as many options. The information involved in the decision-making process is not as diversified and the choice is less determined by personal factors.

Availability of information is crucial to wayfinding decision making. In fact, it is entirely possible that, at a certain point along a route, no information (or only contradictory information) is available. This condition is very common and very specific to wayfinding, and in this situation you have no option other than to resort to trial and error, making decisions by chance or, perhaps, on instinct.

Although we believe that idiosyncratic factors are not as prominent in wayfinding, not all people behave the same in decision-making situations. It has been shown that some will use only a minimum of information to make a decision ("just enough to go ahead"), while others will do a more thorough search of the available information before committing themselves.[6] The reader will have made the link between these cognitive styles of processing information and the decision strategies discussed above.

5.2.2 The structuring of decisions

Let us now examine the nature of wayfinding decisions and their interrelation. The most general wayfinding decision is no doubt "to go somewhere" or "to reach a given destination."

In order to reach that destination in an urban context, for example, you will have to make additional decisions, such as to take a bus, to go downtown, and then to walk to a given shop.

Any of these decisions requires further decisions. To take a bus, for example, may require you to leave the house and to walk to the bus stop. And all these decisions can be further broken down. To walk to the bus stop, for instance, may imply to walk along the footpath to the intersection and to turn right.

If we look at all the decisions that comprise a plan of action, we can see 1) that the plan is structured, and 2) that it is hierarchically structured with the most general decisions at the top and the

satisficing: a technical term coined by Herbert Simon to cover a decision-making situation which is based on the satisfaction of the decider rather than on all relevant criteria leading to an optimal solution

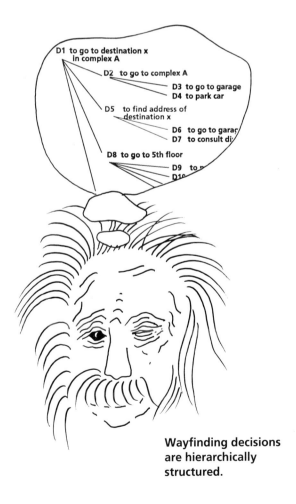

D1 to go to destination x in complex A
D2 to go to complex A
D3 to go to garage
D4 to park car
D5 to find address of destination x
D6 to go to garage
D7 to consult di
D8 to go to 5th floor
D9 to
D10

Wayfinding decisions are hierarchically structured.

29

Chapter 5
How the wayfinding process works
5.2 Decision making and decision executing

decisions leading directly to spatial behavior at the bottom. For convenience, we present the decision plan tipped on its side. The most general decisions are on the left and the decisions leading indirectly to spatial behavior are on the right. The vertical axis represents the chronology of the events.

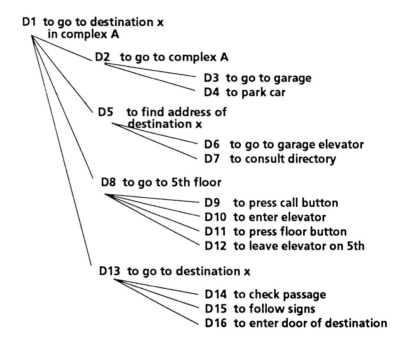

D1 to go to destination x
in complex A

    D2 to go to complex A

        D3 to go to garage
        D4 to park car

    D5 to find address of
    destination x

        D6 to go to garage elevator
        D7 to consult directory

    D8 to go to 5th floor

        D9   to press call button
        D10 to enter elevator
        D11 to press floor button
        D12 to leave elevator on 5th

    D13 to go to destination x

        D14 to check passage
        D15 to follow signs
        D16 to enter door of destination

Diagram of a hierar-chically structured decision plan.

In studying decision plans on an empirical basis, we found that any complex wayfinding problem (and most of them are complex in the detailed analysis) is broken down into smaller problems whose solutions do not exceed three or four decisions.[7] Complex wayfinding problems, thus, become more manageable; a particular aspect of the problem can be treated while still keeping in mind the problem as a whole.

This characteristic of planning is common to all problem solving.[8] The planning of a building may serve as an illustrative example. The most general decision to plan it materializes in a contract. The first level of decisions may then correspond to the overall site planning, the following level to the layout of the building, and the last level to the working drawings.

Most goal-directed behavior can be seen to be structured and guided by plans.

This type of problem solving leads to highly structured plans, which can also be easily remembered. Indeed, structure is a major mnemonic aid. For most people it is impossible to retain even a small selection of random numbers. Some researchers have even argued that magic is associated with the number seven because seven items are the most we can remember in an unstructured fashion. We believe that to remember even seven random units is asking a lot.

Structure is a memory aid.

On the other hand, it is quite easy to retrace the steps of a route involving a great number of decisions. It is also of interest to note that in direction giving, the capacity to describe a route in terms of the necessary decisions to reach a destination is far greater than the capacity of the wayfinder to retain the description. The information-giving person relies on a structured plan of action while the inquiring person receives a string of decisions in a un-structured, and thus unretainable, form.

Although we can recall many decisions if they are structured, we can usually not recall them all. On the other hand, if we find ourselves making a journey that we made once before, we will likely recognize the place where we had to make the most detailed decisions. Recognition (i.e., remembering when actually in the presence of the relevant situation) is far more efficient than recall.

5.2.3 From decisions to behavior°

A plan of action is a mental solution to a wayfinding problem, but it does not in itself take you physically to your destination. Decisions must first be executed, that is, they have to be transformed into behavior. Most importantly, each decision must be transformed into the right behavior at the right place.

It is not enough simply to turn to the right, you will have to turn right at the appropriate intersection. Decision executing is, again, a highly complex process. This process has been well described in other publications. Let us here summarize some of the important points relevant to wayfinding design.[9]

A wayfinding decision is composed of two parts:

1. Behavior, such as turning right, going up, or looking for information
2. An environmental entity, such as the intersection, the stairs, or the billboard

When executing a decision, we match a mental image or idea of something specific in the environment with what we perceive in the environment. If we find the corresponding intersection, stair, or billboard, we execute the behavioral part of the decision. If we cannot find the corresponding part in the environment, we have a very real problem. Because we cannot execute the decision, we have to develop a plan to solve this problem. This suggests how to define a wayfinding problem. A wayfinding problem is a wayfinding decision that cannot be directly executed and that therefore re-quires further planning and decision making.

The workings of decision execution are well illustrated in neuropsychological literature. Brain lesions, we have seen, can lead to spatial agnosia which manifests itself in the inability to recognize spatial features. Everytime the affected patient looks at what should be a familiar sight, such as a street or a building, even his or her own home, it appears to be a first encounter. The patient will be able to describe and understand all the features, but not to recognize them. Some patients have been reported to recall fea-tures from the period preceding a trauma.

The neuropsychologist Pallis studied a case in which a patient reflected that in his "mind's eye" he knew exactly where places were and what they looked like. He could even remember clearly

In the actual planning of a journey, a person may well start with a destination, let us say a specific shop, which is located in a shopping complex, which is in turn located downtown. When the plan is executed, the order will be inverted. The first destination is downtown, then the shopping complex, and then the specific shop.

recognition: (re-cognizing) remembering an item in the presence of the item

recall: remembering an item in the absence of the item

Chapter 5
How the wayfinding process works
5.2 Decision making and decision executing

some of the paths he had taken during his active life. But when he found himself on one of the remembered paths, everything looked foreign to him. He was unable to recall ever having been there and was, of course, not able to find his way.[10] Although he *saw* the relevant environmental features at which to execute the behavioral parts of his decision plan, by not *recognizing* them, he could not make the link with his decision plan.

Even when taking very familiar routes, decision execution is involved. This process, although highly complex, does not require a person's attention. For instance, you can easily drive or walk home from work and engage in a discussion that requires most of your attention. However, if on your drive home you encounter a new one-way street, obliging you to make a detour, you would probably interrupt your discussion until you had made the appropriate decision. While decision execution operates on an unconscious level, decision making generally requires attention.

Taking a familiar route involves executing a recorded decision plan. That the reality is a bit more complex is again illustrated in neurological literature. Let us recall that people suffering from spatial amnesia due to brain lesions are not able to map space cognitively. Although they can learn to get around with a verbal description of the necessary behavior, which is nothing other than a recorded decision plan, their wayfinding efficiency and the ease by which they can find their way is greatly reduced.

In this recorded decision plan, they have access to all decisions and to all environmental features associated with these decisions, but they have no information about the spatial location or about what happens between decisions. In other words, they would not be able to link one decision to the next if it were not for their chronological order.

The cognitive map has the important support function of situating the decision in space. As we have seen, taking a familiar route is executing a recorded decision plan, but a plan that is linked to a spatial representation. Even if the representation is only partial (and may even be rudimentary to the point of being almost non-existent) in certain environmental contexts – even if it is limited to recognition on site rather than to recall – it still provides the wayfinder with a means of locating decisions in space or at least of relating one decision to the next. The relationship and dynamics between decision plans and cognitive maps are a most interesting area of research.

It has been suggested by various authors that cognitive mapping is supported by the formation and execution of travel plans.[11] The hierarchical structure of decision plans helps us to remember not only decisions but also the spatial entities associated with them. This assumption explains the common experience that it is easier for people to remember a route if they make the wayfinding decisions by themselves than if they are following a guide. Although when guided, they are exposed to the same environmental information, because they are not making the decisions, but merely executing them, they are not effectively recording the decision plan.

The hierarchical structure of decision plans: a mnemonic support to remember decisions and to remember environmental features.

Both decision making and decision executing require environmental information. To provide this information at the appropriate place is one of the most important aspects of wayfinding design.

5.3 Information processing

Perception and cognition are the components of information processing. Perception and cognition are interrelated, and it is often difficult to distinguish one process clearly from the other. The distinction is useful, however; one relates to the process of obtaining information through the senses (perception), the other to the understanding and manipulation of information, in particular spatial information (cognition).

Perception has traditionally been a major field of study in psychology, but, as William Ittelson observed in 1973, we know very little about environmental perception.[12] This statement is still true today. We know, in fact, very little about what people perceive in the everyday environment, how they perceive while they are moving and being active, and how they cope with complex situations in which a lot of information has to be processed.

Ittelson argued that the difference between the elementary perception of form, object, and depth, and environmental perception was not just one of scale. Environments are perceived through different sensory modalities. Environments are unbounded and surround a person, calling for exploration rather than passive exposure.

Given their complexity, environments need to be perceived selectively, and the relevance of the obtained information needs to be assessed as well. Most important of all, environments are perceived in the light of activities. Environmental perception is, most of the time, directed and purposeful perception.

In the following few pages we shall outline aspects of environmental perception and cognition. Some come from the professional literature while others have emerged from our studies of wayfinding. Whenever possible we shall refer to conceptual supports in the field of perception and cognition.

perception: the process of obtaining information through the senses

cognition: understanding and being able to manipulate information

5.3.1 Environmental perception

Scanning and glancing

In reading these lines, if you are a patient reader, you will systematically move your eyes from left to right and from the top to the bottom of the page. If you are a speed reader you will have fewer points of fixation but still you will go through the page in a very similar pattern. The environment, however, is not read like a book. Environmental perception is based on a process of scanning and glancing.

When moving through a complex setting, the eye scans the visual field. This pre-attentive perception serves to identify objects or messages of interest.[13] These objects or messages are then focused upon for a short period of time. During this short focus or glance, the eyes rest on the item of interest for some tenths of a second.[14] The image thus obtained is held in a short-term visual memory until it is translated into memory of longer duration.

The short-term visual memory has a limited retention capacity. If it is asked to absorb too many units of information, a bottleneck may occur – it jams the normal glancing mechanisms and interferes with the intake.

Information, in particular graphic information, has to be designed for normal environmental perception, which consists of this scanning and glancing process. People tend to ignore information displays that are not designed appropriately, or to walk away from such displays after spending a minimum of time in futile search. The design of signs with multiple destinations and of map displays must be rethought in these terms.

An adaptation process can block information processing to relieve the cognitive system from information overload. The resulting psychological state is one of general confusion.

Complexity and overload

One of the environment's most striking characteristics is its complexity. The wayfinding person cannot take in everything, but must select that which is useful, in other words, that which is relevant to the decision-making process.

We have been able to document many instances which show that when people are executing a decision plan or part of a plan, they will perceive information directly relevant to that plan. Information that is not directly applicable to the immediate plan, even if it would be relevant sometime later, tends not to be seen. The location of information is therefore a crucial issue. It is not an exaggeration to say that information at the wrong place is as good as no information at all.

In certain complex settings, this selection of information could be more difficult. This is particularly true if wayfinders are bombarded with stimulation of all sorts and if, at the same time, they must plow through this excess to find relevant information. In such cases, a condition of overload could develop in which people reduce their intake of information as an ultimate coping device. The result is that even if they are looking at the relevant information, they are not able to process it.

It should be noted that a lot of stimulation does not in itself necessarily lead to overload. The environment always contains more information than we can process. Overload occurs when stimulation interferes with purposeful information processing. It is only when a person is actively looking for information in a confusing environmental context that the risk of overload occurs. Overload can be averted by design interventions aimed at helping the user to find the relevant information.

Complexity vs. overload.

Sensory modalities

The environment is not perceived through vision alone. Unfortunately, we know very little about multi-sensory perception. In studying people with sensory handicaps, we learn about the potential, and the limits, of certain senses.

Anybody who has worked with blind subjects is painfully aware of the superiority of sight for perceiving the totality of a scene. Visual scanning is fast, efficient, and reliable. Sight is also very versatile. It works both for distance and for close-up views. The perception of distant cues is of special interest to wayfinding. It allows people to perceive and direct themselves towards a distant destination which otherwise would require intermediary points of reference. The perception of distant cues simplifies a great many wayfinding tasks.

Information overload – or just an interesting and exciting setting?

Vision is dependent on an adequate light level. The requirements in this respect increase with aging and reduced eyesight. Optometrists say that a 50-year-old needs almost twice as much light to see clearly as does a 20-year-old. People who are 70 or older need four times as much light.[15]

Some people suffer from temporary blinding caused by strong light contrasts, when moving both from light to dark and from dark to light. It is therefore important to keep a consistent level of illumination throughout the setting and to avoid glare by controlling the direction of the light.

Hearing is probably our second most used sense in wayfinding. It enables us to identify certain characteristics of the setting and to perceive some distant cues. People who cannot rely on sight have two ways of using hearing for such cues:

Messages that have to be read benefit from a strong brightness contrast. The use of color in combination with brightness can optimize reading. It should be kept in mind, when using colors, that 9 percent of males and 2 percent of females are color blind, particularly with respect to red and green. Up to 50 percent of elderly people also have difficulties distinguishing various hues of dark or light colors.[16]

It used to be thought that strobe lights should be used in connection with fire alarms, as a visual signal (see section 15.5.5). Even a simple pulsing 25-watt bulb could be disturbing to elderly people.

- Perceiving an original sound source in the environment
- Perceiving sound produced by the person (e.g., cane tapping) and reflected by objects in the environment (echo-location)

The value of a sound source for wayfinding is often reduced because of the unreliability of the source. You can, for example, see a tree from a given distance, but you can only hear it when the wind blows. Echo-location is more reliable in this sense, but it requires a relatively quiet environment and only works at small distances. You can "hear" a tree through echo-location only if you are directly in front of it.

It has been argued that only blind people have developed the ability to use sound to identify objects. We don't think this is so. In an unpublished study done a few years ago (Romedi Passini), blindfolded, sighted subjects were also found, surprisingly, to be capable of identifying openings, barriers, and even relatively small overhangs through echo-location.

Sounds are perceived regardless of head position. Sounds for that reason are excellent warning cues. Crossing a busy street without being able to hear is quite an unsettling experience for anybody. Indeed, deaf people, because they cannot rely on sound signals, tend to be excessively fearful of accidents. To make things worse, almost all evacuation warning systems (fire alarms, for example) are based on sound signals. Safety is probably one of the major concerns of deaf and hearing-impaired people.

Sound, by the same token, is much more difficult to screen than visual stimulation. Screening, when using a hearing aid, is particularly troublesome. This in itself is a good reason why we should be concerned about the soundscape of our built environment. We are singularly indifferent to noise pollution –even when we know that noise obscures informative sounds and that the effects of noise on stress and health have been clearly demonstrated.

Tactual and haptic perception apply only to proximal objects. The white cane of the blind person is an extension of his or her arm, but that is as far as it goes. The cane serves to identify obstacles and to follow direction-giving lines such as a curb or the edge of a footpath.

Braille and raised letters, raised numbers, and even some raised symbols are read by the blind population. The difficulty with using tactile signage, however, is that blind wayfinders first must know where the information is located before they are able to use it. Furthermore, it has been noted that a social stigma is attached to tactile exploration. At a conference held by the SEGD (Society of Environmental Graphic Designers) in 1988, a blind speaker, Michele Brulé, illustrated this point with the poignant question: "Do you see me exploring the white wall or the impeccable glass door of the corporate office in order to find the company's name?"

Tactile maps have been shown to be useful to blind travellers. Just like the reading of braille and of raised letters and symbols, the reading of tactile maps has to be learned. Researchers have identified characteristics of tactile maps that facilitate their use. They have also developed techniques for producing tactile maps

There are three different types of braille. Grade 1 braille is strict transliteration of the original language; however, grade 2 braille, which includes many contractions, is much more efficient to use. Grade 3 is a type of shorthand and does not concern us here.

Only about one in ten of those registered with blind organizations can read grade 2 braille, although rather more can read grade 1. The assumption that every blind person can read braille is certainly false.

that have a high detection quality and are easy and inexpensive to manufacture.

Few would argue that we have lost the ability to follow our noses, although our sense of smell is not usually enough to get us home. Our perception of odors is simply not fine enough to give us many directional cues. Our sense of smell may have some limited use as a cue for place identification but it tends to be very unreliable in our contemporary environment.

Some research has shown that stimulations, usually associated with one particular sense, could be perceived by other senses as well. A French psychologist by the name of Duplessis, tried to show that discrimination of colors without sight was possible. According to her studies, about 20 percent of the population is able to discriminate colors by what she calls dermo-optic perception. We tried to replicate the experiments in a well-controlled study, but were not able to produce any similar findings.[18]

5.3.2 Environmental cognition

The meaning of cognition is knowing and understanding. Two aspects of environmental cognition can be distinguished:

1. The knowledge people have about the given components of a setting, such as the buildings they remember in a cityscape
2. The understanding of the spatial characteristics of a setting, which has already been described as a cognitive map

The things we remember
It may be of interest to know which buildings people remember best, but more important for the planner is an understanding of the physical and non-physical characteristics that make buildings memorable. Researchers studied these characteristics and arrived at four factors that enhance memory for buildings in a cityscape:

1. The form of the building; its size, contours, complexity of shape, and uniqueness of architectural style
2. Visibility and access; pedestrian access and the possibility of moving around the building
3. Use; if a building had an important function and was used often, it was also well remembered
4. Symbolic significance; elderly citizens were particularly aware of historical and cultural meanings associated with buildings[19]

Cognitive mapping
The representation and mapping of the spatial characteristics of the environment has been a subject of research and debate for many years. Research in the early 70s aimed at developing a typology of cognitive maps. A distinction was made between two types of cognitive mapping:

1. People may structure the environment in terms of routes, that is, the points where they change direction, the angle of directional change, and a measure of the distance from one point to another.

In *Perfume,*[17] a novel by the German author Patrick Süskind, Grenouille is a malevolent genius and master perfumer who is morbidly fascinated by his skills. He conceives the idea of capturing and preserving the fragrance of (not for) a particular girl. By his nose, he locates her – even though she lives on the other side of the city. One day he steps outside his workshop and immediately knows that something is wrong . . .

"The atmosphere was not as it should have been, from the town's aromatic garb, that veil of many thousands of woven threads, the girl's golden thread was missing . . . it was gone, vanished, untraceable despite the most intense sniffing." Even though the girl leaves town, Grenouille, using "the compass of his nose," follows her half-way across France, murders her, and at last successfully captures and distills the essence he has sought for so long.

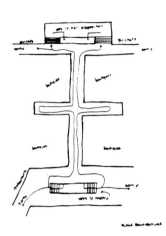

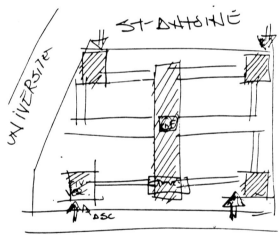

Sketch maps of sequential and coordinate structuring of space.

2. People may record the topographical relationships between critical elements of the explored environment directly, without relying on a specific route or decision plan.

The first type of structuring has been referred to as egocentric and sequential, leading to a representation in the form of a strip or route map. The second type has been referred to as coordinate, leading to a representation in the form of a survey map.[20]

In the process of mapping a new environment, some researchers showed that people tended to start by recording landmarks and used them as anchor-points to subsequently fill in the paths;[21] others have assumed paths and districts to be the original structuring element.[22] The choice may well be determined by the type of environment and the predominance of one or the other of these features as much as by personal preference.

During the last decade, some cognitive and environmental psychologists have made a distinction between two types of representations:

1. *A propositional representation* is seen to be schematic and somewhat abstract in nature; the representation of a setting based on personal exploration tends to be of that order.
2. *An analogue representation* is seen to be figural and Gestalt-like in nature; learning a setting from a physical map can be seen to result in a figural representation.[23]

The distinction is of interest because different characteristics are associated with each type of representation. The representation of a route learned from a physical map (analogue representation) tends to be oriented. One will "see" a map in one's mind's eye, although it may have to be turned to align with the setting. The representation of a route learned while exploring a setting (propositional representation) is not oriented and therefore is more flexible in usage. On the other hand it may be less precise.[24] Research has shown that both representations can coexist even if they contain contradictory information.

It is one thing to have a representation of a setting. It is quite another to manipulate this representation so that it can be used to solve wayfinding problems. In order to study these spatio-cognitive manipulations, we have identified as many basic wayfinding tasks as possible.[25] For each, we have determined the necessary spatio-cognitive manipulation. Seven distinctive tasks and seven corresponding spatio-cognitive manipulations are retained as crucial for wayfinding. They are summarized here.

Basic wayfinding task	Corresponding spatio-cognitive manipulation
1. learning a new route	recording a decision plan and/or developing a cognitive map
2. returning to the point of origin (retracing one's steps)	inverting a decision plan or the mapped route
3. linking known routes to new configurations	combining decision plans or sections of mapped routes into new combinations
4. learning a route from a small display and making the journey	making a transfer of scale
5. pointing to the directions of locations visited on a journey	making a triangulation
6. learning a route from a non-aligned display	making a mental rotation
7. understanding the overall layout of a visited setting	identifying the underlying principle of spatial organization

The basic wayfinding tasks and the corresponding spatio-cognitive manipulations.

This short overview of wayfinding demonstrates how interesting and complex the process is. Considering that every journey we ever make is based on wayfinding, the process works surprisingly well. With the exception of some specific spatio-cognitive operations, such as mental rotation, people are quite skilled at spatial problem solving.

The wayfinding difficulties they have are usually due to particular features of the environment. It may, for example, be difficult to understand the spatial organization of a setting because it is too complex or, more likely, because it is not clearly articulated. On the other hand, relevant information may be difficult (or impossible) to obtain or to understand.

Part Three:
Principles of wayfinding design

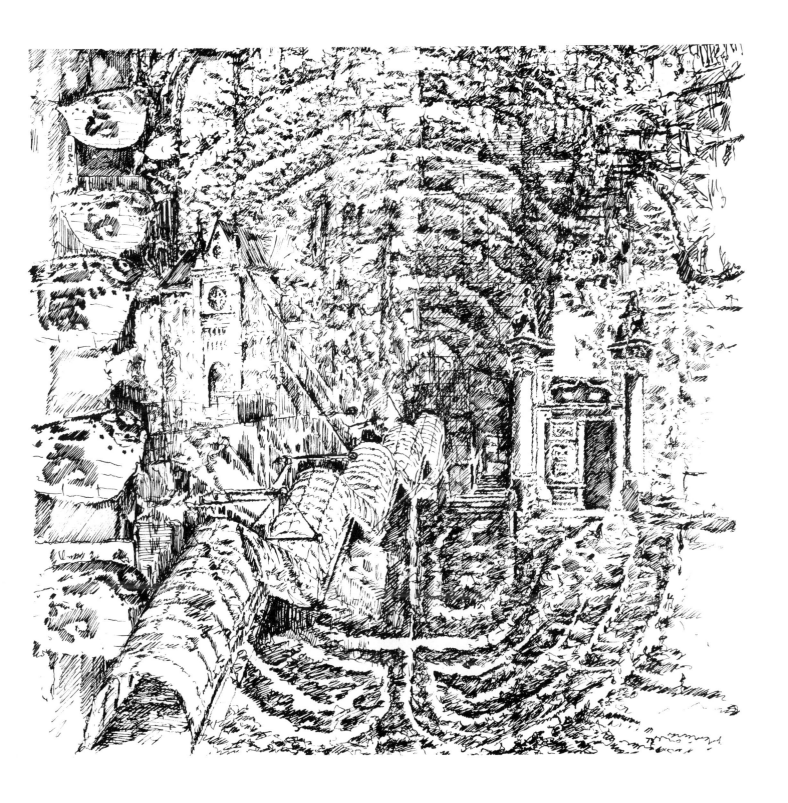

Chapter 6

What is wayfinding design?

Wayfinding requirements, whether they be at the regional, urban, or architectural scale, are integral to the design process – from the most general, overall spatial organization of the setting to the articulation of the form-giving features, and right down to the individual architectural and graphic messages. Wayfinding requirements shape the setting, affect the choice of the circulation system, and contribute to the design of the interior. This is particularly true in large building complexes.

The enormous impact of wayfinding considerations on the outcome of the design of a setting is one of the reasons we feel justified in using the term "wayfinding design."

The other reason is strategic. Wayfinding is a very important aspect of daily life and has been neglected for so long that we want to give it its rightful place on the drawing board. We are totally convinced on this subject. Even if it can be argued that, in the past, the built environment was relatively simple and clear, this is certainly not true of today's mammoth building complexes.

When "wayfinding design" becomes a consideration in its own right (like "HVAC" or "emergency exit procedures"), planners will be made aware that it is a vital part of design, and if they pride themselves on being professionals, they should know about it. Wayfinding design is also a principle. It is user oriented and derives its approach and its interventions from the behavioral and psychological foundations of wayfinding.

Efficient, accessible, safe, and spatially attractive wayfinding environments can be designed only when the principles of wayfinding are understood and when this knowledge is translated into applicable form. The aim of this chapter is to make the link between design and the wayfinding principles introduced previously. Two aspects of wayfinding design will retain our attention: spatial planning and environmental communication.

6.1 Spatial planning

6.1.1 Setting the stage

Wayfinding occurs in space. The spatial characteristics of a site, that is, its size, its organization, and the nature of its circulation systems, all contribute in one way or another to the wayfinding difficulties that confront the site's users.

Spatial planning provides the context for wayfinding and sets the stage for the problem-solving performance. Spatial planning determines the location of the entrances and exits of a setting, the location of the major destinations and, therefore, the nature of its circulation system, the organization of its spaces, and the visual accessibility of its architecture. Spatial planning not only defines the wayfinding problems of the future users, but affects the ease or difficulty they will have in understanding and cognitively mapping the setting. Spatial planning is, therefore, the first major component in wayfinding design.

First wayfinding design component: spatial planning. Setting the stage for the problem-solving performance.

Settings need not necessarily be simple for people to find their way adequately. Wayfinding-efficient environments can be spatially interesting, even complex. It would be erroneous and dangerous to suggest a return to over-simplicity. Boredom is not particularly suited for efficient wayfinding. The challenge for wayfinding design, we feel, is to create interesting settings that allow for gratifying spatial experiences and that are safe, accessible, and wayfinding-efficient, despite any complexity they may have.[1]

Spatial planning has traditionally been the domain of architects and urbanists. Although the spatial layout and the circulation system undeniably emerge from a number of considerations, such as the functions of the facilities contained in the setting, the servicing of the setting, the site, and the neighboring architecture, it is wayfinding and circulation that constitute the prime space-binding factor.

In airports, public transportation terminals, health-care facilities, and many other public settings that have to accommodate large amounts of traffic, the spatial organization is the direct expression of circulation and wayfinding.

6.1.2 The role of decision diagrams in spatial planning

What makes good spatial planning? To answer this question satisfactorily, we have to return to the notion of decision plans. Let's recall that a decision plan is the user's solution to a wayfinding problem posed by the spatial organization and the associated circulation system. We can therefore expect a close relationship between spatial organizations and decision plans.

When planning a new setting, planners should start with a decision diagram representing the desired way for the users to solve wayfinding problems in the setting, and then develop from the appropriate circulation system and spatial organization.

The illustration shows the relationship between a simple decision diagram for a multi-purpose setting, the accompanying circulation system, and a possible spatial organization. In this example, all visitors go first to a central information square; from there they

decision diagram: a diagram established for design or research purposes, showing the desired way for users to solve wayfinding problems

decision plan: the mental solution to a wayfinding problem as it is developed by the user

Spatial planning on the basis of decision diagrams: a first example.

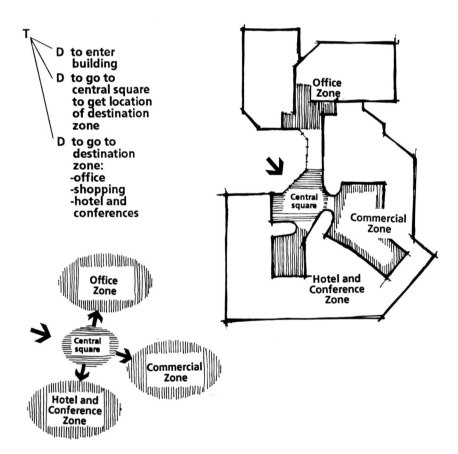

go to the business, commercial, hotel, and conference zones. The same principle can be applied at the level of destination zones. The visitors, when reaching the office zone, find a secondary "business" square, where more detailed information about the location of a particular office is to be obtained. The underlying organization is hierarchical in this case.

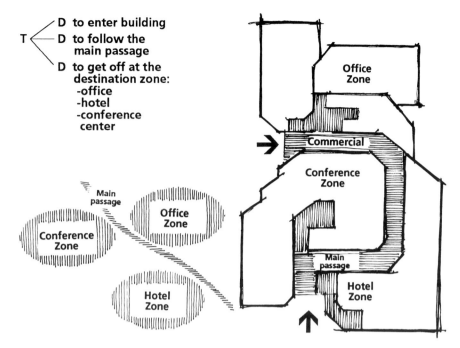

Office Zone

Commercial

Conference Zone

Main passage

Office Zone

Conference Zone

Hotel Zone

Main passage

Hotel Zone

Spatial planning on the basis of decision diagrams: a second example.

In the second example we find a different organization. The visitors are taken along a main passage from which they branch off to the various destination zones. The organization here is linear.

The two examples are intended to illustrate the principle of using decision diagrams in spatial planning. Chapter 10 will provide a more detailed look at this issue.

In an existing building, the spatial organization and the circulation system are givens, and so, therefore, are the basic decision diagrams. The planner should still identify these diagrams, however, to better understand the existing system. Design interventions can then aim at articulating the system and making it perceptually accessible and clear to the users.

The main design task in an existing setting is to develop an appropriate information system. The decision diagrams serve as the basis for the design of the information system.

We are fully aware of the fact that the design process is not as sequential as may be implied here. The designer may first start with a spatial idea and only then think about the circulation and the decision diagram. This may, in turn, affect the original spatial idea.

6.2 Environmental communication

6.2.1 Communication for decision making: the script

The second major component of wayfinding design is environmental communication. Many wayfinding difficulties are due to aspects of information processing. Providing the relevant wayfinding information in the environment is an issue both in architectural and in graphic design.

The design of an information system has to be based on people's wayfinding behavior. It must contain all the necessary information for them to make and execute decisions along a given route. In addition, it must provide the information necessary for gaining a representation of the setting.

Environmental communication not only refers to the visual mode, but also includes the audible and the tactile mode. All environmental communication, in order to be perceived and under-

Second wayfinding design component: environmental communication. Providing the actor with a script to perform wayfinding.

Environmental communication is a design issue. It is responsible for providing users with the information necessary to solve their wayfinding problems.

The positioning of signs at intersections is illustrated in section 15.3.1.

stood, must respond to basic laws of environmental perception and cognition.

The content and location of information
Let us first look at the decision-making and decision-executing aspects of wayfinding.

If, as we have outlined above, information is needed for each wayfinding decision that is made and executed, it follows that the particular information that the wayfinder gathers is determined by the decisions that that person must make.

It is the decisions or, when seen in their totality, the decision plan that is the determining factor in designing an information system. If, for a given decision, we cannot assume that the users have the required information in the form of common knowledge, then the information has to be provided through architectural, graphic, or other, non-graphic means.

It is important to emphasize that wayfinding design should be concerned not only with individual decisions but with a series of them (i.e., the structured ensemble of decisions that leads the wayfinding person to his or her destination).

The logic of the decision plan (or diagram) is the rationale that ties individual decisions into a whole, and this same rationale must tie the information units into the overall system.

Much signage is concerned only with installing signs at intersections. Such a procedure ignores the information needed for decisions that do not directly lead to behavior. In other words, it ignores the higher-order decisions structuring the plan.

An information unit has to be perceived at, or shortly before, a decision point. Otherwise the information tends not to be noticed. In order to establish the *location* of the required information, the designer has to transfer the decisions of the diagram to the route.

By taking note of the physical characteristics of a setting (such as light levels, density of people, heights of ceilings), the designer can identify an acceptable area for placing information at a given decision point.

By superimposing information areas from different routes, it is possible to identify the optimum location of information displays. The decision diagram, in other words, is the logic of combining content and location for the information system.

Let us return to the example of the hierarchically organized multipurpose center introduced above and illustrate the planning of the general information system leading from the entrance of the setting to a particular business office.

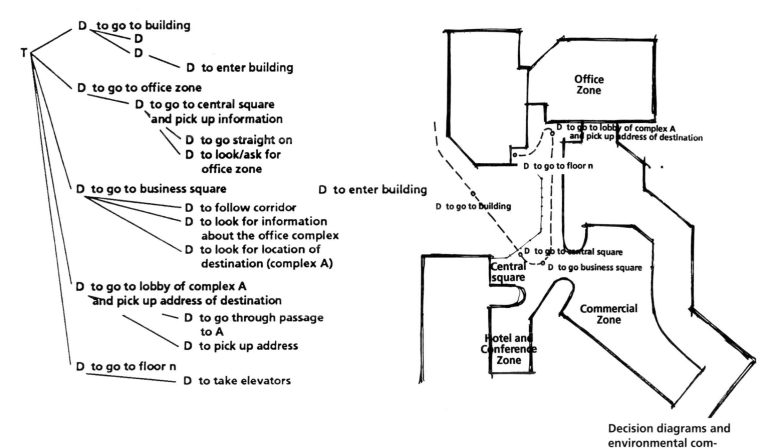

Decision diagrams and environmental communication.

The accompanying decision diagram outlines in general terms the way visitors will solve the problem of going to a particular office. In the layout, the visitors, after having entered the building, find themselves in the central square. They have to understand that this is a strategic spot in which to figure out the organization of the setting and the location of the office zone.

Architectural information can and should communicate the existence and the location of the three destination zones: business, shopping, and hotel (including conference). Graphics can heighten the architectural expression of the three zones and/or indicate their location. In addition, an information center may provide a description of the setting and the location of the zones.

Having reached the office zone in the schematic layout, the visitors enter a much smaller square (the business square). Here

47

they obtain information about the office zone which, for argument's sake, is subdivided into three complexes A, B, and C. The visitors will need to be able to determine

- that there are three complexes,
- where the complexes are located, and
- in which complex their particular destination is located.

Again, we can see the interplay of architectural and graphic information. If the architectural expression of the three lobbies is clear, a minimum of signs will be necessary. If not, the burden of describing the existence of the three complexes, their location, and what each contains becomes a graphic communication issue.

In the elevator lobby of the complex, visitors should find the precise addresses (floor level and office number) of each of the tenants. In this description, we always provide information in sequence. Information about the destination zones appears once the visitors have entered the building. Information about the organization of the office complex is provided once they have reached the office square. The address system is provided once they have reached the elevator lobby, and so on.

This, we know now, is the optimum way to locate information. It always appears when the visitors are in need of it to develop their plan.

In designing the overall information system for the setting, each major route has to be thought through in these terms. Once the system is worked out, the designer will have to fit in the multitude of secondary information which is also essential for the efficient functioning of the setting.

A checklist of specific information needs in public buildings is provided in Appendix 2: Anatomy of a public building complex.

Some practical considerations
The reader at this point may well wonder if our approach, although plausible in principle, is at all practical. It might be thought, for example, that in a complex setting there are as many different decision plans as there are routes, and that for each route there are as many decision plans as there are people. If this were really so, however, we would have to forget about wayfinding design altogether.

It is true that in any large setting an almost infinite number of wayfinding tasks and routes can be identified – if one were to link all possible points of origin to all possible points of destination. It is also true that some routes would be more representative of people's movement in the setting (i.e., primary routes) and that others (i.e., secondary and tertiary routes) would be of lesser importance.

Elsewhere we have described three kinds of primary routes:

- The main circulation between the entrances or exits of a setting and the major destination zones
- The circulation from one major destination zone to another
- The circulation within a major destination zone

The nature and size of the major destination zones will vary from site to site. Examples of major destination zones for large multipurpose urban or suburban complexes may be the office section, the residential section, or the shopping section. The primary routes (even of very complex settings) are quite limited in numbers. If the information system is clear and effective for the primary routes, it will set the wayfinding tone for the whole of the setting. The system will dominate the secondary and tertiary routes. Specific information will still be needed for these latter routes, but they will be integrated into the overall scheme.

Do people who take the same route develop different decision plans? This question is crucial. If everybody were to develop fundamentally different decision plans, these plans would be of no use in the design of wayfinding information systems. Fortunately, however, there is a direct link between the spatial organization of a setting with its related circulation system and the most appropriate decision plan.

Each type of circulation demands its own type of decision plan. Thus, if the appropriate information is provided, people on the whole will develop similar plans. This makes good sense. After all, the wayfinding problem is the same for all people, and if the information to solve the problem is the same, the solution should be the same as well. This does not, however, exclude people's having preferences and choosing one route rather than another for a multitude of personal reasons.

Empirical wayfinding data shows this to be essentially true, but it also points to the need for further clarification.

The information a person seeks in order to solve his or her wayfinding problem is not determined by the environmental setting alone. It also depends on his or her preference for a certain kind of information – whether it is linear and sequential (such as one might find on signs), or whether it is spatial and global (such as that emanating from the spatial organization of the setting itself).

These two wayfinding styles are not exclusive. Most people use both. They will at various times have preferences for one over the other. These preferences are adjusted according to the characteristics of the setting or to wayfinding conditions (i.e., the normal, "everyday," the recreational, and the emergency wayfinding conditions, which are described at length in Chapter 9). The reader may have already made the link between these information preferences and the typology of cognitive maps discussed in the previous chapter.

People who have a tendency to structure information on a sequential basis will also have a tendency to seek this type of information. On the other hand, people who structure information on a spatial basis will seek information giving them an idea of how the setting is organized, and how it is linked by the circulation system.

It should be noted that while the decision plans in both cases may be identical, the information leading to the decisions may vary. It is therefore important that both spatial and linear information be provided to allow for both wayfinding styles.

These matters are discussed again in graphic terms in Chapter 13.

legibility: the ease with which information is able to be perceived

readability: the ease with which information is able to be understood

6.2.2 The form of information

Up to this point we have concentrated on the content and the location of wayfinding information. The third major aspect of environmental communication is *form,* which is concerned not only with esthetics but also with key information processing aspects. Environmental perception and cognition provide the theoretical foundations for the formal aspect of environmental communication.

Legibility and readability

Typically, visitors trying to make use of the information displayed for their benefit may encounter one of two major flaws:

- The information may not be legible in that it is obstructed, badly placed, too small, blurred, garbled, or tactually too mushy to be perceived.
- The information may not be readable in that it can be perceived but cannot be understood.

Many people refer to the terms "legibility" and "readability" as though they were interchangeable. They aren't.

Legibility is a key issue and needs special mention in this chapter on design principles. In the previous section, we saw that environmental perception is based on a process of scanning and glancing. Objects or messages are focused upon for a short period of time. The image thus obtained is held in a short-term visual (iconic) memory which has a limited retention capacity.

The limited capacity of this short-term visual memory has a marked impact on the graphics, in particular on the presentation of written messages. Studies have shown that on signs and maps only a small number of written items, generally three at most, can be read at a glance. If more than three items are presented, they should be grouped into packages not exceeding that desired limit. The wayfinding person will then be able to read the message in a few glances (see also section 13.4.1).

Most written information displays, such as signs and maps, are not designed with this basic perceptual rule in mind. They are hard to read in a glance, and the users, if they think that they need the information badly enough, have to stop and resort to a more linear "book reading" style.

Legibility and readability in complex settings can also be affected by a state of mind often described as general confusion, which is brought about by information overload. This phenomenon of information processing can be averted by design interventions that help the user to find the relevant information.

Consistency in the design of information displays will help a wayfinding person's search by indicating what to look for. The form that the information takes, the material used, and the graphics are all contributing elements. An information display should be able to be identified before it can actually be read. People learn to recognize such displays after having seen them just once or twice before.

Colors, for example, can be used to facilitate the perception of the circulation routes. In a transportation terminal in Switzerland, the vertical circulation is painted a bright yellow. This includes the stairs, the escalators, and the elevators. The effect is very striking. However, the results would have been more effective if the color coding had been included in the signage.

Consistency in the location of information will help a wayfinding person, who must know where to look for information. The haphazard application of such information to columns and walls, or hanging from ceilings, contributes substantially to overload in complex settings.

Structuring information will, furthermore, reduce the chances of overload. Structuring can relate to form and content. *Form structure* is important in facilitating the reading of the information. The criteria of good form emerge from the basic processes of environmental perception and have already been described above. *Content structure* refers to the order of information in the decision-making process. Primary information that directs people to large destination zones should be given more importance than secondary or tertiary information that leads to sub-zones or individual destinations.

In the decision plan, primary information corresponds to the higher-order decisions. The consistent application of this rule creates expectancy, which facilitates the users' search for information and thus reduces the danger of overload.

6.2.3 Communication for cognitive mapping

The importance of a cognitive map as a source of information was demonstrated in Chapter 5. We outline here some of the major design factors that can be assumed to facilitate the process.

Spatial planning affects cognitive mapping in a major way. It creates the space that has to be understood and represented. Probably the most important factor facilitating cognitive mapping

**Administration
Cafeteria
Cashier
Elevators
Information
Maintenance
Pay phones
Security
Washrooms**

**Administration
Cafeteria
Cashier**

**Elevators
Information
Maintenance**

**Pay phones
Security
Washrooms**

Composition of verbal information in signs. Which of the two is the easier to read in a glance?

Information preferences and typology of cognitive maps.

51

imageability: the ease with which the spatial
layout of a setting is able to be understood
and mapped

and thereby contributing to the imageability of a setting is the
clarity of the spatial organization and the architectural expression
of the underlying principle. Once people have understood the way a
setting is organized, they also have a pretty good cognitive map of
the setting.

Environmental communication affects cognitive mapping. The
legibility of key architectural elements (such as entrances, circulation both horizontal and vertical, major landmarks) is a prerequisite to understanding the spatial organization. It is obviously not
enough to have a clear spatial organization if it is not understood.
The principle of the organization has to be communicated to the
wayfinding users.

The first thing that comes to mind when one thinks about
cognitive mapping and graphic information are map displays and
models. Indeed, map displays, if they can be read, provide users
with a bird's-eye view which they cannot otherwise get. But map
displays are not the only form of graphic information facilitating
cognitive mapping. The structuring of the information on signs
according to the decision diagrams will also contribute to a better
understanding of the underlying spatial organization. In some
cases, the use of color and memorable terms to designate certain
areas may help to structure the setting.

In summary, we have identified two major components of
wayfinding design: spatial planning and environmental communication. Environmental communication can be broken down into
information concerning the decision-making and decision-executing process on the one hand, and the cognitive- mapping process
on the other. In Chapters 10 through 15, we shall be looking at
these aspects of wayfinding design from architectural and graphic
perspectives in order to identify the relevant design components.

6.3 An integrated view of wayfinding design

The diagram of the wayfinding pyramid summarizes the design
principles discussed so far. The user is the ultimate reference of
wayfinding design and is therefore represented at the top of the
pyramid. Of course, we are not interested in any personal aspect of
the user, but in the wayfinding process. It is an understanding of
how users solve wayfinding problems – of how they make decisions, how they execute these decisions, and how they perceive
and understand the environment – that should affect the planning
of the layout and the designing of the wayfinding information
system. It is therefore in respect of the wayfinding process that a
setting can be judged to be wayfinding efficient, accessible, and
safe.

Spatial planners are responsible for designing the layout of a
setting and its circulation system. Graphic designers are responsible for designing the information system. That is the conventional
wisdom, but it is only partly accurate.

Less obvious is the fact that because spatial planners cannot
avoid communicating wayfinding information about their buildings,
they are also designers of the information system. Graphic designers, on the other hand, do more than just design the signs. They

have an important role to play in interpreting and expressing the character of the setting. While both disciplines have their own specific functions within this process, the overlap is so large that a close relationship at an early planning stage is of paramount importance in good wayfinding design.

What do spatial planners have to know about the wayfinding process to design efficient, accessible, safe, and interesting layouts? They have to know about cognitive mapping and assure themselves that their layouts can be spatially understood. More than that, they have to know about wayfinding in terms of problem solving, because in designing the layout they determine the wayfinding problems that future users will have to solve. (In Chapter 10 we shall be looking at this issue in some detail.) They also have to communicate relevant architectural wayfinding information to the users. (This will be addressed in Chapter 11.)

What do graphic designers have to know about the wayfinding process to design efficient, legible, and readable information systems? All of the above and more. They have to provide all the information for the users to be able to make and execute their decisions. This includes information about specific tenants, facilities, and special events. It also includes the nuts and bolts of graphic communication (which will be covered in Chapters 12 through 14).

Unfortunately, coming in as they generally do at the end rather than the beginning of the design process, graphic designers are frequently called upon to apply their bandages and cosmetics to provide the simulation of order when, in fact, none may exist.

We propose an integrated approach to wayfinding design. The layout of a setting and the wayfinding information system contained in it have to be intimately related. For the users, this translates into a coherent correspondence between their wayfinding problems and the information available to solve them. If this coherence is achieved, the design of the layout of a setting and its environmental communication will be mutually reinforcing.

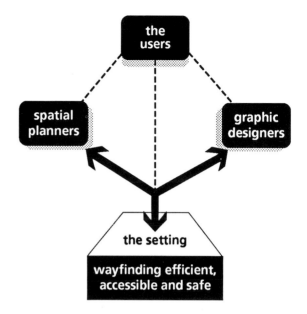

The wayfinding pyramid.

Chapter 7

Who is involved in wayfinding design?

The faithful reader who has followed the argument so far will be well aware of the fact that much more is involved in wayfinding design than merely putting up nice-looking, inoffensive signs and that graphic designers are not the only professionals involved. In this chapter, we identify other members of the cast – all of whom, from their various perspectives, have major influences on how visitors to a building will ultimately find their way about in it.

This chapter also serves to point out another significant fact which is that "design" (as in wayfinding design) involves more than architects and graphic designers. Management plays an important role too.

7.1 The design profession

No, signs would not have done the trick. They needed a master builder like Daedalus to create the most confusing and disorienting labyrinth, one fit to imprison the Minotaur. If the mythical architect were able to build a perfectly disorienting building, he should also have been able to build a perfectly orienting one. Able or not, today's architects, including urban planners, have an enormous impact on the wayfinding success or failure of a setting.

In planning the layout, they are creating the setting and the wayfinding problems future users will have to solve. In articulating the setting, they are providing the users with much of the necessary information to solve the wayfinding problems at hand.

The notion of wayfinding is relatively recent, and it is only fair to say that architects and urban designers have always been aware of the importance of the spatial organization of a setting and of the ensuing circulation system. This, after all, touches on the essence of architecture and city planning. In focusing attention on wayfinding, spatial planning is brought into a new light – one that is user friendly and has all the potential for stimulating new creative thinking.

Architectural practice in the last decades has gone from one crisis to another, and much has been said about the underlying crisis of meaning. Some ask whether architecture is deprived of all meaning or whether it still has something to say about our contemporary society. It may, or it may not, have something to say about contemporary society, but what is certain is that architecture has to say something about itself. It has to communicate its content, its spatial organization, its circulation system, entrances, exits, horizontal and vertical paths. Architecture has to have distinct and memorable features and destination zones. In other words, it has to communicate wayfinding information. We feel this to be a solid basis for architectural design and that new thinking and new forms and, above all, a new coherence of expression can emerge through wayfinding design.

Architects and urban planners have to work with other professionals at all stages of the design process, from preliminary conceptual drawings to detailed working drawings. Given that graphic designers are usually responsible for an important part of wayfinding communication in complex settings, they become the architect's natural collaborators in wayfinding design.

The role of architects and urban designers is not to supervise the graphic designer but to collaborate with him or her in order to arrive at a coherent information system. The earlier the collaboration begins, the smoother the process and the better the chance of creating a quality building in terms of people's efficiency of movement, in terms of their accessibility and safety, and in terms of their general appreciation.

Chapter 7
Who is involved in wayfinding design?
7.1 The design profession

The logo of the Society of Environmental Graphic Designers (SEGD), Cambridge, Massachusetts.

7.1.2 Environmental graphic designers

Environmental communication is a blanket term that embraces architectural information as well as graphic and verbal (or audible) communication within a given setting. Environmental graphic design is a relatively new calling, dating only from the early 60s. Until recently, it recruited its members exclusively from the ranks of graphic designers.

In the early 70s the Society of Environmental Graphic Designers (SEGD) was formed with offices in Cambridge, Massachusetts, and ever since has assumed a leading and influential role in raising professional standards and in broadening an understanding of the graphic designer's function in the environmental and architectural contexts.

The SEGD has also taken a lively and intelligent interest in education – so far, however, in the face of a less-than-lively response from the groves of academe. The institutions of learning claim that their curricula are already full and that they cannot, therefore, accommodate new courses on subjects like environmental communication.

This raises a problem in that increasingly in future, architects and graphic designers will have to be forming closely knit collaborations in the development of environmental communication and very few institutions are interested in preparing them for this.

The role of the architect in wayfinding design has been described in the preceding section. In any case, the role of the architect has always been well established and we all know what architects do. What, however, does the graphic designer do in this new context of collaboration on environmental communications projects? His or her prime contribution is a thorough knowledge of the effective planning and organization of two-dimensional space.

This knowledge must be tempered by a more than nodding acquaintance with industrial design and the requirements of public safety.

In addition, it must be assumed the graphic designer on the team is thoroughly up to date on developments in the sign industry, which, with the advent of computer-driven equipment (such as computerized cutters and plotters), have been advancing very rapidly.

The graphic designer also brings an extensive knowledge that includes the following graphic techniques:

- hand graphics
- typographics
- pictographics
- photographics

Although a knowledge of environmental psychology is not generally to be expected from the graphic designer, knowing about the processes of environmental perception and cognition is more than "a help." Environmental psychology is an essential part of wayfinding design and, therefore, needs to be considered a part of the graphic designer's education.

Finally, because environmental communication is not limited to architectural and graphic information, but comprises audible or verbal information as well, some member of the team must be conscious of the important role that voice will play in the context of wayfinding design.

We now know for certain that some forms of information within the environment are most effectively communicated through sound. People would, for example, much rather (if they had the choice) be *told* how to get to their destination than have to figure it out from a sign or a map.

It therefore becomes incumbent on the team to provide for verbal and audible information, and in our experience it is generally the graphic designer's function to do so. (It is also his or her function to provide guidelines for training the personnel who will staff the information desks.)

All of this is a far cry from the role the graphic designer is prepared for in most of our art and design schools. As Edward Carpenter (writing about wayfinding in *Print* magazine) put it so well: "With the complexity of today's mammoth building projects, the need to design buildings friendly to the user is more urgent than ever. Graphic designers who perceive the problem should do more about it than take an architect out for lunch."[1]

7.1.3 Landscape architects

Landscape architects are involved in wayfinding design when planning large areas for recreation and work such as parks, golf courses, athletic facilities, promenades, and bicycle paths. Wayfinding design in architecture and in landscape architecture have many aspects in common. In planning the layout, they set the wayfinding stage; in articulating the landscape, they communicate the necessary information to the wayfinding person.

In terms of wayfinding design, landscape differs from architecture not so much in content as in the vocabulary used. Landscape architects also compose with paths, landmarks, and destination zones. They also organize space and communicate a circulation system.

One of the underestimated functions of landscape architecture is site planning. In the conception of a campus, a large residential area, or a large exhibition complex, it is landscape architecture that defines the spatial organization and the circulation system at the extra-building scale.

If we focus on the building itself, the landscape can put its form into perspective. It can make the building visually accessible and can emphasize the location of its entrances. In certain cases, where the doors are hidden, it may well be that the landscape provides the only available information about where to enter.

Special features of the landscape can help users to distinguish one part of the setting from another and thus assist the cognitive-mapping process. Landscape features can even announce the spatial organization the visitor will find inside the building. Vistas

Chapter 7
Who is involved in wayfinding design?
7.1 The design profession

from the building towards remarkable features in the landscape can be memorable landmarks. The same can be said about interior gardens. Landscape architects must be part of the team.

7.2 Management

7.2.1 The owners

This book was not planned with members of the design profession as its sole audience. The person who hires these consultants in the first place assumes a large responsibility for the final product. Without getting into the contentious subject of whether or not there are both "good" and "bad" architects and graphic designers, there certainly are practitioners who are concerned about wayfinding, and those who are not. It is our contention, of course, that the former can do a "better" job for the building owners than can the latter.

By "better" we don't mean just prettier. We mean to imply that the wayfinding component is at last being seen as an essential (and not just a peripheral or "nice to have") element in any building complex.

In the commercial real-estate business, there are influential consultants whose function is to advise their clients, from a totally independent perspective, whether a given building is worth the rental costs being charged for it – or not. These consultants have developed over the years an extensive list of several hundred criteria on which they base their evaluations of individual commercial buildings.

Until 1990, wayfinding was not one of these criteria, strange as it may seem. But it is not really so strange when taken in the context of "normal" building practice, which is to hire a designer or sign company to "do" the signs just prior to opening day to provide a series of "grace-notes" for embellishing the building. This, however, *is* fast changing. Wayfinding (in its true sense) is now one of their criteria and is just about as important as any of the others.

After all, when one comes to think of it, why shouldn't it be vital from a tenant's viewpoint that visitors should be able to

- single out and identify the building itself from its neighbor,
- know how and where to enter the building,
- park their vehicles easily, and find their way back to them when they have finished their business,
- understand where they are in the building,
- develop an action plan on the route that they will take to get to the tenant's office or facility,
- execute that plan easily and effectively,
- if redirected, find other offices or facilities in the complex just as easily, and finally,
- quit the premises at the exit of their choice.

The difference between such a building complex and one that has none or only a few of these advantages is that the former has a distinct marketing edge because visitors will feel that it was a pleasure doing business (or shopping or whatever) there and will want to come back again. There is real evidence to show, by contrast, that people will deliberately avoid, if they have the choice, building complexes that ignore the wayfinding component.

7.2.2 Building managers

The proliferation of signs is to no one's advantage. Not the designer, who is invariably blamed for lousing up a building with "too many" signs. Not the architect, who regards them as "unnecessary." Not the owner, who must pay for them and maintain them. And last, but far from least, not the public, which, at best, is merely bemused when confronted by "too many" signs.

The question of why there are so many signs (if indeed there are) is rarely asked, and just as rarely answered. Here are a few topics on this subject that relate to the way the building is managed (as distinct from the way it was built and whether the wayfinding component was considered in its planning):

- At every decision point en route to destinations that requires a sign, the question to ask is whether visitors are routed in a manner that requires the minimum number of decisions; are they, in other words, being routed inefficiently?
- If the wheelchair route is different from the pedestrian, will that account for even more signs?
- In an office building or a hospital, are departments, branches, or divisions that provide analogous services grouped together? Is "X-ray" all over the building? Are the "employee benefits" offices all in more or less one location or are they not? If they are, they form a series of "destination zones" and wayfinding is much easier (and efficient in terms of the number of signs required) than when this is not the case.

It may, however, not always be "convenient" to create logical groupings of services, departments, or facilities within a complex. Frequently, it is much more convenient to allocate space to each of them according to what is available. This is, however, bad practice from a wayfinding viewpoint. Management should recognize that the cost for this is more signs – and less efficient wayfinding.

This then identifies the trade-offs. To opt for the "convenient" in terms of what is available may result in lost time by staff in constantly redirecting visitors to correct addresses, and lost time by clients and visitors in missed appointments, all of which results in people avoiding the building altogether if they can.

Such pathetic little notes are anathema to building managers who generally have them speedily removed. They are, however, cries for help which should be heeded. Something is radically wrong with the whole system when these signs start to proliferate.

7.2.3 Security personnel and fire marshals

Fire and security officers have their own rules and expertise. In cases of emergency, they have the prime responsibility for getting people to safety.

Judging by most contemporary research however, some safety and emergency procedures are based upon assumptions of behavior that are not always supported in reality.

The insistence on "special" fire exits is a case in point. Another is the continuing insistence that the color of safety is red. Given the extraordinary symbolic potency of color in our everyday lives, the idea that the same color (red) will serve equally well for STOP, Danger!, and prohibition, as well as for fire protection is illogical to the point of perversity and flies in the face of many national and international standards. (These issues are dealt with in more detail in Chapters 9 and 13.)

For whom do we plan?

Architects and graphic designers have tended to see the user of their settings as a stereotyped, physically fit, attentive individual, with only one preoccupation – to explore and enjoy the settings they have created. The reality, however, is quite different. Many users have impairments in respect to perception, cognition, and mobility (physical behavior), which affect their wayfinding abilities. Some of these impairments are permanent, some are temporary; some are slight, some are profound.

This chapter provides an overview of user groups and reviews some of the major impairments affecting wayfinding. It concludes with a philosophical position in respect to designing for the handicapped and the so-called normal population.

8.1 User groups

The idea that there are user groups is in itself a fairly new one. In the "old days" (which, in fact, by any other standard would be called recent), we used to treat "users" as a single homogeneous group. Researchers, however, have known for a long time that there is nothing homogeneous or uniform about users of the built environment – particularly in terms of their abilities to assimilate and process environmental information.

It is therefore time that we stopped designing for some vague (and imaginary) able-bodied "user" and started to concern ourselves with a much broader but more realistically focused view of user groups that are the ultimate consumers of everything that we design, build, fabricate, and install.

The accompanying definitions give a short description of the user groups to be considered in wayfinding design. Without doubt, it would be instructive to be able to attach precise numbers to each of these user groups. In this way we could develop some impressive statistics in support of why we should be designing in order to satisfy the needs of all the people and not just some of them.

Hard data, however, are virtually unobtainable. What we have tends to be unreliable and frequently contradictory. Information on numbers of persons with multiple disabilities is even more difficult to get. In any case, statistics are not really the issue. Even a humble statistic (e.g., .05 percent of the population), when related to 275 million people, is no mean statistic. It relates, in the case of persons with speech impediments for example, to 137, 500 persons in North America.

8.2 The unimpaired user

The category of "unimpaired" is difficult to define. Some elderly citizens who have reduced vision and hearing may be on the borderline. A person who is angry, confused, or distraught may momentarily show signs of cognitive impairment. The user who is pushing a stroller or a cart or carrying a heavy load may classify as mobility impaired. Nobody is always "unimpaired."

8.3 Perceptual impairment

Visual impairments and blindness are the most obvious and most severe perceptual impairments affecting wayfinding. It is estimated that close to 1 percent of the population is visually impaired and that about 20 percent of these are totally blind. Nearly a third of persons with low vision are over the age of 65. Many of them also suffer from other impairments associated with aging. About one in ten men and one in fifty women have color deficiency, in most cases in the red/green range.

People with a hearing impairment (approximately 4 percent of the population, according to the Canadian Health and Disability Survey) also have specific wayfinding difficulties, which, however, are less well documented. According to the Canadian Hearing Society, 2 percent of the hearing impaired are deaf, which repre-

Unimpaired
unimpaired: adults without serious perceptual, mental, or physical disabilities

Perceptual impairment
sight impaired: persons with poor eyesight, partial vision, or anomalies of vision such as color deficiency and reduced field

blind: persons without useful vision

hearing impaired: persons who have a moderate to severe hearing loss, and have to rely on hearing aids

deaf: persons who have a profound hearing loss

Cognitive impairment
situationally impaired: persons who are in a temporary state of anger, apprehension, confusion, or distress caused by a particular situation or environment; persons overloaded with information

developmentally impaired: persons who are learning-disabled, mentally retarded, or mentally disturbed; elderly persons who have reduced cognitive abilities

Literacy impaired
literacy impaired: persons who are functionally illiterate in the language in which the message in an information display is expressed

Mobility impairment
mobility impaired who can walk: persons who have impaired strength, endurance, dexterity, balance, or coordination; persons using crutches or other walking aids; persons with strollers or carts; persons with heart or other conditions that reduce mobility but are not apparent to others

mobility impaired in wheelchairs: persons who are permanently or temporarily restricted to wheelchairs

sents about .08 percent of the population as a whole. Speech impairment can also result from hearing impairment, particularly if hearing loss occurred at a very young age.

Both perceptual impairments can lead to wayfinding difficulties of such magnitude that the persons concerned do not use difficult settings. These wayfinding difficulties become a form of barrier, not as visible as an architectural barrier is for a wheelchair user, but just as effective.

8.3.1 Visual impairment and blindness

A recent series of studies on mobility and wayfinding of the visually impaired and blind population found that only about half of the visually impaired population in the Montreal area consider large public buildings to be accessible to them. The accessibility rate for the blind population falls to about 10 percent.[1]

Interestingly enough, a wayfinding assessment study of large public buildings found that the staff responsible for the overall functioning of the setting thought that blind people did not have any wayfinding difficulties in their building because, as they observed, the blind never come alone; they are always with a person who guides them. This vividly demonstrates that the plight of the sensory-impaired population is still far from being understood. Of course, it is always much easier to say that something does not work, while it is so much more difficult to make it do so.

In respect to the visually impaired and blind population one could ask what information is needed for their wayfinding requirements[2] and, even more importantly, whether they need a specially designed environment in order to get around independently. A specially designed environment can be justified only if a particular user group (such as the visually impaired or blind) has to engage in a special wayfinding process or has to rely on totally different environmental information in order to make and execute wayfinding decisions. Research (by Romedi Passini) in the last few years has been aimed at addressing some of these matters.

Concerning the decision-making and decision-executing process, we found decision plans of the congenitally totally blind – who are the most handicapped group in the sense that they have never had a visual experience – to be quite similar in nature to those of a sighted control group. They differed only in the sense that the blind group prepared for a journey in more detail and that during the journey, they also *made* more decisions than the sighted control group and used more environmental information.

This difference is explained by the blind person's reduced distance perception. While a sighted person can actually see a destination, such as the end of a corridor, a blind person has to refer to a series of intermediate reference points which he or she can perceive only by ear or touch.[3]

Of course it can be, and has been, argued that a congenitally blind person has no visual imagery and therefore is not able to have any conception of space. It should be noted that the term

Legal blindness is defined as a visual acuity with the best corrective lenses of 20/200 or less. A person with 20/200 vision would have to be within 20 feet (or less) of a particular scene to see what a person with normal vision can see 200 feet away.

Tunnel vision is an angle of vision of 20 degrees or less, as compared with the 55 degrees for normally sighted people.

64

imagery (a common alternative to cognitive map) has a distinct visual flavor. In accordance with what is called a deficiency theory, cognitive mapping of large spaces during wayfinding is not possible for such people. This argument extends the perceptual handicap to that of a cognitive handicap.

Numerous studies have, however, shown that even a congenitally totally blind person is capable of reproducing a path learned in a wayfinding experience.[4] We were able to corroborate this result and to show furthermore that the congenitally blind were also able to perform all of the spatio-cognitive operations necessary for wayfinding. They were able to learn a route and to invert it to reach the point of origin. They could combine learned routes into new journeys, learn a route on a small model, and then execute the journey in the actual setting. They could point to locations visited earlier on a journey, make shortcuts, and make spatial rotations to fit a non-aligned map with a setting. Finally, they could identify spatial organizations, such as symmetries, in a real setting.[5]

Blind travellers have to rely on auditory and tactile cues. Only in rare circumstances can they use olfactory or heat perception. All of the senses compensating for sight are generally less informative, less reliable, and less efficient. Nothing replaces sight in gaining a global understanding of the environment or in perceiving distant cues which are so important for wayfinding.

Hearing is the prime mode of perception for the blind, but the objects composing our physical environment tend to be silent. They become audible only through direct contact or reflecting sounds. This in itself reduces the compensatory value of sound perception for the blind.[6] In addition, sound is not as informative as sight. It is often difficult to localize a sound source, especially if the cue is of short duration. Sounds work very well as warning signals, however; even a small cracking sound can have a startling effect.

Even with its shortcomings, however, auditory perception is most important to the mobile blind person and it has to be optimized as much as possible. Background noise has to be controlled as it is enemy number one of auditory perception.

The blind person entering a public setting, such as a commercial or transportation center, often finds it very difficult to extract any useful information from the generalized noise that is so common to these places. Background noise drowns auditory cues coming from an original sound source and renders echo-location impossible. Background noise has also been described by blind people as having a generally disorienting effect. They observed that such noise makes walking in a straight line even more difficult. The same is said for strong air currents, which are often encountered at the entrances of underground subway systems.

Public settings should be designed so that people, including the blind, can find their way around efficiently. A supplementary service of personnel trained to guide blind travelers to their destinations will, however, always be appreciated. It is important to the blind person's autonomy to be able to reach a setting independently. Once there, additional help for those who require it is a bonus.

The warning message carried by certain sounds tends to impose an emotional dimension on auditory perception for the blind. The sighted person can always visually check what the warning is about and whether it has to be taken seriously or not. The blind person, however, has to guess and wait for an additional signal – just like somebody being frightened at night.

To give verbal wayfinding information to a blind person is not as easy as it might sound. It has been our experience that it works much better the other way round. Blind people usually remember street names, and their descriptions of places are often much clearer and more precise than are the descriptions given by the sighted. Quite apart from using visual cues, the sighted population puts less effort into understanding settings in order to get around, and this affects information giving. It is therefore suggested that training for people working in information booths include wayfinding communication to the blind.

The energy and attention required from a mobile blind traveler is enormous. Many blind people, when reaching middle age, feel drained of energy and exhausted by the tasks of wayfinding in unfamiliar as well as in familiar environments. Even just from a humane point of view, architects and graphic designers ought to take into consideration the needs of this population, both to facilitate mobility and to reduce the risks of accidents.

"Visual residue" is a generic term that covers various visual handicaps. Individuals may have a low acuity of the whole visual field, such as blurred vision due to cataracts. They may perceive only part of the visual field. Some may experience "night blindness" in poorly illuminated settings. Some may be temporarily blinded from strong light contrasts.

Certain design criteria can facilitate the perception of relevant wayfinding information for the visually impaired, among the most important:

• The use of strong color and brightness contrasts in signage
• The avoidance of contrasts as well as of glare in the general level of illumination
• Visual and tactile definitions of main circulation routes to set them apart from open areas
• The pairing of visual with non-visual sensory information

These criteria for facilitating visual perception will also benefit the population at large and the elderly in particular.

Up to this point, it could be argued that if a setting is well designed for the population in general, it will also work reasonably well for the visually impaired and blind population. We say "reasonably well" because there are still some minor interventions that will greatly benefit the blind population. Blind people, for example, have difficulties traversing large open spaces without some form of directional guide. They need warning signals in order not to collide with obstacles or fall into openings. These are, however, minor design interventions and do not need to affect the overall design approach.

8.3.2 Hearing impairment and deafness

The wayfinding difficulties encountered by the hearing-impaired population are not commonly known. Over 1 percent of the population uses hearing aids. They have two types of physical problems in public settings. The first is due to magnetic interference; motors and transformers, for example, cause static interference, which can render the use of a hearing aid just about impossible. The other problem is caused by the difficulty in separating background noise from the desired message. The discrimination of useful from useless sounds is more difficult for those using a hearing aid.

A deaf person, in order to communicate, has to rely on written messages, sign language, or lipreading. The last of these would seem to be most used when obtaining information from a non-deaf person. Lipreading can be made difficult by insufficient lighting or by the physical and behavioral idiosyncrasies of the person giving the information.

Some of the deaf might have difficulties understanding the sense of spoken and written words. Their vocabulary tends to be more action oriented. Abstractions and words describing concepts may not be readily understood. The common saying that it is worse to be deaf than to be blind (although who would want to have to choose?) is rooted in the difficulty not only of communicating but also of understanding. It should be noted, however, that a study comparing the spatial understanding of deaf and non-deaf people demonstrated that the deaf had a *better* spatial knowledge than the non-impaired control group.[7]

One of the major problems common to all handicapped groups, including the deaf, is of a psychological nature. Some people feel ashamed of their handicap or find the emotional effort to get information too great for the reward. A concerted effort on the design and educational sides will probably lead to a reduction in the problem. Confidence is built up over time by the feedback of rewarding experiences. Wayfinding design can contribute to the reinforcing effect and thus affect the well-being of everyone.

8.4 Cognitive impairment

Cognitive impairments, again, range from temporary confusion due to information overload or stress, to more or less severe incapacities which can be due to disease, accident, age, or mental retardation. Cognitive impairment can affect linguistic abilities independently from spatial abilities.

The nature and the gravity of the impairments are too diverse to be covered within the framework of this book.

8.4.1 Situational cognitive impairment

This category includes persons who, by reason of their psychological state, may experience difficulties in processing environmental information and making appropriate wayfinding decisions besides those directly related to vision, hearing, or literacy.

Everybody by virtue of being human is "situationally impaired" at one time or another. People who are visiting public buildings by reason of being unemployed or having their taxes straightened out may be more likely to be distracted or distressed by their anger, confusion, or apprehension. A particularly important issue is possible situational impairment as a result of stress, as it might be experienced when facing danger or when having to evacuate a setting during an emergency.

8.4.2 Developmental cognitive impairment

Development refers to the whole life span. Its impairment may affect the learning abilities of the young child or result in the loss of cognitive abilities in the elderly.

Most people have heard about dyslexia. However, the full range of learning disabilities is very much larger than that, including the impairment of the ability to calculate or do math, dysgraphia (impairment of the ability to write), and a host of other conditions, some of which (such as difficulty in left/right discrimination) have a direct bearing on our subject, while others do not.

Estimates on the number of learning-disabled persons go as high as one in ten; however, accurate figures are impossible to obtain because many learning disabilities are never recognized as such, and few people acknowledge that they have them.

Dementia caused by Alzheimer's disease and related disorders affect an important section of the elderly population. It is estimated that approximately 1 percent of North Americans suffer from dementia which is considered to be the fourth leading cause of death. Alzheimer's is an irreversible degenerative disease of the brain which disables various cognitive functions at different rates.[8] Some of its earliest manifestations are confusion, memory loss, and disorientation with respect to time and space. Alzheimer's patients tend to forget recent events while keeping some of their longterm memory. They tend to wander and easily get lost. Wandering is particular to Alzheimer's. Gilleard (1984) identified three causes: activity seeking, habitual walking behavior, and disorientation.

What is the cause of disorientation? Some researchers explain it as a general loss of memory and cognitive abilities; others assume that the degeneration is selective and that the spatial abilities are particularly prone.

Among the spatio-cognitive abilities, it is those requiring higher-order representations that are struck first. Alzheimer's patients may still be able to operate efficiently, although at a more elementary level. It is also assumed that Alzheimer's patients are not able to process high levels of information. If they do operate at the limits of their capacities, they can experience stress and overload.

The therapeutic objective in institutions, on the other hand, is to support the highest level of functional utility in order to reinforce competence and self esteem. These considerations point to an optimal middle ground in which the environment is stimulating without being overbearing. Alzheimer's patients seem to require a specialized environment, which, as we have indicated, can have therapeutic functions. For example, rather then trying to eliminate wandering, the provision of safe and well-defined wandering paths has been suggested.[9]

In order to facilitate wayfinding, the design of a setting should include clearly defined paths to destinations and should incorporate striking landmarks. Visual accessibility of the site itself is also important. In planning the wayfinding concept, additional design ideas should be introduced on an experimental basis. In order to facilitate the wayfinding task, the designers should attempt to reduce the number of decisions along the paths and, even more importantly, they should provide environmental information that does not require higher-order manipulations.

8.5 Illiteracy

8.5.1 Functional illiteracy

Many more people are functionally illiterate than one would like to think. Hard statistics based on actual ability are virtually impossible to obtain because illiteracy, in our society, is generally considered a shameful subject.

If we describe a person who cannot read and write sufficiently well to fill a job application as illiterate, we may estimate the illiteracy rate at 20 percent. Typographic signs are by no means completely useless to this group. Many of them are able to read a little, or at least to recognize certain key words from their shape or their first letter.

We all are illiterate in some ways and in some situations. If we expand the meaning of illiteracy to include an inability to read a written message in a given language, we have to include in the illiterate group anybody visiting a foreign country who does not speak its language and we also have to include children of pre-school age.

Symbols and pictographs are the obvious alternative to written messages. They have demonstrated their usefulness in coping with international visitors in settings such as world fairs, airports, and public transport terminals – provided their content is limited to very simple concepts such as washrooms, phones, or baggage claims.

Pictorial language, like any other, has to be based on a set of recognized elements, and this implies a certain level of standardization of content. For years, European railway stations have used the same sort of pictographs to identify baggage claims, money exchange, waiting rooms, and other facilities. These signs are now well understood by everyone and they are as effective as verbal descriptions.

Symbols and pictographs also have their shortcomings, however. There are limits on what can be described or identified in a pictograph and there is also a limit to the number of different pictographs that can be used in a sign. This issue is discussed in further detail in Chapter 13.

8.5.2 Multi-lingual illiteracy

As observed earlier, we are all likely to find ourselves functionally illiterate at one time or another. Visiting a foreign country is one of them; living in an officially bilingual country like Canada is

During a recent visit to Japan, I (Romedi Passini) was made painfully aware of what it means not to be able to rely on written messages. Looking for a railway station, for example, I could read neither the directional signs leading to it nor the inscription identifying it. I had to rely on features of landscaping and on the architecture of the buildings. Some buildings expressed their function quite clearly, while others did not even arouse any suspicion of their being railway stations.

Architectural language becomes one of the major means of communication for the illiterate wayfinder.

Japan is a very well-organized country. Having traveled by train for ten days, I discovered punctuality and found the trains to be so reliable that all I needed to know for boarding was the time and the platform of departure. Arriving at the destination was even easier. The time table and a watch were all I needed. This works only if the traveler finds a reliable alternative to the unreadable written messages. I don't suggest that anybody try to use the bus service in North America on such a basis.

another. It is, therefore, appropriate to discuss the design of signs that must display more than a single language within the context of "illiteracy."

Given that there is a limit to how many "chunks" of information a sign may contain, how can all the "extra" messages be accommodated? The answer, in many cases, is that they can't.

Bilingual traffic signs are considered a political necessity in Canada's capital city, Ottawa – but they are dreadful. They manage to be both illegible *and* unreadable (which in itself is no mean feat).

Ottawa, like other cities, has streets that must be designated as east or west, north or south. These descriptions are invariably translated in full (nord, sud, etc.), but in an awkward manner: in letters that are less than half the size of the street name, over and under each other. To make everything worse, words such as street, drive, and parkway are also translated. All of this must be somehow miraculously assimilated by motorists (who may be tourists from somewhere else) at highway driving speeds.

The problem is that a wrong-headed attempt is made for simultaneous translation which, however praiseworthy in political forums, is ludicrous (and potentially dangerous) on a sign.

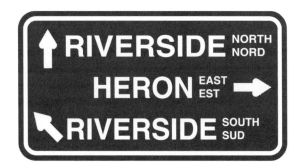

A typical Canadian attempt at bilingualism in highway signs – with altogether predictable results.

The original sign on the left demonstrates all that is hopeless about attempts to combine bilingualism with readablility.

There is too much copy, too many arrows on the French side, and none on the English.

Given, however, the need for such signs, the sign on the right is at least better.

By contrast, the signs in Gatineau Park (erected by the National Capital Commission), across the river from Ottawa, make no such attempt. They are bilingual, but they separate the languages into localized areas on the signs, generally side by side.

Even so, these Gatineau road signs may contain up to six or more destinations (some requiring several words each), in three directions, and the result is too much of a muchness for anyone – particularly as each sign is entirely black with white letters and arrows.

Even when it is a part of the designer's intent that signs must be black and white, it would make an enormous difference if one language were white on a black field, with the second language in the reverse order, black on white, and if the two were side by side, or, when necessary, over and under. Then, providing there is consistency in the presentation of the material with one or the other language version always being on, say, the left and the other on the right, the viewers would have a chance to focus on the left or right side of the sign for their information.

By extension, it would even be possible to imagine trilingual signs with the language versions alternating consistently across the signface in positive and negative form. It would not be good signage, but it would be tolerable at least.

There is, however, another method for a bilingual situation, which is simply to double the numbers of signs (never a popular idea) and dedicate each to providing information in one language only. This may be practical in pedestrian situations, but on highways it would mean separating the signs by a minimum distance of some 750 feet (225 m).

Something that must be considered when reversing type out of a dark background is the halation effect. Halation (see section 13.1.7) is the visual phenomenon by which shapes viewed in

US Border Station
El Paso, Texas

US Customs Service   US Immigration Service

Estación de Inspección
fronteriza de EUA

Servicio de Aduano   Servicio de Inmigración

A bilingual sign in which languages are separated by color (blue on white or white on blue). Note how much bolder the negative letters appear to be than the positive ones. They are, in fact, the same weight. General Services Administration, Washington, DC, 1974, Paul Arthur.

reverse or negative form seem to swell, while those viewed in positive form seem to shrink. The undesirable result is that one message will appear to be in a medium weight of type, while the other will appear to be in a bold weight of type.

The problem of directions (of which there may be three: left, right, or straight ahead) must also be addressed in bilingual signs. We are always in danger of overloading the viewer with information, and while two separate language versions in one sign is bad enough, it is immeasurably complicated by having to cope with three directions as well.

We deal elsewhere (see section 13.4) with the issue of layout for directional signs. It is enough here to remark that it is desirable (if not always feasible) in all signs, unilingual and even more so bilingual, to separate pedestrian-related directions into individual signs. At decision points in corridors, for example, it is better to have left-pointing information in one sign and right-pointing in another, if it can be managed.

← Departures   Départs
Arrivals   Arrivées →

Even in bilingual countries designers have trouble with messages in more than one language. This Canadian classic was eventually withdrawn after someone noticed that what it *seemed* to be saying was that French- and English-speaking passengers had to use different facilities.

8.6 Mobility impairment

8.6.1 Persons in wheelchairs

Governments have a special responsibility in trying to create a favorable atmosphere for the barrier-free design of buildings. In the United States, leadership has been shown in setting up a regulatory body, called the President's Committee on Architectural and Transportation Barriers Compliance Board (ATBCB). In Canada, our prime ministers have shown no such interest, and we must look for leadership at considerably lower levels. The federal departments of public works and of transport have both taken active interests in barrier-free design.

In a wayfinding assessment study of public buildings the authors did for Donald Henning of Public Works Canada, we found that, if wheelchair users did not have access through the main door, not only were their access routes much longer but their journeys required up to twice as many decisions when compared to their pedestrian counterparts.[10]

The number of decisions that have to be made is a rough indicator of the difficulty of a wayfinding task. Each decision requires a mental effort and involves the risk of making a mistake. To make the situation even more difficult, wayfinding information required by wheelchair users was often missing. These extra routes tend to escape the designers' attention.

In this study, as might be expected, we came across a lot of minor design problems. Access to information from the height of a wheelchair, for example, was shown to be difficult when horizontal displays are used. In addition, reflections are often accentuated from a wheelchair perspective, which creates a screening mirror (or veiling glare) effect. Control buttons are often inaccessible from a wheelchair, a problem that is still common in elevators.

Probably the major problems facing wheelchair users, however, are still physical architectural barriers such as stairs, overly steep ramps, and heavy doors, all of which pose problems of accessibility.

It can safely be said that if mobility-impaired users in wheelchairs have access to a setting by the same routes as able-bodied users, their specific wayfinding problems are reduced to relatively few and minor considerations, such as the access to information displays, as mentioned above.

8.6.2 Mobility impaired who can walk

We tend to forget that the largest number of mobility-impaired persons are those who can actually walk, although with difficulty. They may, for example, be on crutches or in walkers. Then there are obese and elderly people whose mobility is also impaired.

A common denominator for all mobility-impaired persons, whether in wheelchairs or not, is that their cones of vision are restricted, or lowered. People in wheelchairs, for example, share the problems children have in that their eyes are closer to the ground than are those of standing adults. Hence, their cones of vision are considerably lowered. Crutches, on the other hand, tend to alter posture in a radical way, so that instead of looking straight ahead as they walk, people on crutches in all probability direct their vision downward. For these and other reasons we strongly recommend a maximum height for signs to be off the floor (see section 15.4) in an attempt to strike a reasonable compromise that will accommodate everyone.

Access to information is crucial for the mobility impaired. Signs that are up even a small flight of stairs (and that are not duplicated at the bottom) are, of course, useless. Signs that are not legible from the distance at which they are intended to be seen may not be useless, but they do require additional (and unnecessary) movement.

Veiling glare off signs (which effectively renders them illegible) may be worse at the eye level of persons in wheelchairs than for standing people. And whereas the able bodied can usually maneuver about to avoid the effects of glare, persons in wheelchairs have much more difficulty doing so. People on crutches may have even less maneuverability.

Signs are routinely obscured on the ground by planters and on the ceiling by ductwork or even by other signs. Again, the unimpaired can make efforts to cope with this (assuming that they see the signs are there at all), but the disabled have much more difficulty in seeing that the signs are there or in doing anything about catching a glimpse of them.

8.7 Macro- and micro-approaches to planning

"Access to information" is what it's all about and, in the light of the new-found interest in, and concern for, the problems of the disabled, the question arises: How do we go about planning environmental communications in the first place?

Selwyn Goldsmith distinguishes two different design approaches.[11] The "macro-approach" sets a high standard within which the disabled are treated as "normal." Their needs, in terms of physical requirements, are accounted for as a matter of course. The usual provisions for the whole population become accommodating for them as well. The macro-approach tries to make all buildings accessible to all types of users.

In the "micro-approach," however, the disabled person is treated as a special case with specific requirements which can be accommodated only by provisions made especially for them. This approach leads to the creation of selected settings, specifically designed for the very special needs of the handicapped.

Discussions about the wayfinding requirements of the disabled population tend to favor the macro-approach for the design of public buildings. It is only for very severe cognitive disabilities, such as Alzheimer's disease, that a specialized environment becomes necessary. To plan for the population as a whole helps the general public and especially the majority of elderly persons who may have several different impediments.

Chapter 8
For whom do we plan?
8.7 Macro- and micro-approaches to planning

The macro-approach assures a higher overall standard of planning; moreover, it does not create artificial barriers between population groups and does not ostracize the handicapped.

The design of accessible and safe settings is now a political issue. It is only thanks to pressure groups, spearheaded by wheelchair users in the early 70s, that the population as a whole and politicians in particular have been made aware of the issue.

From the political point of view, the macro-approach would seem to be more acceptable than the micro. It is always easier to ask for a provision that benefits the population as a whole than to ask for one that benefits only a specific group because, even if that group has every right to make such a request, it tends to be perceived as a special favor.

The macro-approach to planning does not preclude small adjustments when they are needed. Although planning standards should be based on the requirements of the population as a whole, circumstances may require that minor interventions be initiated for a given disabled population.

In line with our own support for the macro-approach, the authors have chosen not to write a special chapter on "wayfinding and the disabled population." Rather, we incorporate references to their normal and some of their specific requirements in the body of the text.

Chapter 9
Planning for wayfinding conditions

In terms of the strictest orthodoxy, wayfinding conditions are described as normal (or "resolute"), recreational, or emergency. Normal wayfinding conditions are those in which the provisions for wayfinding in a given setting are measured exclusively in terms of their efficiency and utility. Recreational wayfinding conditions, by contrast, call for the ability to explore and enjoy a given setting. And hanging like a pall over both are the emergency conditions that can and do happen at any time, anywhere.

9.1 Day-to-day conditions

It is not, of course, as though the planning for "normal" and for "recreational" conditions can be considered to be mutually exclusive. The actual conditions at a given time may be one or the other, but in the planning and design of a setting the designer cannot opt for one over the other.

For example, take something as purely "utilitarian" as a highway. It must be planned to accommodate the business person, who has the sole objective of getting there fast, *and* the family, who wants to get out to explore the beauties of the local countryside. Or take something that seems, at first, to be at the other end of the scale: a park or a zoological garden. These recreational facilities must also be planned to accommodate both conditions. Visitors to a zoo may have come for a day's (or an afternoon's) outing with no particular aim in mind except to enjoy themselves. On the other hand, some visitors may have very definite ideas in mind. They want to see the polar bears, for example. They will be most disappointed if, at the end of their stay, they still haven't found them.

We should no more plan a system for the use of the general public exclusively around "efficiency" or "enjoyment" than we should develop such a system around the disabilities of any one group. The routines that make up our daily lives suggest a less orthodox and possibly more fruitful way of looking at wayfinding conditions. We know that we need wayfinding information to cope with the four major settings, aside from home, that we deal with every day. These are:

- The travel setting, when we are in transit from one place to another
- The work setting
- The recreational setting, when we are at play
- The retail setting, when we are shopping

Each of these environments or settings requires its own kind of wayfinding information.

On the most superficial level, for instance, the conditions of traveling at 90 to 100 feet (30 m) per second on a highway are very different from those of walking along a city street.

But it is more complex than that. However, to deal with each of the four major sets of conditions identified above in any detail is the subject of another volume and must, therefore, be dealt with very superficially here.

9.1.1 Travel conditions

Terminals

Airports, bus, train, and marine terminals, and subway stations are all characterized by a combination of confusion, apprehension, and disorientation. Passengers are, in nearly all cases, deprived of the clues that normally assist them in orienting themselves when they are outside. Added to this is the anxiety of being wrongly directed and thereby missing one's flight or bus – or subway stop. Another factor is the effect of bigness. The sheer, non-human scale

Chapter 9
Planning for wayfinding conditions
9.1 Day-to-day conditions

of some of these transportation facilities is a further condition that needs to be coped with by the designers of such wayfinding systems for passengers.

Major roads
On highways and byways we may be traveling at high speeds. Such conditions impose their own disciplines on the designers of the highways themselves and of the information beside or over them.

Travel information
Travel information systems are the manner in which information is conveyed to motorists in motion (by means of signs), as in Vermont, or at rest (inside information centers), as in Oregon. This could well be the subject of another book. How much information can be effectively conveyed under these conditions? And of what type, and how should it be organized?

City streets
City streets pose problems for motorists or pedestrians when there are no street names at intersections. Inconsistencies of sign placement at intersections, illegibility of street names, and frequently the total lack of visible numbers on houses and buildings are just a few of the conditions that people have to contend with in using the streets of their own cities. When they travel to a strange city, these conditions are more difficult to contend with.

9.1.2 Working conditions

Industrial buildings
In factories, laboratories, and the occupational environment generally, in addition to wayfinding, the condition of what is euphemistically called "loss prevention" must be provided for.

Office buildings
Public or office buildings were at one time just that: discrete buildings that housed offices. Now they are, as often as not, huge complexes, with multiple uses, and they baffle most wayfinders. For example, how do you find the way into buildings for which the architect has, seemingly, provided no doors? How do you tell which building to enter (assuming you can find a door) in a complex comprising not one but five or more absolutely identical – and probably black – buildings?

Health-care facilities
Health-care facilities, from medical clinics to hospitals, create their own special conditions for wayfinders. What makes these conditions in a hospital different from those in an office building? And why, so frequently, do designers treat them as if they were the same?

Educational institutions
Wayfinding in the groves of academe is normally considered exclusively an open-air activity. Signs and other wayfinding devices may be in evidence outside campus buildings. However, the interiors are most frequently labyrinthine in their architecture and without signs. Why?

9.1.3 Playing conditions

Sports facilities
Sports stadia get ever bigger, which in turn creates the condition of hordes of people all attempting to find their individual seats in a vast coliseum in a few minutes before the event commences – and then to find their way back through the vomitoria to transportation home, again all at the same time.

Public parks and zoos
Wayfinding in parks and zoological gardens may not, as we have already observed, be exclusively exploratory. People may have an objective (the polar bear) or they may have time limitations. They may, for example, have only a couple of hours to spend. How can they best enjoy the setting in that amount of time? How can professionals best provide them with information about their options?

Theme parks and fairs
Amusement or theme parks and world fairs create their own conditions also.

9.1.4 Retail conditions

Underground pedestrian malls can be five or more kilometers in length and comprise in excess of a thousand individual enterprises of all kinds from shops to theaters to restaurants to fitness centers and so on. The conditions of being underground and deprived of all the visual clues that we take for granted above ground make their own demands on the wayfinding designer of such spaces.

In a mall setting the designer will be dealing not with any single authority but perhaps with many – all of whom cannot be counted upon to have the same objective. Added to this is old-fashioned, although now largely discredited, notion that people are stimulated to purchase things in direct proportion to the extent to which they don't know where they are. This notion dies hard and explains why there are no clocks in shopping malls and why wayfinding is generally discounted in mall settings. (A well-known Toronto retailer until recently had "COME IN AND GET LOST" emblazoned in huge letters on the front of his store.)

This very cursory review of the myriad conditions that wayfinding designers (and their constituents, the public at large) must cope with is a plea for sensitivity to something we admittedly don't yet know enough about. What, in fact, *are* the effects of these different

Chapter 9
Planning for wayfinding conditions
9.1 Day-to-day conditions

conditions on the planning and design of wayfinding in these settings?

9.2 Emergency conditions

It is commonly assumed that in serious emergency situations people will panic. Jonathan Sime, who has done extensive research on peoples' behavior in fire, has determined that this assumption is basically wrong.

Investigating the behavior of people who had survived fires, Sime found that they tended to behave in a controlled and rational way – as long as they had a hope of getting out and being saved. The rationale for their behavior was not necessarily that of the planning architect or the fire marshal, but of people who had to deal with whatever information they had about the building. It is not, therefore, a sign of irrationality that they tend to move along previously experienced routes and to ignore fire exits.[1]

Any fire marshal will confirm the fact that the single most important factor in saving people's lives in a fire is time. Through the production of combustible (and toxic) gases, fires expand in leaps and bounds. Seconds may make all the difference between life and death. Therefore, to delay the announcement of a fire in a public building for fear that people will panic is not only ill advised, but irresponsible.

Panic is not usually part of wayfinding behavior in emergencies. However, stress is, and stress does affect performance in one of two ways. Depending on the context and the level of stress, stress can either reduce or improve performance.[2]

If stress leads to a high level of anxiety, the effect always tends to be negative.[3] Worrying also consumes energy. Psychological and cognitive resources have to be allocated to deal with anxiety, and these resources are therefore not available for wayfinding.

Furthermore, information that is processed to control anxiety may compete with the relevant wayfinding information, thus creating a condition similar to that of overload. Thus, even if information were available, a person might not be able to absorb it. Consistency in the form and location of environmental communication is the best way to reduce overload.

Stress can be caused by the perception of danger (for example the sight of smoke), by time constraints, and by uncertainty. The danger may be real and the time limitations important.

The only cause of stress that can be reduced is uncertainty. Uncertainty about the person's safety is reduced by keeping people informed of the nature and location of the danger. Uncertainty about escape can be reduced by providing the necessary wayfinding information. Information is the best means of lessening stress.

The overall knowledge people have about the spatial characteristics of the setting with its entrances and exits will probably be their most valuable information. If the setting is well understood by the users – that is, if they have a clear cognitive map, they will not only have all the decision-making information at their disposal, they will also be able to develop alternative options should a particular exit turn out to be barred by hazards.

Fire drills, intended to familiarize people with escape procedures, also make them familiar with fire exits in the building. This advantage has to be counterbalanced by the progressive loss of effectiveness of the fire alarm through repeated drills. People may mistake an emergency situation for a drill and decide that they have more important things to do. Drills, furthermore, can only be used in a setting that houses permanent employees or residents. It would be difficult indeed to imagine a fire drill in a department store or in a large shopping complex.

With increased accessibility of public buildings to the disabled population, new questions of safety emerge. If one advocates a macro-approach to access, then it follows that settings should be designed to standards that allow easy escape for everyone. Of course, we have to make some special provisions so that all the people in a building can be adequately warned of an emergency and have the information at their disposal that will enable them to make – and execute – appropriate wayfinding decisions.

Complex settings, even if they are well designed in terms of wayfinding and have the necessary provisions for the disabled population, still need a plan for evacuation. Large settings usually have fire officers in residence who are responsible for evacuation.

In some countries, such as the United Kingdom, great importance is given to assisted escape. Certain occupants of a setting will be assigned the responsibility of helping an impaired fellow worker to escape. Sime and Gartshore, for example, analyzed the time required to evacuate a wheelchair user through a stairway and have commented on the interference this has with evacuation in general.[4]

Several European countries (France and Italy, to name two) require the frequent and prominent display of *green* (note the color!) "Safe exit arrows" in all public spaces – from department stores to museums to hotel corridors. These point to the closest exit from the building.

To sum up: in terms of emergency wayfinding, information is the answer. It can reduce anxiety, and it can reduce the effects of overload. Finally, information can lead to more efficient escape behavior. However, an important point should be made here: we do not need more information (certainly not more signs). We do, however, need information that is more accurate and relevant to wayfinding.

Settings should be planned with all three wayfinding conditions – normal, recreational, and emergency – in mind, and special escape routes should be eliminated or kept to a minimum. If a setting works well under normal conditions, it will have a better chance of working well in emergency conditions. Special provisions and controls will still be needed, but they are not the key issue. The prime insurance for public safety is good wayfinding design.

Part Four:
Architectural components of wayfinding design

Chapter 10
Spatial planning

The difficulty of a wayfinding task is affected by two major physical factors: the layout of the setting and the quality of the environmental communication. The layout is defined by its spatial content, its form, its organization, and its circulation. Environmental communication includes all of the architectural, audible, and graphic expressions that provide the essential information for wayfinding.

In this chapter we look at the first item, the layout and its planning. The layout of a setting is conceived at a very early stage in the planning process. Wayfinding problems are intimately linked to the configuration of the layout. It is therefore never too early to think about wayfinding.

10.1 The process of planning a layout

Seen from a wayfinding perspective, three phases of spatial planning stand out:

- Identification of the constituent spatial units
- Grouping of spatial units into destination zones
- Organization and linkage of units and zones

Whether planning a new setting or renovating an existing layout, the process is similar, although the relative importance of each phase varies according to the extent of the intervention.

10.1.1 Identifying spaces and their identity

Planners are usually given a design program which specifies the general aims and objectives of a building as well as its content. The content is expressed in terms of general and specific functions. For each function, a spatial area is defined and performance specifications are outlined, such as the control of lighting, temperature, desired levels of social interactions, and ambiance. Wayfinding, unfortunately, is rarely included in performance specifications although it certainly is a function – one that should not be ignored.

People finding their way in complex settings will try to understand what the setting contains and how it is organized. In order to form a mental map of the setting, they have to identify things to map. Among the basic building blocks of cognitive mapping are spatial entities. People can only map these spatial entities if they are distinct, if they have an identity that distinguishes them from surrounding spaces.

Similarly, decision making can only be sustained if destinations and intermediate sub-destinations have an identity distinguishing them from other places. The same applies to decision execution. A place has to be recognized before a decision can be transformed into behavior. Distinctiveness giving places their identity is, thus, a major requirement for wayfinding. This can be achieved by the form and volume of the space that defines architectural and decorative elements and by the use of finishes, light, colors, and graphics.

A rather curious example of distinctiveness is the house within the house of the architectural museum in Frankfurt (see p. 86). The house within takes on a particular meaning by its surprise value. It also symbolizes the elementary habitat which can be seen as the source of architecture. Meaning and symbolic expression clearly reinforce distinctiveness.

Activities and the atmosphere created by people's behavior can create a form of distinctiveness. Although this may be a strong factor to which people are sensitive, it has the disadvantage of not being permanent – of disappearing with the flow of the key occupants. Open-air markets, for example, can give a very strong sense of distinctiveness to an urban square or street for the time of their occupation. Once the stands are taken away, however, the square might not be recognizable to the casual visitor.

Designers have at their disposal a variety of means to create distinctiveness. It is important to note, though, that users will

In designing a home for a new Department of Environmental Graphics and Wayfinding Design, for example, the aims and objectives of the department should be considered. The aims might be to form skilled wayfinding designers and researchers, while the objectives might be for students to acquire a certain knowledge base and design skills. The aims and objectives are achieved by curriculum activities as well as support behaviors of the members of the organization, which might include atelier work, courses, seminars, conferences, library services, and maintenance. It is in respect of these activities that spaces are identified.

A main reason for the difficulty in understanding labyrinths is their absence of spatial identity. When a person walks through a uniform labyrinth, each zone looks just the same as the one visited before. The absence of spatial identity leaves the user without building blocks to construct a cognitive map or to form an overall image of the layout.

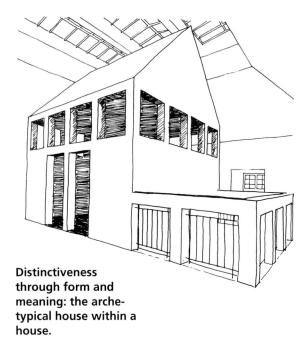

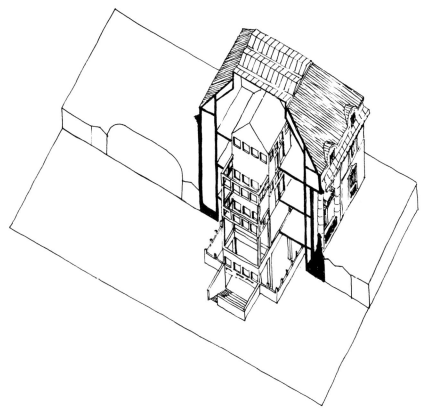

Distinctiveness through form and meaning: the archetypical house within a house.

Museum of Architecture, Frankfurt, Germany,1983, Oswald Matthias Ungers in association with Heinrich Klotz.

Excessive zoning laws at the urban scale have been associated with the often over-planned, sterile environments of new towns. It should be noted that even in mixed planning, a certain grouping is necessary. The early new towns can be seen as an excessive application of the functional principle.

Grouping is also an act of classification that helps the designer to gain an initial understanding of the setting to be planned.

probably not notice them all. For this reason, the redundancy principle, which advises us to use multiple means to express important information, is important in wayfinding design.

10.1.2 Grouping spaces into destination zones

In the second phase of the planning process, similar functions tend to be grouped together according to the following rationales:

- The need for human contact or privacy
- The necessity for information exchange
- The sharing of certain services

This basic grouping in respect to functions establishes a primary order in a complex setting. The bubble diagram and its derivations are traditional tools for establishing this functional order among the required facilities.

Let us now slip into the wayfinding shoes of some potential users. When visiting a setting, users do not think in terms of functions, nor do they have access to a bubble diagram. Users think of destinations and see them as specific facilities – a particular office, a type of shop, the washrooms, or whatever. Each individual space in a setting is a potential destination.

Any complex setting has a great number of destinations, and if it were not for the grouping of similar destinations into zones it would be very difficult for people to find their way. Just imagine a building, such as a hospital, in which each room was allocated by chance. Clearly it would be total chaos, and even with the most sophisticated information system it would be impossible to guide staff, patients, and visitors to their destinations.

Destination zones operate at different levels. Let us introduce this notion with the help of an everyday example: a person shopping for a particular food item in an urban context. In order to buy, let's be extravagant, a rare Russian caviar in a complex multi-purpose downtown facility, the person will probably consider the shopping area as a first destination zone which distinguishes itself from other zones such as office or residential. Within the shopping zone, the person will look for a sub-zone that groups food products, for example, a supermarket. Even at that level we can consider the speciality counter to be a sub-zone of the supermarket. Destination zones are therefore composed of sub-destination zones which are in turn composed of sub-sub-destination zones.

The proper articulation of destination zones affects wayfinding in two ways. It facilitates the cognitive mapping process by emphasizing the spatial units to be mapped, and it supports the decision-making process. Looking at decision diagrams, we find that in complex buildings, "to reach a major destination zone" is a higher-order decision.

It is crucial that wayfinders be able to identify certain spatial characteristics that allow them to group destinations into zones. Like any other grouping or classification, two forces are at work: identity and equivalence.

Identity, as we have already outlined, is the characteristic that allows us to differentiate one space from another. *Equivalence* is the characteristic that allows us to group them into zones along some common traits. In order to distinguish one destination zone from another, the zones must have distinct features, but the spatial units within a zone have to have some common characteristics.

The spaces needed for a particular function usually share certain physical characteristics. All shops, for example, have something in common. By grouping spaces according to their functions, the designer creates destination zones which distinguish themselves from other zones.

Large unifunctional settings, on the other hand, may not have distinguishable destination zones. Visitors tend to be faced with almost insurmountable difficulties in mapping the setting because everything looks more or less the same. Uniformity does not favor decision making.

In a previous chapter we said that spatial planning sets the stage for wayfinding. The truth of this statement is brought out again. The development of an adequate signage system depends on a clear identification of destination zones. Where else can you direct people?

In some large commercial complexes, designers have successfully introduced "artificial" destination zones by giving each zone a particular character that is not necessarily related to its function. Metro Centre in Newcastle, England, with its "three miles of spacious shopping malls," over 350 shops, and "free parking for 10, 000 cars," is one of the world's largest commercial complexes. Although it is essentially unifunctional, it contains (and advertises)

Identity and equivalence: the laws of classification.

87

Chapter 10
Spatial planning
10.1 The process of planning a layout

special areas such as the Mediterranean Village, the Roman Forum, the Garden Court, and the Antique Village. These zones are planned to be attractions but they also fulfil the function of destination zones.

Destination zones in unifunctional settings; Metro Centre, Newcastle, England.

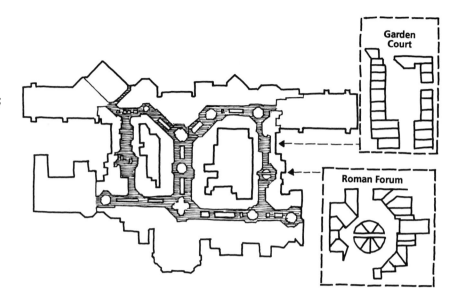

Destination zone: the Garden Court.

Destination zone: the Roman Forum.

While most new settings are planned by grouping similar functions, this order is often not maintained during the lifespan of an existing setting when adjustments are made in response to changing needs. An expanding department, for example, may want to relocate facilities to where more room is available, which may be on a different floor in a different wing.

If this "filling in vacancies" policy is adopted over the years in an unrestrained fashion, the setting will deteriorate into a wayfinding nightmare. It has been our experience that the administration in such cases tends to blame the signage – not realizing that their own chaotic planning is the main source of the problem.

The breaking up and diffusion of destination zones is a major problem in complex and dynamic organizations.[1] To intervene retroactively once such diffusion has occurred is often very difficult as it implies moving departments from one area of the setting to another.

The administrators of these settings have to be made aware of the danger of indiscriminate space allocation. They have to understand that reorganization may well be necessary and that redesign of the signage system alone will not solve the underlying problem.

It might be suggested that such reorganization of a setting be considered a long-term goal. There is, however, always the danger in such cases that "later" turns out to be "never."

10.1.3 Linking and organizing spaces

The third planning step – and by far the most difficult one – is to link the spatial units that have been identified as having functional relationships. This, of course, is the big creative quantum leap.

The leap, metaphorically speaking, can go in one of two directions. It can take off from the circulation system and end up with an overall form, or it can start with the form and end up with the circulation system. Whichever way, form and circulation are closely related.

In respect to wayfinding, the form of a building's volume is particularly instructive. It provides the users with cues about the internal organization and the circulation system.

Underground settings, because they lack an accessible exterior form, are known to be difficult to map even when their internal organization is relatively simple. Exterior form gives a setting an objectlike quality, which is easy to grasp and to retain. Even the names of famous buildings such as the Empire State Building in New York or St Peter's in Rome immediately evoke objectlike images. The issue of providing the user with adequate information through the form of the setting is discussed in Chapter 11, Architectural Wayfinding Communication.

The circulation is, without doubt, the key organizing force of a layout. We like to think of the circulation system as the bone structure of a setting. The bone structure is the organizing feature of a body. The circulation system is equally determining for the layout of the setting.

A bone structure is also very informative. By looking at the skeletons of dinosaurs in a paleontology museum we can usually determine much about what the animals looked like, how they moved, what they ate, and so on. Similarly, if we understand the circulation system, we can also understand the spatial organization of the setting and its architecture.

The circulation system is also the space in which people move and in which they have to find their way. Thus it is this space that we try to understand and it is in this space that we have to make our wayfinding decisions.

In the following section we present an overview of the basic types of circulation systems and their related spatial organization. This will serve as a basis for discussing the features that make these organizations wayfinding-friendly.

Down to the bare bones.

10.2 A typology of circulation systems
The typology is based on the physical characteristics of circulation systems which may be categorized as follows:

- Linear circulations
- Centralized circulations
- Composite circulations
- Circulation networks

For each type we shall identify the underlying organizational pattern.[2]

10.2.1 Linear circulation systems

Single paths

Moving through a setting is a linear affair. The most fundamental circulation space, not surprisingly, is the path. But there are paths and there are paths. They may be wide or narrow, short or long, straight, angled, or curved.

In terms of wayfinding, we must distinguish between the ordered path responding to a geometric form and the freely disposed, random or shoestring path, which has no particular geometric order.

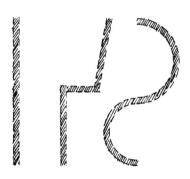

Linear circulation.

Ordered paths (Gestalt).

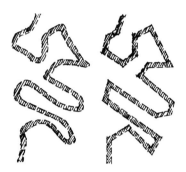

Random paths (shoe-string).

The use of repetitions, rhythmical arrangements, and compositions based on the variation of a basic theme, is sometimes referred to as an organic principle of organizing space. The term is used here in reference to organic substances, in particular plants, which reflect similar characteristics.

Single ordered paths.

If the geometric form of ordered paths is relatively simple, like the schematics in the illustration, we refer to the circulation as being based on a Gestalt pattern. Gestalt, let's recall, refers to the basic visual processes of perceiving form.

The Royal Crescent at Bath is an example of an urban setting; it is organized on the basis of a Gestalt pattern and takes the form

Urban setting organized on the basis of a single ordered path. Royal Crescent at Bath, 1767, John Wood.

of a single elliptically curved path. The highly repetitive arrangement of the Ionic columns as well as the symmetry of the whole give it an additional unity that reinforces the Gestalt quality of the setting. Both the elliptical form of the layout and the order of the façade are unencumbered and easily perceived from all positions.

It must be noted that if identical units are repeated in great numbers, the compositional rule becomes somewhat useless to wayfinding persons. Although the rule may be understood, it does not allow us to organize space cognitively. The lack of distinctiveness is the culprit.

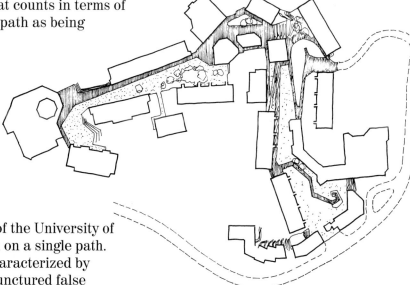

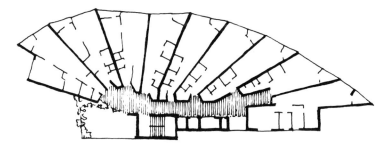

The layout of the apartment building designed by Alvar Aalto in Bremen, Germany, is also based on a simple Gestalt pattern. The form here is reinforced by the changing angles of the separating walls which can be seen to create an internal coherence. It has been likened to musical composition in that the repetitions and the variations in the repetitions give it a rhythmic quality.

Many, if not most, small settings are based on single ordered paths. The examples show how the underlying form can be enhanced by introducing an additional order to express a relationship among the constituting units.

Single random paths.

We call the form that emerges from a random path a shoestring because it resembles the form of a dropped shoelace. Single random paths in their purest form are most easily found in nature, but even there they are not absolutely random. What counts in terms of wayfinding is that the user should perceive the path as being random.

Kresge College on the Santa Cruz Campus of the University of California comes close to a random distribution on a single path. The layout, which evokes a village setting, is characterized by distinctive architectural features. Irregularly punctured false façades emphasize the street. The landscape also has been articulated. An arch, a promenade, and different plazas give strong identities to various parts of the site.

The corridor in the Baker House, designed by Alvar Aalto for MIT, is not a purely random path, although it might be perceived as such by some users. The building form on one side clearly expresses the form of the single corridor, which reinforces its Gestalt nature. The same path in an otherwise undifferentiated layout would be much more difficult to understand.

The scrambling of an ant carrying a crumb through the encumbering grass looks just random to the observer. Rest assured, though, the crumb will in all probability find its way to the colony. What looks like random movement at the small scale may add up to an ordered path.

Architectural layout organized on the basis of a single random path. Baker House, Massachusetts Institute of Technology, Cambridge, 1948, Alvar Aalto.

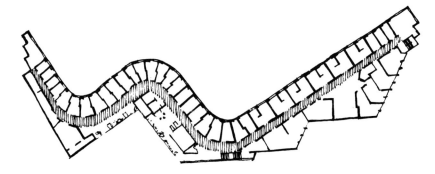

Cores

The core is also a single path although it has a more clearly expressed structural and unifying impact on the setting. The core gives a certain importance to the setting. It is not only a circulation path but it represents a place in and by itself.

Scarborough College, University of Toronto (West Hill, Ontario), is organized along a core that is formed into a narrow, high, canyonlike space. This is clearly the backbone of the setting. The regularly placed staircases reinforce the core idea. The form of the core, in this case, is not far from a shoestring pattern.

View of the organizing core.

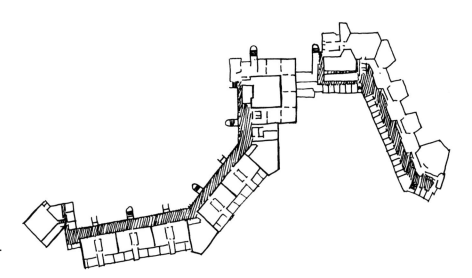

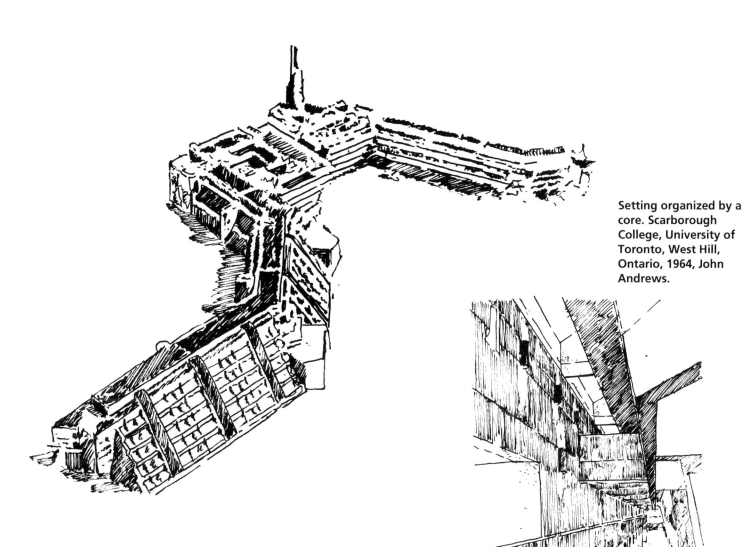

Setting organized by a core. Scarborough College, University of Toronto, West Hill, Ontario, 1964, John Andrews.

Cores are quite common in large urban public settings. Many interior and strip malls use the concourse as a distinguishing core to give a look of prestige to their organization.

Axes

In an axial circulation system, the spatial elements are symmetrically reflected by a key axis. Whereas in the single-path arrangement discussed above, the path merely links spatial units, in core and axial arrangements, the path *is* the dominating and controlling spatial element.

Axial circulations have always flourished in urban design. The most obvious, and probably also one of the most imitated, examples of classical city planning is the Champs-Élysées in Paris. Apart from its inherent symmetrical pattern, the beginning and the end of the axis are emphasized. This also gives it a very strong Gestalt expression.

The axial arrangement is commonly found in religious architecture. Gothic cathedrals, in particular, express symmetry through the plan, the building volume, and the façades. Here also we find emphasis at both extremities in the architectural expression of the entrances and the choir.

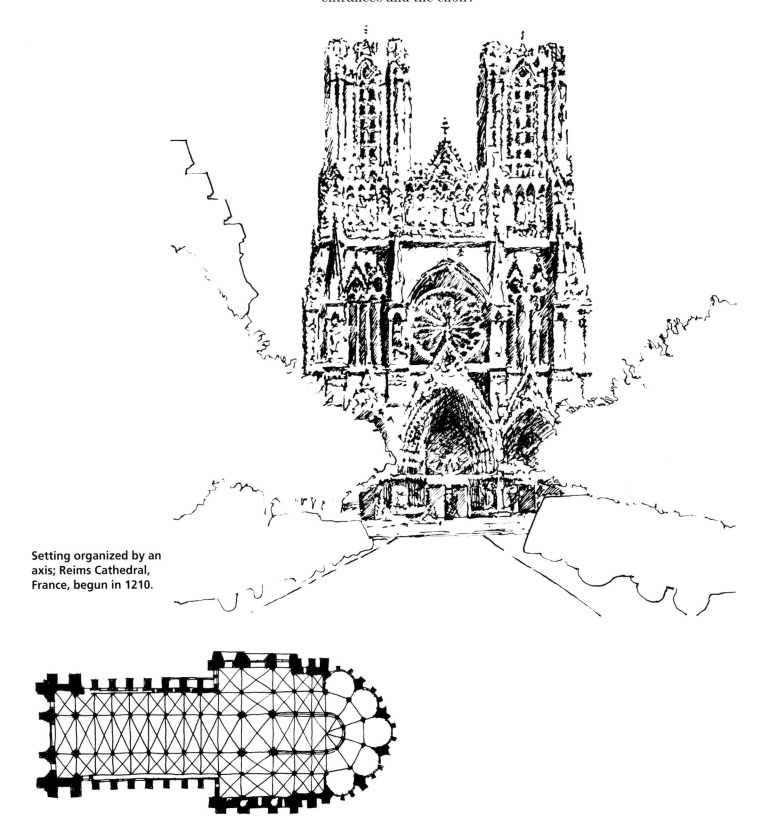

Setting organized by an axis; Reims Cathedral, France, begun in 1210.

94

Bouygues World Headquarters, a massive complex composed on strict axial symmetry, is even aligned with a new super-highway on the outer edge of Paris. Visitors are assured a full view of the symmetry. The landscaping also reflects this symmetry in the classical French tradition.

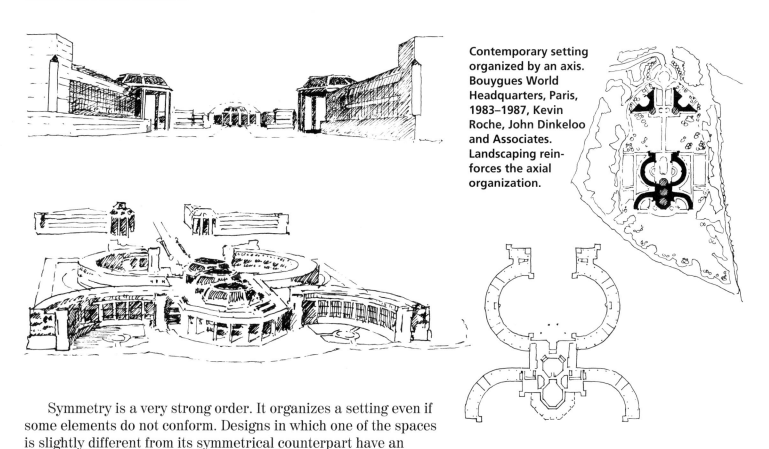

Contemporary setting organized by an axis. Bouygues World Headquarters, Paris, 1983–1987, Kevin Roche, John Dinkeloo and Associates. Landscaping reinforces the axial organization.

Symmetry is a very strong order. It organizes a setting even if some elements do not conform. Designs in which one of the spaces is slightly different from its symmetrical counterpart have an additional tension.

San Vitale, Ravenna, Italy, completed in 547.

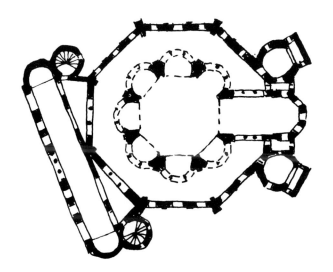

Focal circulation

The square, like the single path, is another basic circulation space. At a more structured level are central symmetry and rotation.[3]

Focal circulation: Square.   Central symmetry.   Rotation.

The square can take many forms. The important characteristic is the underlying organizational principle. It is the center around which space is organized. Piazza del Campo in Siena is a major organizing feature of the urban layout. The tower gives it a distinctiveness and an orientation.

Urban focal square. Piazza del Campo, Siena, Italy.

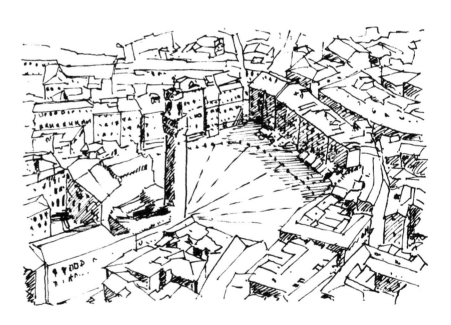

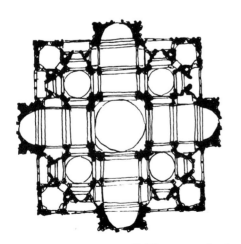

Setting organized on the basis of a central symmetry. Plan for St Peter's, Rome, 1506, Donato Bramante.

The square is also used in public buildings and commercial centers where it is perceived as a strong organizing feature. A well in a multistorey building creates concentric circulation for the upper levels.

Layouts based on a central symmetry are naturally associated with Renaissance architecture. The plan for St Peter's by Bramante is a central symmetry; it also reflects on four axes. Furthermore, a hierarchical relationship between the central and the four peripheral cupolas provides an additional order which is well reflected in the building form, both in the layout and in the volume.

The plan for the St Mark's Tower in New York by Frank Lloyd Wright is based on a pure central symmetry; it cannot be reproduced by a single axial reflection.

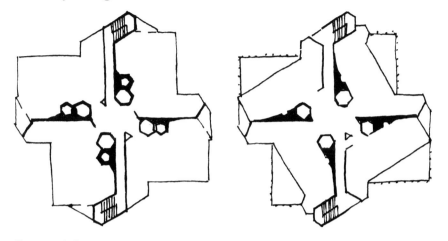

Central symmetry: concept for St Mark's Tower, New York, 1929, Frank Lloyd Wright.

Concentric

Concentric patterns of circulation systems are related to focal organizations. They are characterized by circulation around a focal square which has to be perceptually accessible at least in parts. If the center cannot be perceived and the path returns to its original position after having circumscribed an area, we refer to it as a loop.

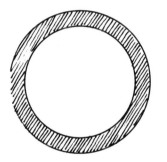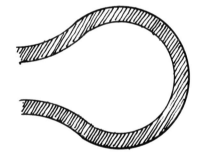

Concentric circulation.

Fontenay Abbey is a good example of a concentric organization. All the buildings are connected by the cloister, but more than that, the concentric circulation becomes the organizing center. The well in the corner of nearly all cloisters creates a distinctive feature which provides people with a sense of orientation.

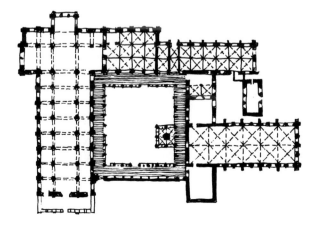

Setting organized on the basis of a concentric pattern. Fontenay Abbey, Burgundy, France, begun 1139.

The Town Hall in Säynätsalo, Finland, designed by Alvar Aalto, is a contemporary, less strictly applied concentric solution which, however, has kept the power of the central organizing force. Distinctive features are created by the architecture and by the landscaping.

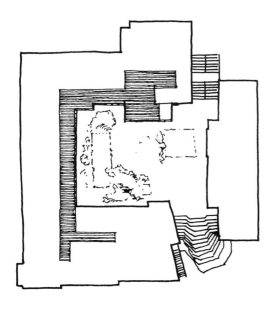

Setting organized on the basis of a concentric pattern. Town Hall, Säynätsalo, Finland, 1949–1952, Alvar Aalto.

Spiral
The spiral pattern, a much less common spatial organization, can be seen as a rotation with a regularly increasing radius.

Spiral patterns.

98

The Italian city of Palombara Sabina near Rome is planned on a spiral circulation. On rare occasions a view towards the exterior is provided, which periodically allows visitors to get their bearings after having lost all references because of the spiral movement of the path.

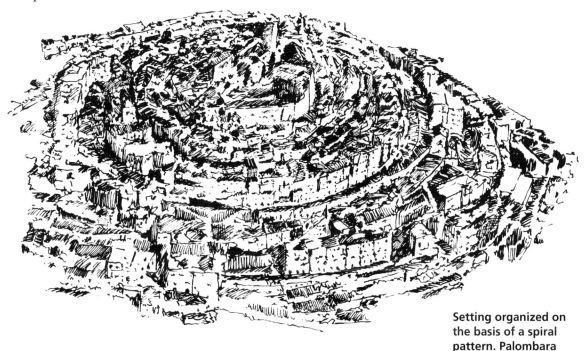

Setting organized on the basis of a spiral pattern. Palombara Sabina, Italy.

The spiral plan of the Guggenheim Museum in New York allows constant visual contact with the center. If that center were totally uniform, people would soon lose all directional reference. The presence of particular architectural features on the ground floor and in the spiral layout allows for directional reference. The Guggenheim is not a disorienting building.

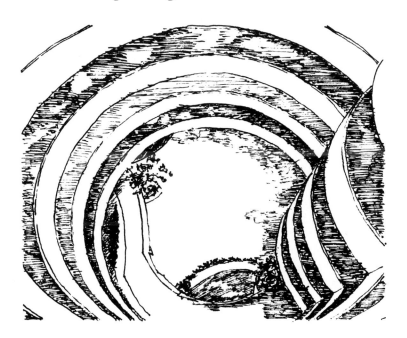

Layout organized on the basis of a spiral pattern. Guggenheim Museum, New York, 1956–1959, Frank Lloyd Wright.

The situation would have been radically different in the spiral museum planned by Le Corbusier. Without any perceptual contact with the center and without any distinctive reference points, visitors would surely have become spatially disoriented after only a few turns.

Concept for the Museum of Endless Growth, Philippeville, Algeria, 1939, Le Corbusier.

10.2.3 Composite circulation systems

Complex settings are not usually based on a single path or on a single focal square but involve a combination of the basic circulation systems. The main distinguishing features of composite circulations are the intersections, which create alternative possibilities of movement. This is where we get down to wayfinding and decision making. Composite circulations reflect all the organizational patterns introduced above.

If paths and squares are assembled on a more or less random basis, they reflect the shoestring pattern. If they are organized, they may conform to a geometric form or a geometric law. The geometric form leads to a Gestalt pattern and the geometric law to a systematized pattern. Central symmetries, axial symmetries, and organic relationships compose the systematized pattern.

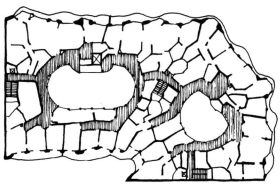

A composite concentric pattern with shoestringlike paths. Plan of typical floor of the Casa Milà, Barcelona, 1905–1910, Antoni Gaudi.

Composite circulations can be based on paths only, squares only, or a combination of the two. In certain cases a person is confronted with two or more competing organizational principles. This tends to lead to ambiguous layouts which can be interpreted in different ways.

Place Bonaventure is one of the first large multifunctional settings built in Montreal. It includes a hotel, offices, an international trade center, a large exhibition hall, and a vast shopping complex on the ground floor. The shopping complex is directly accessible by the underground Metro at a square (Place de la Concorde).

In a cognitive mapping study of Place Bonaventure, it was found that subjects tended to extract a single organizational pattern and that they organized the whole setting according to it. This led to gross distortions.[4] The illustrations show that some subjects organized the setting as a function of the central square (Place de la Concorde), others organized it according to a Gestalt pattern

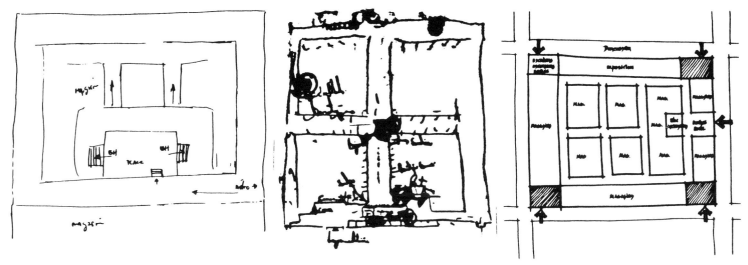

(the central paths forming a cross), while still others organized it according to an imposed rectangular grid.

Circulation networks are characterized by the application of a dominant, repetitive pattern over a large area. We distinguish three types of networks:

- Scatter-point network
- Grid network
- Hierarchical network

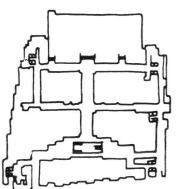

Plan of Place Bonaventure in Montreal with interpretations of the layout by three subjects in a cognitive mapping task.

Scatter-point network
All points in the scatter diagram can be linked together, which creates a network of paths. The network composed of straight lines or curvilinear connections can be as random as the distribution of the points.

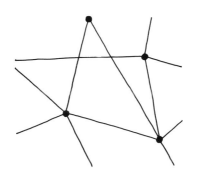
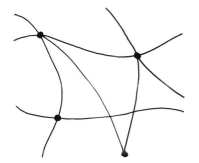

Scatter-point network.

101

Urban setting organized on the basis of a scatter network. Toledo, Spain.

The perception of organization, however subtle, can be learned and is therefore culturally determined. *Medinas,* in the eyes of their inhabitants, are structured. This structure usually escapes the eye of the uninitiated visitor. The *medina* has three types of streets, each with a particular function and expression. In the main street, the *chari,* which is one of the few streets traversing the city from one end to the other, one finds the political and religious establishments as well as public institutions like the main market. The *durub* is a secondary road which often leads from the *chari* to a dead end. It is semi-public and gives access to shops and residences. The *zuqaq* is a tertiary road, starting at the *durub* and also leading to a dead end. It usually leads to residences only.

In the *medina* of Islamic cities, which comes closest to a random distribution, housing units are joined together to form an urban cluster. The circulation merely fills the gaps between the housing units. As can be seen from the plan of Toledo, although paths tend to straighten when running towards the center, the overall impression remains totally labyrinthine.

Grid network
Grids in the built environment usually are orthogonal, but they may

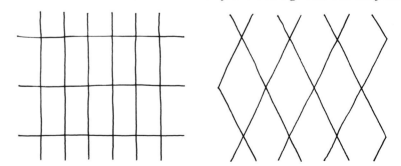

Grid network.

also be based on some other recurring geometric form.

Spatial units arranged on the basis of an orthogonal grid conform to a coordinate address system. That is to say, they are arranged in a fashion such as to be described by two or three coordinates and can be reached by moving the appropriate dis-

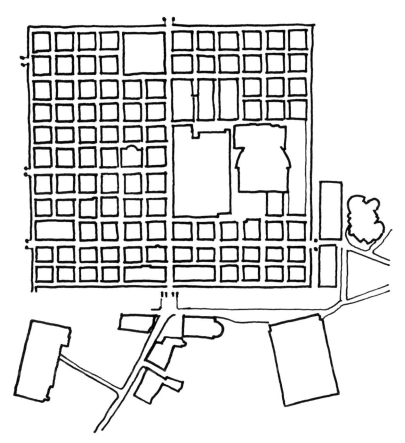

tance along the coordinate lines. From the Roman military camp to
our contemporary cities the arrangement of buildings and streets
tends to correspond to a coordinate system.

By contrast, the Japanese urban address system is quite different. Rather than being organized by coordinates, it is based on a
nested space system. It describes a destination by a sequence of
areas going from the large city scale (the *shi*) to the small
neighborhood scale (the *machi*). Although the system is difficult in
terms of independent wayfinding, the Japanese have resisted
changing it. The nested system is more than just a way of describing a destination, it reflects the socio-spatial reality of the Japanese semi-autonomous neighborhood.[5]

Hierarchical network

The hierarchical system assumes units of different values linked

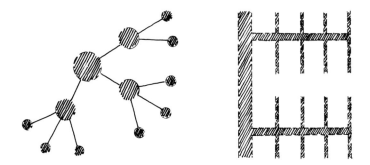

Hierarchical network.

103

from a higher to a lower order. Contrary to the grid network, which imposes a certain, mostly orthogonal, arrangement of spaces, the hierarchical network allows for a free arrangement. The only prerequisite is a differentiation in the order of spaces (or paths) and a linkage of these with a space (or a path) at a superior level. In complex buildings, the hierarchy is established among distribution nodes. The circulation system is composed of the links among nodes.

Hierarchical circulation patterns are particularly suited to large complex settings where random arrangement is impossible and composite arrangements are often inadequate. The layout of Place Desjardins, a large multifunctional center in Montreal, can be seen to be hierarchically organized. You enter a vast plaza from which you can reach four sub-centers, the hotel and three office complexes. The sub-centers are again broken down into smaller units.

Setting organized on the basis of a hierarchical network. Place Desjardins, Montreal, 1976, La Haye and Oulette.

In terms of hierarchical clarity, it would have been preferable to have had one larger office distribution node leading to the three office complexes. It is interesting to note that this hierarchical ambiguity has in fact led to signage problems. Having reached one office complex, you may be told that two other office complexes also exist and that your destination may lie in one of them. In a pure hierarchy, you would be given all this information *before* reaching any specific complex.

10.3 Circulation patterns and wayfinding
Each of the four types of circulation systems has features that make it wayfinding-friendly.

In this section, we identify the features that make circulation systems easier to map and that facilitate decision making and decision execution. Both cognitive mapping and decision making are affected by the patterns of the circulation systems. These patterns have been identified as follows:

- Shoestring
- Gestalt
- Systematized
- Network or repetitive pattern

10.3.1 The shoestring pattern
The shoestring pattern, which is based on a random or a quasi-random distribution, does not have an underlying organizational principle. Users would be ill advised to search for something that is not there.

Mapping a shoestring
Recalling that cognitive mapping is, by definition, a process of organizing spaces, one may wonder whether people can actually map a shoestring arrangement. The answer is that they can. People are able to map these random arrangements, within certain limits, with respect to their size and complexity.

Probably the most efficient strategy is to take note of landmarks and use them as mental anchors. These anchors can then

Major events in a person's life are used as anchor points in time. Most people can remember even minor things that happened just before or just after major events.

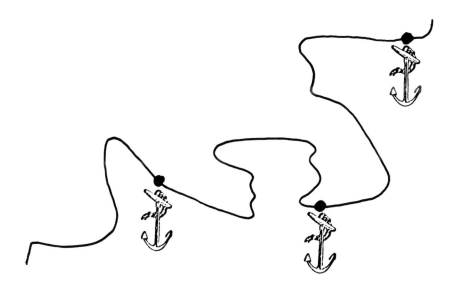

Mapping a shoestring arrangement of the circulation.

serve to attach segments of the route and the surrounding space. Anchor points in wayfinding can be distinctive physical features, events, and or distinct destination zones.

Distinctiveness, we have seen, can be achieved by outstanding features and by compositional characteristics. The repetitions of spaces or architectural features, their rhythmic arrangements, and other proportional relationships can be considered distinctive and thus gain anchor-point quality.

Memorable features or events are not necessarily the same for everybody; what may be a landmark for one person may not for another. Again, it is by planning with redundancy that communication will be most effective.

In many cases a path *is* structured, but for a variety of reasons having to do with the architecture or with the state of mind of the user, the structure is not perceived. In such a case it is illegible. The user will see the path as a shoestring and will revert to the anchor-point technique in attempting to understand and cope with it.

We therefore recommend that anchor points be introduced as a failsafe device even in the best-planned settings to allow for the eventuality that the circulation pattern may *not* be perceived.

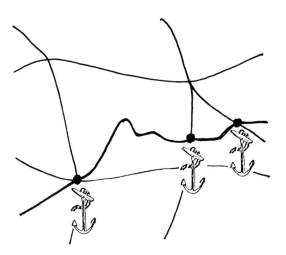

Mapping a scatter network.

The scatter network has no discernible organization and is therefore very difficult to map. Users have no choice other than to map the routes independently. Given that the routes are of the shoestring type, anchor points become the cognitive structuring information.

This cognitive strategy has limits, as can easily be seen from the crowded impression given in the illustration. In a complex scatter-point network it remains quite possible to map certain paths, but not the whole network.

Deciding within a shoestring pattern
The decision-related processes are based on information. It is therefore not surprising to find a close link between cognitive mapping and decision making.

106

When there are no intersections, a single path does not require much decision making. Still, at some point you must decide to terminate a journey – after having recognized your destination, for instance. If the destination has not been reached, you may have to decide whether or not to go on. This is purely a safety valve. People do not keep on walking endlessly until they are exhausted.

We have argued that some distinct features along a shoestring path are necessary to serve as anchor points around which people can build their representations. Anchor points can also serve to break down a long journey into manageable units. This gives them the additional function of intermediate destination points along a path.

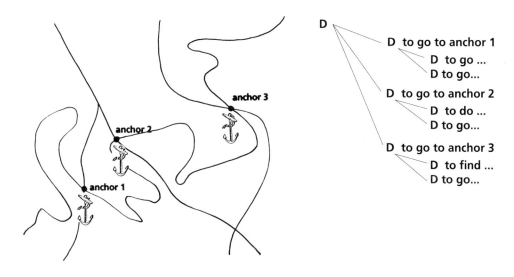

Decision diagram corresponding to a shoestring pattern of circulation.

To reach such destinations is a higher-order decision of the corresponding wayfinding plan. In other words, the information system for any shoestring circulation is based on anchor points.

While directional changes make it more difficult to map a path, it is the number of intersections (decision points) that affects the difficulty of decision making. For each decision, people have to obtain and process environmental information. Furthermore, at each decision point there is the potential for a mistake.

Of course, there is nothing wrong with decision points. After all, wayfinding is problem solving and decision making. It is the combination of too many decision points and not enough information that gets people lost.

The difficulty of mentally mapping a scatter network manifests itself in decision making also. Anchor points will be the key references of the decision plan, but they have to coincide with decision points in the setting for the plan to be efficient.

A unicoursal labyrinth will disorient people in the sense that they become incapable of knowing where they are and where the direction of the exit is. They are not disoriented in the sense of not knowing how to get out. To do this, they just have to turn around and walk in the opposite direction. It is in the multicoursal labyrinth, in which paths intersect, that people get lost in a wayfinding sense.

10.3.2 The Gestalt pattern

The organizational principle in Gestalt patterns is the form. The difference between a path that is perceived as a Gestalt and a path that is perceived as an amorphous shoestring is not always evident.

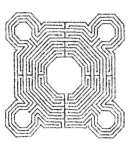

Unicoursal labyrinth.

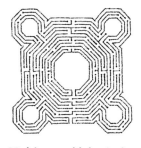

Multicoursal labyrinth.

107

Mapping a Gestalt

According to Gestalt theory, *Prägnanz* is a major determining factor in the perception of linear form. There is no precise translation for *Prägnanz*. It refers to the ease with which a form imprints itself on the mind. Simplicity (or goodness of form, as a Gestalt psychologist would say) is the most important factor. Additional factors are symmetries and other regularities in composition.

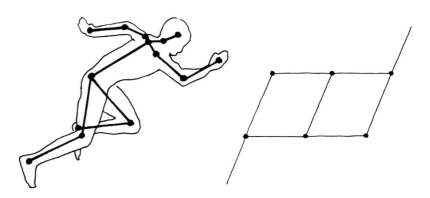

Mapping a Gestalt circulation.

It must be realized, however, that the wayfinding public rarely sees the overall form of the paths. Quite the contrary. The Gestalt has to be mentally constructed from partial views.

Even a form as complex as that of a running figure is grasped – and communicated – mainly through lines and joints. In buildings with Gestalt-type organizations, it is suggested that designers emphasize straight or curved lines and, in particular, junctions or joints of the form.

Mapping a constellation with the help of a bear Gestalt.

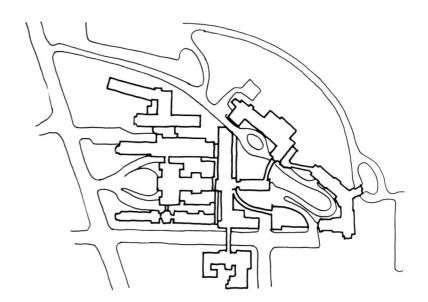

Organization too complex to be recognized as a figure. Royal Victoria Hospital, Montreal.

The perception of the exterior form of a setting, if it corresponds to the form of the circulation, will be an additional clue for understanding Gestalt-type layouts.

Settings that expand indefinitely by having wings added to the original structure are notorious for creating wayfinding problems.

The basic figure of the circulation system often becomes too complex to be recognized, and people have to map the setting without the aid of any underlying organizational principle.

If people perceive a setting as a random distribution of spaces they can map it only on a shoestring basis. This task rapidly becomes more difficult as the setting increases in complexity. Shoestring patterns are not suitable for complex settings.

Deciding within a Gestalt pattern

The Gestalt organization is characterized by the intersections or joints of the form. The joints play a similar role to anchor points in a shoestring organization.

In a Gestalt-patterned circulation system, it is the joints that structure the decision plan. The joints, however, are not just scattered randomly. They are part of a Gestalt which, if perceived, organizes them into a form.

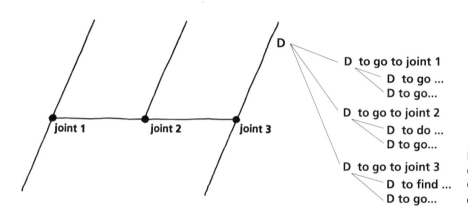

Decision diagram corresponding to the Gestalt pattern of circulation.

10.3.3 The systematized pattern

A systematized arrangement is one characterized by a unique compositional rule. Focal, rotational, and spiral arrangements, as well as axial and central symmetries, are systematized patterns.

Mapping a systematized pattern

If the compositional rule is identified, cognitive mapping of the setting is greatly simplified. Many systematized arrangements also lead to a relatively simple form that provides the users with a complementary or an alternative organizational principle.

The focal composition of buildings in which spaces are organized around a center or an open well are among the easiest to map. An open well has the additional advantage of giving visual access to the floors from the center, thus simplifying the cognitive mapping process.

Rotations and symmetries are also concepts that tend to be easily understood. One promenade from Place de la Concorde to

Place de l'Étoile in Paris will suffice for anybody's image of the axial arrangement of the Champs-Élysées.

Perception of the symmetrical disposition of spaces is vital information about the spatial organization of the setting, which, in turn, facilitates cognitive mapping.

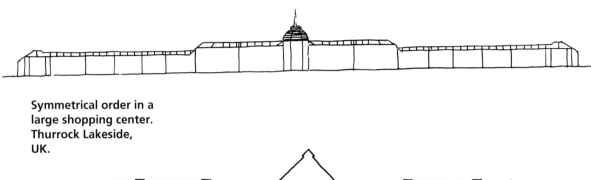

Symmetrical order in a large shopping center. Thurrock Lakeside, UK.

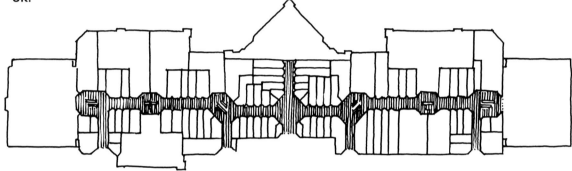

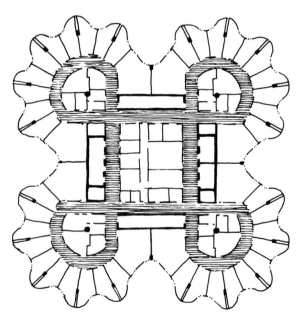

Saint Mary's Hospital, Milwaukee, Wisconsin, 1975, Bernard Goldberg.

The large shopping center in the illustration is an axial arrangement. It is easily mapped, but it also suggests the drawback of symmetrical arrangements. Although you may get an overall image of the setting's layout without difficulty, you may just as easily mix up your position in space. You may know that you are in a wing but the question as to which one may go unanswered.

The symmetrical layout of Saint Mary's Hospital in Milwaukee must have disoriented more than an occasional visitor. The plan has no distinguishing features, not even a reference to the outside.

In organizations with central symmetry or rotations, it is important to provide wayfinders with some distinct features that will allow them to situate themselves in the setting. A uniform circular or spiral path is sure to get people disoriented. Although the central organizations are generally understood in themselves, they can lead to confusions in orientation.

Deciding within a systematized pattern

Although symmetrical layouts are easy to map, there is the difficulty of situating yourself in space. Not knowing where you are also affects decision making. If you are lost, you might want to return to a known base to get your bearings and to rethink the decision plan. The base can be the axis or the focal point in a symmetrical arrangement. If distinctive features are introduced to facilitate orientation, they will also appear in the decision plans of the users. In layouts with additional Gestalt characteristics the distinctive features should correspond to the joints of the form.

Mapping networks

Networks are based on a recurring rule of arranging spaces over a large area. This section refers to the coordinate and the hierarchi-

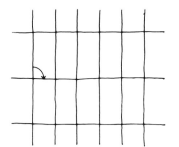 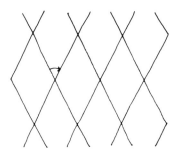

Mapping a grid network.

cal network, the scatter network having already been discussed in section 10.3.1.

If the organizational principle is not perceived the users may have to figure out a partial Gestalt organization for a given path or they may have to regress to the shoestring strategy of cognitive mapping, which, in all situations, is a last resort.

The cues necessary to perceive the grid network are few. The users have to understand the angle of the intersection of the paths and the repetition of that basic arrangement.

The grid network contains the most evident structure of all the networks. Once the grid is understood, it has a most forceful mental structuring effect. Many visitors to Manhattan get lost when they enter the zones at the southern tip which are no longer organized according to the central grid.

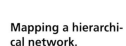

New York City, Manhattan.

 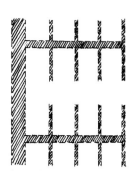

Mapping a hierarchical network.

The hierarchical network is more complicated to perceive. Users have to understand that spaces and paths are linked according to an order that is repeated throughout the network.

The hierarchical network may also be more difficult than any other organization to express by architectural means. In complex settings, where the hierarchical organization is particularly suited, spaces are grouped around paths or circulation nodes, and it is the paths and nodes that should express the hierarchical order.

In a hierarchical organization, everything, from the spatial composition to the articulation of circulation nodes and paths, from the descriptions of the destinations to the graphic communications, ought to be hierarchical. It is only then that designers can rest assured that people will be able to discover the organizational principle so important in cognitive mapping.

Deciding within repetitive patterns

Wayfinding in an orthogonal grid network, whether in a two-dimensional city layout or a three-dimensional building layout, is usually quite simple. If your New York destination is 5th Avenue and 42nd Street, you know that, once you figure out the direction of your destination, you can walk any way you want as long as you do not cross 5th Avenue or 42nd Street. Fifth Avenue and 42nd Street are your limits; they are the stopping point in the grid.

Decision diagram corresponding to a grid network.

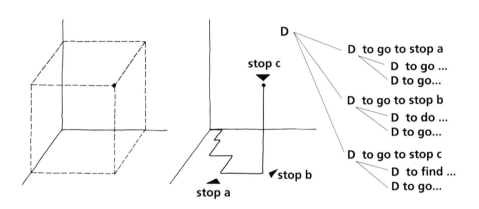

In more abstract terms, a person who needs to reach point P in a coordinate system will have to know not to go further than (a) in direction of the coordinate A and not further than (b) on the coordinate B, and not higher than (c) on the vertical coordinate C. These stopping points represent the intermediary decision for operating in a grid system. For any point P (a,b,c) the decisions are to go no further than a, b, and c.

Wayfinding in a hierarchical network relies on the nodes or paths of the system. Once the hierarchical arrangements are

Decision diagram corresponding to a hierarchical network.

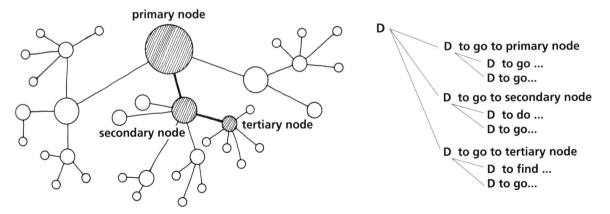

understood, the user has to work his or her way up or down the hierarchy. The user may go from the central plaza of an urban

112

complex to a business center, then to an office building lobby, and finally to a suite of offices.

In a hierarchical network, a person moves from node to node (or path to path) in respecting the given hierarchical order. At each node, the wayfinding person has to make sure that the correct branch is taken to reach a lower- or higher-order node.

Nodes, thus, correspond to the decision points: they have to contain the architectural and graphic information for decision making. Nodes are responsible for intermediate decisions when operating in a hierarchical network.

10.4 Planning the layout: a summary

We have seen that planning the layout of a setting involves three basic design phases which all have an impact on wayfinding:

1. Identifying the spatial units of the setting and their identity
2. Grouping the units into destination zones
3. Linking the spaces and destination zones into a designed ensemble

The linking of spaces is made possible by the circulation system, which in turn organizes the setting in spatial terms.

Circulation systems fall into two major groups: those that reflect an organizing principle and those that do not.

Systems that do *not* reflect an organizing principle and are arranged randomly are based on a shoestring pattern. A layout based on a shoestring pattern must contain distinct features that can serve as cognitive anchor points. These are essential for both the cognitive mapping and the decision-making processes.

Patterns that *do* reflect an organizational principle also fall into two types: those that are organized by a geometric form (Gestalt pattern) and those that are organized by a geometric law (systematized pattern and ordered repetitive patterns).

Layouts based on the Gestalt pattern have to be relatively simple in order to be perceived as a form. From an interior perspective, it is important to emphasize the joints of the circulation form, and from the exterior, the corresponding configuration of the setting. Maps and other displays that can communicate the form of the circulation and the building are of particular importance here. In the event the form is not perceived, the joints can serve as anchor points and the user can revert to a shoestring strategy.

Layouts based on a geometric law will be simple for cognitive mapping and decision making only if this law is perceived and understood by the users.

The patterns of symmetrical layouts tend to be easily understood and mapped, but in such settings, situating oneself, wayfinding, and decision making may all be more difficult. In large and complex symmetrical layouts, difficulties can be reduced by introducing unique landmarks to serve two aims: to allow users to distinguish one side from the other and, if everything else fails, to serve as anchor points.

The scatter-point network is composed of shoestring patterns and can be understood only on the basis of anchor points. In a network, anchor points should coincide with intersections. This might, in certain cases, facilitate a partial understanding in Gestalt segments. It must be said clearly, however, that random networks are hard to cope with.

Grid networks reflect a recurring geometric pattern. The orthogonal is the most common grid and is known to be easily perceived and understood. Combined with coordinates, it establishes an efficient address system which is reflected in the decision plans of the users.

Hierarchical networks are less constraining in form than the grid. Care, however, has to be taken to communicate the underlying organizational principle.

The layout of a setting has a strong influence on wayfinding. Of course, there is no *ideal* circulation system. What is best for any given setting will depend on the function of the setting, its size, and its environmental context. But for each system a structuring order and/or structuring information has to be expressed so that members of the wayfinding public can develop their decision plans and can thus map the setting cognitively.

The following table lists the organizational patterns and their representative circulation types. It also summarizes the structuring order and the information that makes them viable.

Organizational pattern	Circulation type	Structuring order	Structuring information
shoestring	single path	none	anchor points
	core	none	anchor points
	composite	none	anchor points at intersections
	scatter network	none	anchor points at intersections
Gestalt	single path	form of the path	joints of path and building form
	core	form of the path	joints of path and building form
	central	form of the path	center of path and building form
	composite	form of the path	joints and intersections of paths and building form
systematized	axial	symmetry	axis
	central	symmetry focal order	center focal point
network	grid	grid pattern	stopping points
	hierarchical circulations	hierarchy	hierarchical order of nodes or paths

114

What all this adds up to is that an important aspect of wayfinding design is already in operation when planners think of their first organizational and spatial ideas. Those sketches on the napkin during the business lunch with the client are full of wayfinding implications.

Chapter 11
Architectural wayfinding communication

Many people think that signs are the most important means of providing wayfinding information in an urban or architectural setting. Without downplaying the importance of signs, it is nevertheless easy to show that the natural and built environments provide the wayfinding person with a great variety of basic wayfinding cues.

If you see a road you understand that you can walk along it without having to see a sign saying that you can do so. You can enter a building through a doorway even if it is without an entrance sign. You may even know what is in the building and how it is spatially organized just by looking at it. You can use a nature trail, a park, a square, an avenue, an elevator, or a stair, because wayfinding information is contained in these elements.

People in their daily movements have to pick up circulation information in order to find their way. They have to find out where to enter a setting and where to exit it. They have to recognize destinations. They have to identify the paths of horizontal and vertical circulation systems. To be fully efficient, they have to understand circulation systems.

This chapter is about architectural wayfinding communication. It outlines the architectural features that define the circulation and it proposes means to communicate the relevant wayfinding information.

11.1 Entrances

Entrances give access to places. But what makes an entrance? The doors. Yes, but…

Even if, in most cases, the door is the ultimate sign of an entrance, people first have to find the door. Doors may not be visible from a distance, and some entrances do not even have doors – gates, for example, tend not to have doors. In this section we outline the factors that enhance the legibility of an entrance. Let us first look at the way we approach an entrance and how this affects its legibility.

11.1.1 Approach and legibility of entrances

The legibility of an entrance or a gate varies with the angle of approach. Entrances can be approached in a frontal, an oblique, or an indirect way.[1] The frontal approach gives the greatest visual

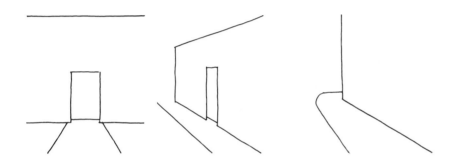

Frontal, oblique, and indirect approaches to an entrance.

access to an entrance. Visual access diminishes as the approach becomes more oblique and finally disappears when the approach is indirect.

Piazza d'Italia, New Orleans, 1975–1980, Charles Moore with V.I.G. and Perez Associates.

The frontal approach can be considered ideal in terms of legibility, but this is not intended to mean that all entrances should

117

be approached frontally. As we shall see throughout this section, designers can express an entrance through architectural or landscaping means even when the approach is oblique or indirect. People over the years have learned to detect and read a variety of entrance cues.

The projection (or recess) of an entrance in a façade is just one of the means of giving additional prominence to the entrance. Projections and recesses are particularly effective if the approach is oblique.

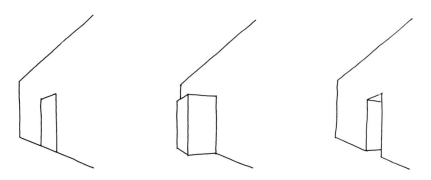

Flush, projected, and recessed entrances.

11.1.2 Gates

The gate is an entrance to a domain, a site, or a place. One of the oldest functions of gates (such as those found in the walls of fortified cities) was to control access. At the same time, they expressed the character of the city, usually wealth and glory, which made it imperative that they be embellished with all the architectural and decorative art of the period.

In terms of wayfinding, gates also marked the entrance to an important destination zone. In addition, they tended to become major reference points and, thanks to their design, often acquired landmark quality.

Typical Roman gate.

The Brandenburg Tor (or gate) is a rather interesting case. Although now located in the heart of the city, it did become a true gate, albeit a closed one, through the separation of the two Berlins.

Gates to cities. Brandenburg Gate, Berlin.

Contemporary cities have lost the defining shape that used to be provided by walls and with it they have also lost their gates. Some exceptions remain, mostly cities that were able to retain their fortifications or that have natural borders.

In cities whose boundaries are defined by water, bridges tend to become gates. The Golden Gate bridge to San Francisco, for instance, still retains all of its meaning as an entrance to the city. Moreover, it has become one of the city's best-known symbols.

The alternative to a bridge is a tunnel. If it is an access to a city, it could also be described as a gate. Tunnels, however, don't have the same strong quality as reference points and generally don't feature as major landmarks in people's understanding of a city.

Gates also exist at a smaller urban or semi-urban scale and that is where they are most important to us. Parks tend to have gates; prestigious estates and important organizations have gates; but often "ordinary places" like municipalities, shopping centers, and parking lots have gates too. These smaller gates have functions similar to those of historical city gates:

- They mark the transfer from one domain to another.
- They signify the nature of the residence.
- They impose a certain control on accessibility.
- More importantly, they communicate to visitors where to enter a destination zone.

A gate can be an extension of a building's entrance. For example, the gate to the Canadian Centre for Architecture, designed by Peter Rose, is in close visual contact with the entrance and announces the architectural vocabulary of the door.

The gate or proscenium arch of the Opéra de la Bastille, designed by Carlos Ott, is almost stuck to the entrance. It certainly heightens the legibility of the entrance and advertises the importance of the building. It may even signify the function of the building, but probably only to the initiated visitor.

Golden Gate Bridge, San Francisco.

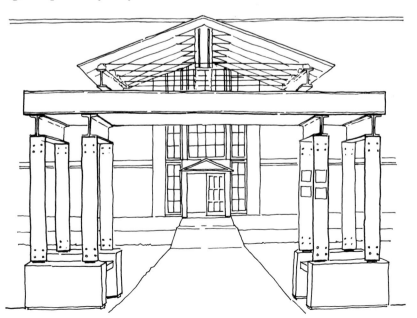

**Below left:
The Canadian Centre for Architecture, Montreal, 1989, Peter Rose.**

**Below:
Opéra de la Bastille, Paris, 1988, Carlos Ott.**

The gate to the Glasgow School of Art has retained much of its strength and elegance. As gates go, it is quite minimal. Nevertheless it clearly demarcates the public from the semi-private zone and reinforces the entrance to the building.

Glasgow School of Art, 1897–1909, Charles Rennie Mackintosh.

11.1.3 Colonnades and marquees

The colonnade at the Capital High School in Santa Fe helps to emphasize the circulation and gives it a public character. The curved section at the entrance is used to welcome visitors and to indicate the entrance to the most public building, the auditorium. The message is reinforced by the central tower and the surface treatment of the plaza, an example of the value of redundancy in wayfinding communication.

The use of colonnades. Capital High School, Santa Fe, USA, Ralph Johnson of Perkins and Will.

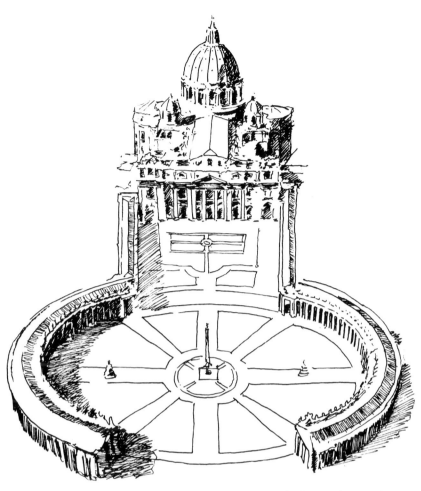

Aerial view of
Bernini's colonnade to
St Peter's, Rome.

Colonnades have also been used to give a feeling of containment and protection and to lead the visitor to the entrance of an important place. The example that best expresses these ideas is Bernini's colonnade to St Peter's in Rome.

Marquees, porticos, and other similar building elements can be part of the original design. More often, however, they are post-occupancy interventions. Their function apart from weather protection is, again, to draw attention to the organization and to give significance to the entrances.

Marquees and porticos are useful in strengthening an otherwise architecturally weak entrance message. Marquees are most effective from an oblique approach, which is no doubt why they are so common in large cities where the line of vision from the sidewalk is almost parallel to the building façade.

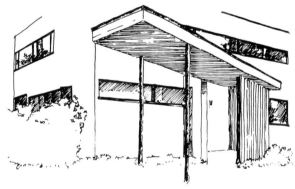

Marquees marking
entrances.

121

11.1.4 Landscaping

One of the most effective preludes to an entrance is the landscaping. The entrance can be put into perspective by the arrangements of paths, the lead-in walls, and the border plantings that mark the path.

The location of the building entrance may be emphasized by a prominent feature such as a group of trees, a water display, or a sculpture seen from a distance. Raised platforms, stairs, and ramps in front of the entrance are additional cues.

**Paths and vegetation
marking an entrance.**

Landscaping will emphasize the location of the entrance not only from the oblique but also from the indirect approach. Apart from the building form, which is not always visually accessible, features of the landscape may be the only cues able to lead people to "hidden entrances."

11.1.5 What buildings say about entrances

How does the building itself communicate the location of the entrance? If the form of the building layout can be grasped, the viewer may already have some cues about the main entrance.

Symmetrical layouts have a long tradition in public buildings and houses of worship.[2] The layout is usually perceived without difficulty and the assumption is that the entrance will be found in the axis of the bilateral symmetry (see illustration 1, opposite).

Asymmetrical layouts are generally more difficult to interpret. Their form requires some special features to distinguish the entrance (compare layouts of illustrations 2 and 3). Buildings with

**Below:
Layout of Villa
Trissino, Meledo, Italy,
1553, Andrea Palladio.**

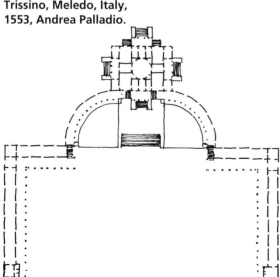

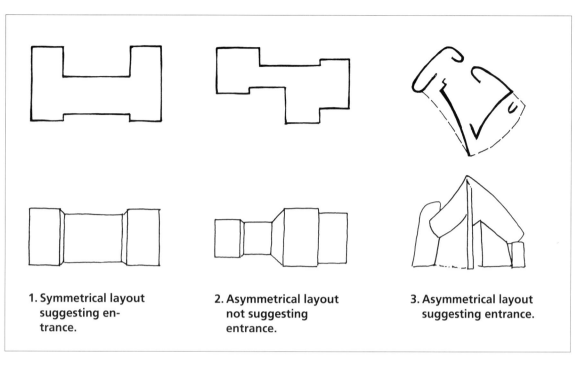

The composition of a layout can suggest the location of the entrance.

1. Symmetrical layout suggesting entrance.

2. Asymmetrical layout not suggesting entrance.

3. Asymmetrical layout suggesting entrance.

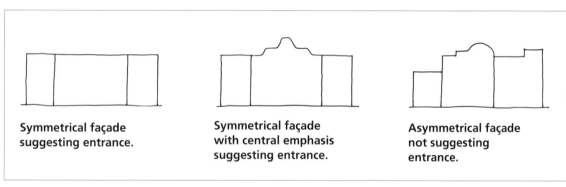

The composition of the façade can suggest the location of the entrance.

Symmetrical façade suggesting entrance.

Symmetrical façade with central emphasis suggesting entrance.

Asymmetrical façade not suggesting entrance.

asymmetrical layouts usually rely on additional cues to indicate the location of the entrance.

From the viewpoint of the users, façades are more easily perceived than the building layout. Given that the façade often expresses the building layout, it is not surprising to find that symmetrical façade compositions also provide entrance cues. Even in the schematic drawings without doors, it is not difficult to point to the probable locations of the entrances. The message is even clearer if the central section is emphasized. In the asymmetrical façade the location of the entrance is much more ambiguous.

Façade of Villa Trissino, Meledo, Italy, 1553, Andrea Palladio.

The strictly functional requirements for letting people in and out of buildings necessitates relatively small doors even for large public settings. Architects and designers, throughout history, have tried to enlarge the expression of the entrance.

Doors and the space around them have been emphasized in all architectural styles. Nowhere, however, have door settings been treated as lavishly as in baroque and rococo architecture. You just

Baroque and rococo door settings.

Sankt Johannes Nepomuk, Munich, 1733–1746, Egid Quirin Asam and Cosmas Damian Asam.

San Fernando, Madrid, 1722, Pedro de Ribera.

Door setting to a machine hall. Sollern coal mine, Dortmund, Germany.

can't miss such an entrance.

The art nouveau example of an entrance to a machine hall in Dortmund speaks the language of its period, but it is by no means modest. In considering the function of the building, one may well assume that machine shops have lost some of their prestige over the years.

The same need to emphasize entrances can be seen in contemporary architecture where sculptured decoration has given way to compositions with different materials. The effect can be quite convincing, for example, Ott's Opéra de la Bastille and Venturi's Philadelphia Orchestra Hall.

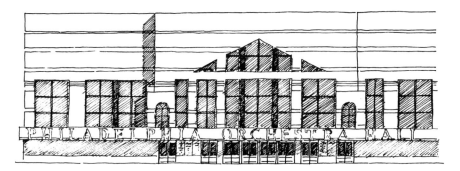

Philadelphia Orchestra Hall, Philadelphia. To be completed in 1993, Venturi, Rauch, and Scott Brown.

Pediments used in classical architecture have always been associated with the identification of doors. In post-modern movements the pediment has reentered architectural language. Even if it is used for decorative, rather than for wayfinding, reasons its impact can still be useful.

The elements introduced above are not new. It is, however, of interest to review them in the perspective of communicating important wayfinding information. Designers have multiple means at their disposal and there is not really any excuse for designs in which people have difficulties locating the entrance. Nonetheless, entrance problems, unfortunately, are not as rare as one might think.

The classical pediment.

125

**Out-patient entrance
to a large hospital.**

The problem of entrances is quite typical in this hospital. When the hospital was expanded, existing and new buildings were linked together. The administration has not been able to decide whether to organize the hospital as one complex, with a main entrance, or as a number of semi-autonomous sections, each with its own entrance. The situation shown reflects that ambiguity.

A major hospital in Montreal has one entrance that looks like a small service entrance. It is small, but it is certainly not a service entrance. It is the most direct and most used entrance for out-patients in the hospital, with about a hundred people an hour entering and exiting. Both architectural and graphic communication are almost totally absent. Needless to say, the entrance is notoriously hard to find.

The cues indicating the location of a gate or an entrance are mainly visual. The blind visitor, having no visual access to the building volume or its façade, will not be able to perceive the architectural treatment of the door either. The cues the blind will be able to perceive, therefore, will be so much more important to them. A recess, an overhang, landscape features, a decorative articulation of the entrance, the use of different textures – these are all cues that can be picked up by the visually impaired.

In addition, directional guidance can be given by distinguishing the access path from the surrounding area. This may be achieved through texture or by a guiding shore line. It must be noted that a well-articulated path usually has these distinguishing characteristics in any case. The designer just has to be careful that these cues are not exclusively visual.

Entrances to certain buildings may also be marked by a sound source. This directional cue can be very efficient as long as it is not drowned out by background noises. It is, of course, not feasible to have all entrances marked by a sound; but the solution is a reasonable one for buildings that are frequently used by the visually impaired population.

Sound sources have been designed to be activated by a small pocket-size device. This is an interesting solution to eliminate competing sounds and the possible nuisance value of permanent sound.

11.2 Exits
The exit of a building requires particular consideration. Although it is the same architectural element as an entrance, from the user's point of view it is certainly not seen the same way. The perception of the exit is often limited to the actual doors and most of the time they are seen only at short range. Exits are important when wayfinding – they represent sub-destinations when people are leaving a setting.

11.2.1 Exits in complex settings
The wayfinding tasks of reaching an entrance are quite different from those for an exit. For the unfamiliar visitor, the entrance has first to be found, while the exit in most settings requires a simple return to the point of entry. If people are able to map their entrance route, they will require only limited environmental information to return to the exit. In a recent wayfinding experiment in a labyrinth, we were able to show that most people were able to point

to the entrance of the labyrinthine layout even after having taken a relatively complex route inside it.[3]

If the setting is too complex for users to map their route, and that does happen too, they will have to search for the exits. In essence, they will do the same searching operation that was required to find the entrance.

It should be noted that in large *urban* shopping complexes, people tend to enter and exit the site at different points. In such cases, exits should be given the necessary emphasis to make them easily detectable. (In *suburban* shopping centers we try to exit by the same door we entered, as this is the only way we'll be able to find our vehicles again. The same principle applies, however. The exit must be detectable.)

The door, even when seen from the inside, can be emphasized by the architecture of the door setting. Limited by height, visual access will not be as easy as it is on the outside, but distinctiveness is more important in terms of legibility than size.

The limitation in size can be easily compensated for by making efficient use of the outside light. As can be seen from the examples, natural light in the right context signifies the possibility of an exit. Most blind people retain a certain light perception of which they make as much use as they can. The use of light as an exit cue is therefore useful to most people.

Emphasizing an exit by architectural expression and the use of light.

11.2.2 Emergency exits

Exits also have to be used in emergency conditions. In a previous chapter, we noted that in emergency situations people move towards the familiar, while fire exits, if they are reserved just for emergencies, tend not to be used. This finding has far-reaching consequences for the design of these emergency exits. In fact, it challenges our fire regulations and building codes in their present form.

People's behavior in a fire can easily be interpreted in terms of wayfinding. Moving towards the familiar is nothing other than applying a decision plan that has already been worked out and proven successful. In a stressful situation, the person is not inclined to experiment with the unknown. The unknown is a synonym for risk.

Movement towards the familiar is psychologically comforting and sometimes even justified. The narrow little passage of many fire escapes does not leave many alternatives for escape and the door at the end might just be locked. The sight of fire doors, which cannot be opened from the outside, is not always very reassuring.

The notion of emergency exits, we suggest, ought to be rethought in the light of these observations. In order to increase the use of emergency exits, one of two conditions must be fulfilled. Either the exit route must be familiar to the users, or the exits must be directly perceived from the inside. People may not use a fire exit sign, but it can be assumed that they will use an exit if it clearly leads to the outside or to another safe place.

Besides, it may just be a false alarm, we convince ourselves.

Familiarizing people with emergency exit routes through fire drills is an option that may work for some settings but not for others. While it is possible to have fire drills in office buildings, it would be virtually impossible to do the same in a large shopping complex or an airport. Furthermore, fire drills, like all drills, are a nuisance, and people cannot be blamed if they ignore them, although this attitude might lead to truly catastrophic consequences in a real fire.

A more efficient and elegant solution in public buildings that cope with a high volume of visitors is to design a number of normal entrances/exits which are used in both senses under normal conditions. There is no reason why buildings cannot be designed in these terms and at the same time respect constraints imposed by security and maintenance. This might be more difficult when retrofitting an existing structure, but there is no doubt that a good argument can be made that the security of people *in* the building might just be more important than the security *of* the building.

The direct perception of exits from the inside is only possible in settings with large open spaces such as shopping malls, airports, and stadia. The argument here is to do away with the notion of fire exits as much as possible while still respecting the safety requirements of having alternative escape routes.

11.3 Paths

In discussing wayfinding communication related to paths, we should distinguish between two aspects:

- Perception of a path, its use, and its accessibility
- Understanding the configuration of the circulation system

Let us first consider information on paths – it tells people where the path is, whether it leads to somewhere worthwhile, and whether or not they are allowed to take it.

 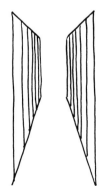  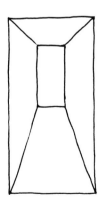

Basic elements defining paths.

11.3.1 Legibility of a path

A path is perceived by markings on the ground, a guiding structure on the side or above, or by a combination of these elements. The path-defining elements can be continuous or repetitive.

In the first example, a museum exhibition hall, the path is marked by the design of the ceiling. The solution incorporates the lighting to provide directional guidance and assures a uniform floor-cover. In the bottom illustration, the path of the main circulation route is marked on the floor by using a material that has a different texture and tone from the surrounding areas. The textured marking improves the legibility of key paths and allows them to be used by the visually impaired population for whom open-space arrangements are particularly difficult.

Paths and their physical articulation are at the heart of architectural, urban, and landscape design. The vocabulary provided by the texture of the materials, by the structural and decorative elements of walls and ceilings, by columns and light, vegetation and water, is almost infinite.

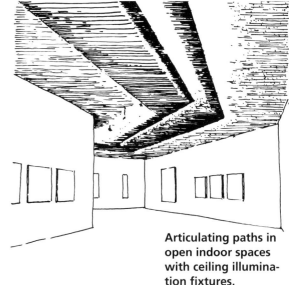

Articulating paths in open indoor spaces with ceiling illumination fixtures.

Articulating a path by using different materials and textures for the wall, the colonnade, and the ceiling.

The articulation of paths is a fundamental aspect of wayfinding communication. Proper articulation not only indicates the direction of movement and facilitates an understanding of the circulation system, it also gives users an indication of the importance of the destination and whether or not they have access to it. In this respect, paths and gates communicate similar information.

Articulating paths in open indoor spaces with floor textures.

Hiking and nature trails or promenades are expressed by the nature of the surface covering, the treatment of the edges, and the planting along the path. How often have you taken a path that had all the trimmings of an access to a worthwhile destination only to find it just led to a garbage dump or to a garage door? How often have you been walked into a dead end?

Articulating a path by the use of landscaping.

The design of a path can tell the user whether he or she has access to the destination or not. Subtle clues make a difference in interpreting whether a path is private or public. Sometimes the message is confusing. A wayfinding study for a large hospital in Montreal found that people who entered a pavilion through what clearly appeared to be a main public entrance found themselves in a corridor that they perceived not to be public at all. They all hesitated and some of them even began looking for an alternative entrance.[4]

By introducing decorative elements, like a photo exhibition on an appropriate theme, it would have been quite feasible to have communicated a message of public access.

11.3.2 Finding a path

The urban fabric and the layout of a building incorporate different systems of paths. Finding a path becomes an issue when people transfer scale or when they move from one type of circulation pattern to another.

In a typical urban wayfinding example of reaching a public building, each of the following wayfinding decisions requires information about the location of a path:

- To go from the public city street to the semi-public parking lot
- To go from the parking lot to the entrance of the building
- To go into the building
- To go from the entrance to the appropriate corridor

Entrances/exits and gates are the transition points from one scale and circulation pattern to another. In the previous section we outlined the means at a designer's disposal to communicate entrances and exits of buildings. The same architectural features, with appropriate adjustments, are used to express all transition points.

It is therefore recommended that access to a corridor from an interior square, for example, be considered like an entrance and emphasized according to its importance to allow for easy detection.

Interior transition point: "entrance" to a new circulation system. Union Bank of Switzerland, Zurich.

The difficulty in finding good examples of well-articulated transition points between different circulation systems may well indicate that this is a neglected aspect of architectural communication.

11.3.3 Vertical access

Given that the vertical circulation is a must when you need to change levels, stairs, escalators, and elevators should be directly perceived upon entering a setting. They can be strong architectural features and there is absolutely no reason why it should be necessary to install signs leading to them.

The issue here is not to do away with signs for esthetic or purist reasons. However, as we shall see in the chapters on signage, one of the most common problems in perceiving and understanding signs is information overload. In terms of environmental communication, fewer signs makes for better signage.

Main stair of the Paris Opera, 1861–1874, Charles Garnier.

Lloyd's Bank, London.

The intention behind the design of the main stair of the Paris Opera by Charles Garnier was no doubt more than just getting people from one level to another. Quite apart from its social intention, it expresses clearly its original function, it is certainly not difficult to find, and, thanks to its distinctive architecture, it is also both a reference point and a landmark. Contemporary "Garnier escalators" for Lloyd's Bank translate the importance of the vertical circulation into a technological language. In terms of wayfinding design, both examples clearly express the same information.

The two illustrations opposite impress by the importance given to the vertical circulation in terms of size and design. While space may be limited, design is not. Even small vertical accesses can be communicated efficiently, and even small vertical accesses can be of landmark quality.

Weak architectural expression of an escalator.

The examples shown here are testimonies to inadequate design. The illustration above shows an escalator in a shopping complex which does not communicate its presence sufficiently strongly, and typically, the added sign does not contribute much to solving the problem either. The elevators in the example below, although architecturally clearly expressed, are tucked away out of sight when entering the setting.

Hidden elevators. Insufficient architectural expression of vertical access.

133

Chapter 11
Architectural wayfinding communication
11.4 The circulation system

11.4 The circulation system

In the previous chapter we outlined a typology of circulation systems from which we identified four circulation patterns (shoe-string, Gestalt, systematized, and network or repetitive patterns). For each pattern we were able to describe the information needed by the users to map the circulation system. In this section we look at building form and its relation to the circulation system.

11.4.1 The circulation system as architecture

The form of the circulation system may be more or less visible to the users of a setting. Buildings organized around an open well have the advantage of providing the users with a visual and sometimes auditory access to the form of the circulation system.

Recently, architects and urban planners have rediscovered that circulation also has a form that can enhance the setting and give it a special character.

In terms of wayfinding design, this is a happy development. The architectural expression of the circulation system makes for a building that is much easier to understand. The Centre Pompidou in Paris is characterized by its exposed circulation system. There is the "backbone" of the building, in full view.

The Transport Canada headquarters in Montreal, with its interior circulation system, gives a strong formal expression which immediately provides everything the users need to know to get around efficiently.

The circulation system as a form-giving element. Centre Pompidou, Paris, 1976, Richard Rogers and Renzo Piano.

Transport Canada headquarters. Dorval, Quebec, 1987, Fichten-Soiferman.

11.4.2 Communicating the circulation system

Among the most difficult settings to understand are those underground, including parking garages, subway stations, shopping malls and multifunctional urban complexes. Two major reasons can be given to explain the difficulties we have understanding these settings.

Underground settings may be less well organized than buildings. The underground network in downtown Osaka, which links two main railway stations, a number of smaller railways, and the subway stations through shopping concourses, defies any organizational principle. With over fifty exit stairs, it is confusing for foreign visitors and Japanese alike.

Underground settings are difficult even if the circulation system is simple. We have data to show that even a layout essentially rectangular in form is difficult to understand if it is underground. The only distinction with an equivalent building above ground is that the latter has a building form that gives it an objectlike character and that tells people something about what is going on inside.

Building form can express the spatial organization of the setting and the linking circulation system. It can, but it does not do it automatically. In the pairs of illustrations below, the square

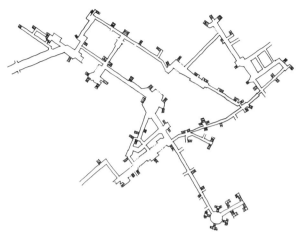

Underground shopping network in Osaka linking railway and subway stations.

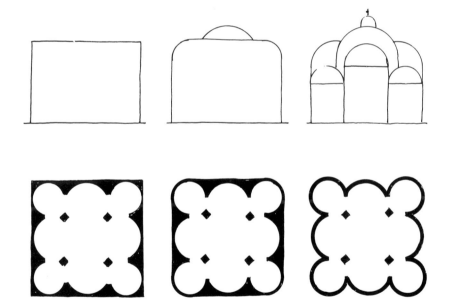

The forms of buildings as a means of revealing the layout.

building shown in elevation on the left probably expresses a rectangular layout, but theoretically it could house a Renaissance-type, centrally organized layout with a focal circulation, as shown underneath. The building form in this case would not reveal any of the content. It might even be seen to express misleading information. Moving to the right, building forms illustrated become progressively more revealing. The fully articulated building tells us everything about its internal central organization. Clearly, a person perceiving a well-articulated building is in possession of valuable wayfinding information. The perceived spatial organization serves as a framework for building a cognitive map and for integrating information that will be obtained inside.

Chapter 11
Architectural wayfinding communication
11.4 The circulation system

The Banyoles Hotel for the rowing competition of the 1992 Olympics in Spain contains 150 rooms arranged on a linear circulation pattern apparently inspired by the movements of oars. The linear layout is taken up in the building form. The plans of the layout and the elevations are so similar that they may be confused.

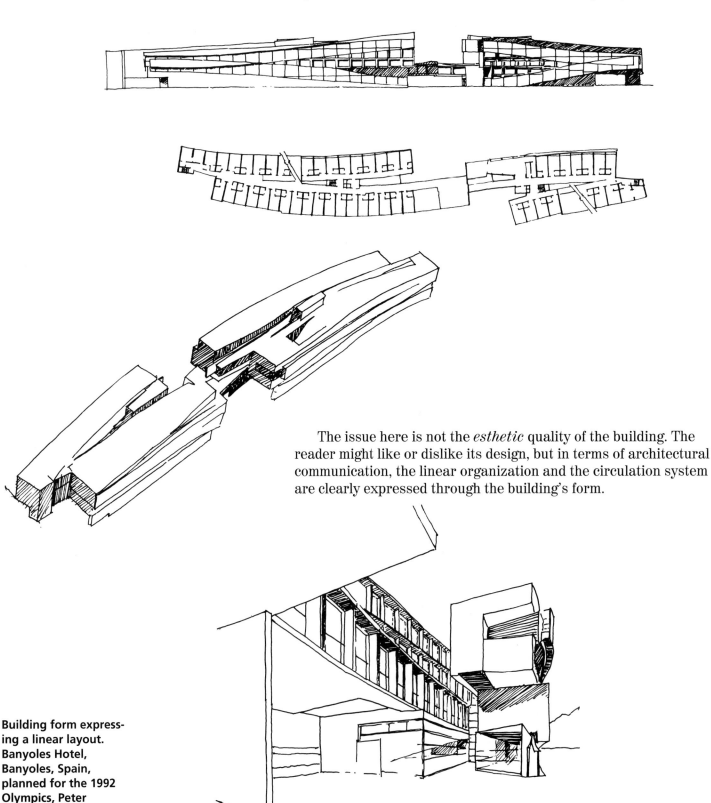

The issue here is not the *esthetic* quality of the building. The reader might like or dislike its design, but in terms of architectural communication, the linear organization and the circulation system are clearly expressed through the building's form.

Building form expressing a linear layout. Banyoles Hotel, Banyoles, Spain, planned for the 1992 Olympics, Peter Eisenman.

A circular auditorium is the organizing force of the cultural center for Avezzano. The circular layout finds an echo in the overall form of the building, the almost full circle of the auditorium, and the broken rings containing exhibition spaces, libraries, and lecture rooms. The elevations reinforce the building form. They are composed of uninterrupted ring-slabs. The positioning of the entrances and the windows in the breakages of the rings strengthens the communication of the central organizational principle. Even the landscape architecture reflects the organizational principle in the circular pergola and path system.

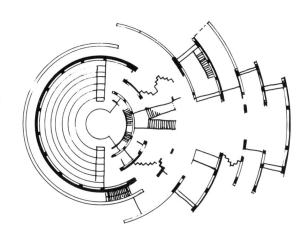

Building form expressing a centralized layout. Avezzano Cultural Center, Avezzano, Italy, 1985, Paolo Portoghesi and Vittorio Gigliotti.

Using landscaping to further emphasize the centralized layout. Avezzano Cultural Center.

Chapter 11
Architectural wayfinding communication
11.4 The circulation system

In the addition and renovation of the College of Architecture and Landscape Architecture of the University of Minnesota, the layout is composed of two major forms, a circle and a square. The circular part is the addition to the older square building. Both forms have strong Gestalt qualities and reflect the concentric circulation system. The towers in the old and new constructions contain studios.

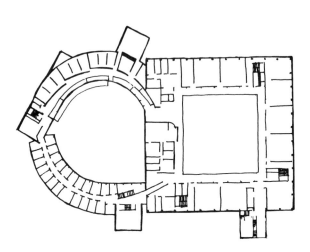

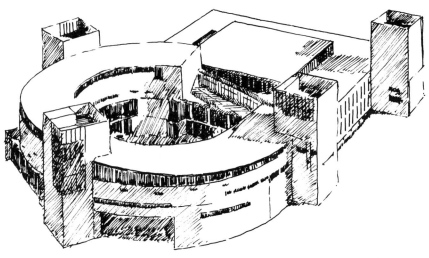

Building form expressing a composite layout. College of Architecture and Landscape Architecture, University of Minnesota, Steven Holl.

By way of contrast, what does the building below contain? How is it spatially organized? What does it say about its circulation system? The answer is, not very much.

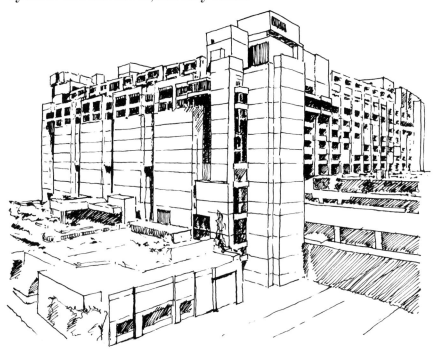

The mute building form. Place Bonaventure, Montreal, 1962–1966, Ray Affleck and Partners.

Place Bonaventure is a large urban multifunctional center containing a hotel, office spaces, trade centers, a large and fashionable commercial center, one of the largest exhibition halls in Montreal, parking garages, a railway connection, and subway connections. Although the spaces are generally considered to be agreeable and of high architectural quality, none of the content of this complex is communicated through building form and façade.

Not to use building form to express the spatial organization and the circulation of a building amounts to poor wayfinding design. A mute building is like a book without a title and without a table of contents. It does not say what it contains and it does not say how it is structured. It deprives the users of a unique opportunity to gain an overall understanding of the setting.

11.5 Planning the architectural information system: a summary

Architectural and graphic information systems go hand in hand. The basic information about entrances, exits, the location of paths and vertical accesses, and the nature of the circulation system are all in the realm of architectural communication. Graphic information may well reinforce and describe the circulation in more detail but it can rarely effectively replace missing or misplaced architectural information.

The legibility of entrances and exits is affected by the angle of approach. The decrease of legibility imposed by the steepness of the angle of approach can be compensated for by the architectural treatment of the entrance. Projected and recessed entrances heighten legibility from an oblique approach. Marquees, porticos, and colonnades have a similar impact.

Landscaping and the arrangements of paths provide strong cues to locate an entrance. If the entrance itself is not visually accessible, such as in an indirect access, the communication task falls on landscaping – or on signs.

Apart from the architectural and decorative expression of the entrance itself, the form of the layout and of the corresponding façades can indicate the locations of the entrances.

Gates communicate transition from one domain to another. They also communicate the point of entry into a destination zone, but they signify in addition the nature of the domain, as well as who may enter and under what conditions. Transition points, it is recommended, should be expressed at all levels from the largest unit (the city) all the way down to a specific place or destination zone.

Communicating the circulation system is probably the most difficult aspect of architectural wayfinding design. At the same time, it is most useful for efficient wayfinding. The circulation system can be communicated through both the form and the volume of the building. Spatial articulation is the key to understanding a setting.

In addition, we recommend that circulation be considered as more than just a link between spaces. Circulation is space and is therefore also architecture. All of its elements (gates, entrances and exits, paths, vertical access, and even the configuration of the circulation pattern) can have architectural expression. They can be given autonomous form which can make for interesting and

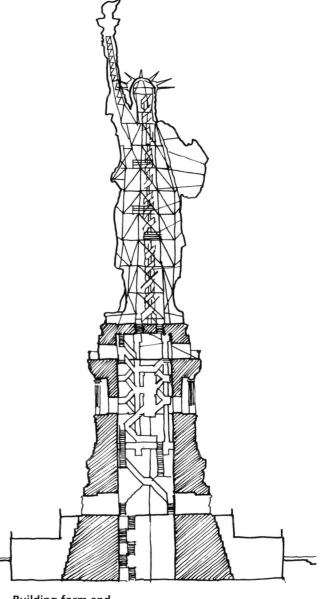

Building form and circulation: the Statue of Liberty.

Chapter 11
Architectural wayfinding communication
11.5 Planning the architectural information
system: a summary

esthetically pleasing buildings and, at the same time, for excellent wayfinding design.

Proper articulation of the circulation system coupled with the expression of destination zones will create distinctiveness, thereby giving landmark quality to these architectural elements.

Finally, we reiterate the importance of redundancy in wayfinding communication. The use of multiple means to communicate the same information is the best guarantee that the message gets across. In considering the needs of the perceptually impaired population, redundancy ought to be extended to include different sensory modalities. Rather than relying exclusively on visual means of communicating information, we should use auditory, tactile, and kinetic means as well.

Part Five:
Graphic components of wayfinding design

Classification of graphic information

Our ability to classify, and therefore to structure, information is at the basis of all knowledge. If it is not mankind's greatest gift, it is certainly one of them.

The ability to recognize and articulate the components in a signage problem puts us already close to its solution. We have found the classifications that comprise this chapter very useful in practice.

12.1 Functional information types

Graphic information should be designed in conjunction with architectural information. In wayfinding it does not matter whether information is obtained by graphic, architectural, or other means as long as it is legible and readable.

In the most basic terms, there are three things that people need in unfamiliar settings:

1. Information to make decisions, that is, information about the setting, the way it is organized, where they are in it, and where their destination lies
2. Information to execute decisions, that is, information directing them to their destination
3. Information to conclude the decision-making/executing process, that is, information identifying the destination on their arrival

Information type	Description	Examples	
Orientation and general informatiom about the setting. (This is decision-making information.)	• Information that gives users an overview of what "shape" the building has (E, H, T, L, etc.), where they are, and where the destination lies, as well as other relevant information about the general setting.	• Maps, floor plans, exploded views, and models, all with you-are-here arrows on them, and clearly identifying corridors and destination zones. • Building directories. • General dos and don'ts that affect behavior in the building, including safety information.	**?**
Directional information to destinations. (This is decision-executing information.)	• Information that guides people along a designated or pre-selected route to a destination.	• Signs with arrows or plain-language descriptions involving the use of building features or landmarks. • Floor directories in elevator lobbies. • Colored lines on walls or ceilings leading to destination zones.	**→**
Identification of destinations. (This is decision-executing information.)	• Information provided at the destination.	• Signs with names or pictographs at entrances to destinations. • Sometimes safety colors will help to identify equipment. • Signs identifying local hazards.	**id**

Chapter 12
Classification of graphic information
12.1 Functional information types

This description of functional information types may be criticized as being simplistic because the decision-making and executing processes are ongoing with people frequently changing their plans in mid-route.

Nevertheless, we must start somewhere and even if the plan is changed halfway to a given destination for a quite different one, the sequence and the information needed, particularly the graphic information, is still the same.

The signage aspect of wayfinding is frequently regarded as a hopelessly complex matter. We submit it isn't any such thing and if it is broken down into its components, it is all relatively simple.

12.2 Formal information types

Another helpful classification concerns the means available to the graphic designer for communication. There are four main classifications:

- Typographics
- Hand graphics, computer graphics, photographics
- Pictographics
- Cartographics

In addition, designers have a handful of miscellaneous tools, including, of course, color.

12.2.1 Typographics

Typographics rely mainly for their comprehension on letterforms, digits, words, or phrases. (They also rely upon the viewer's ability to see and understand them, but this is another matter and is dealt with elsewhere.) Conventional (static) signs or electronic displays

This way to the egress

Typical static verbal (or typographic) legend or message.

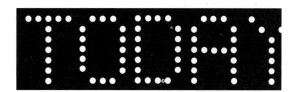

Typical electronic display. Message scrolls quickly across the signface.

of varying types all make use of typographic messages. The words appearing on the screen of a video unit or a Telecommunications Device for the Deaf (TDD) also fall into the static category.

While typographics are probably the most used means of communication in signs, their use is based on the assumption that the viewer is literate and can (if the letters are big enough) see and comprehend the message. This may frequently be too big an assumption and it is therefore best to combine pictographic with typographic messages.

There are many letterforms that are equally efficient in signs. It is false that only sans serif faces can be effective, although many low-vision people prefer them.

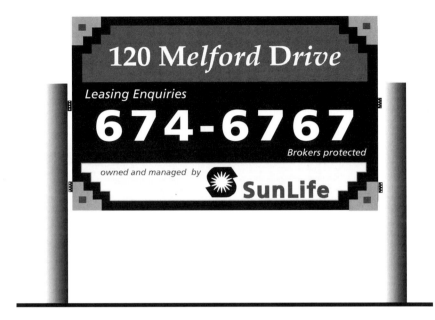

Typical static post-mounted sign. SunLife Toronto, 1990, Paul Arthur, Lawrence Burak.

12.2.2 Hand graphics, computer graphics, photographics

Drawings and diagrams in the form of hand graphics, computer graphics, and photographics are incorporated on occasion into signs. More and more frequently these are being computer generated. Video displays rely heavily on computerized graphics.

Another effective use of drawing (however generated) on signs is the replacement of a map by an illustration of the reality that the viewer is looking at. Words inserted into the drawing identify buildings and other elements that can not be identified by signs – or that are too far away for the sign to be read. In such cases, the natural features or building shapes *become* the signs. One sees signs like these in places such as the mountains or Niagara Falls where features that are unsignable can be readily identified.

Drawing may also be very effectively used to illustrate or to explain a given process in a sign, for instance, the correct method for inserting a form into a machine.

Photographics fulfil the same function as drawings on video displays: they explain a process or portray reality in lieu of maps.

Photographs taken from a 60-degree oblique angle (or a 90-degree, overhead) can also form most effective bases for maps. Their inherent realism tends to overcome the difficulty so many people have with drawn or stylized maps.

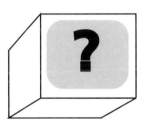

Video displays are effectively replacing signs in interior spaces.

12.2.3 Pictographics

While pictographs are drawings that may be hand or computer generated, they belong in a classification of their own because they are essentially symbols or icons representing reality. While efforts are made to strive for "realism" (the dial as a pictograph for a phone, for example, is avoided because this no longer a proper representation of the telephone), they are frequently quite abstract (see section 13.2.2).

A typical "realistic" pictograph.

Chapter 12
Classification of graphic information
12.2 Formal information types

Pictographs, glyphs, or symbols (all more or less synonyms) are used in symbol signs which can, through the combination of color and shape, provide a richness of information that transcends the simple meaning of the glyph itself.

While the use of pictographs is an effective method of cutting across linguistic and literacy barriers, it is doubtful that more than

Three typical "abstract" or conceptual pictographs to identify "information," "enter," and "no entry" respectively.

a relatively small number of symbol signs can be presented without the support or clarification of words.[1]

12.2.4 Cartographics

Maps are also now generated mainly by computers, although there are still cartographers who draw their maps.

Section of a computer-generated map. George Brown College, Toronto, 1990, Paul Arthur.

Like so much to do with graphics in environmental communication, the effectiveness of a map is hard to evaluate. While everybody says they find a map helpful, many people experience great difficulties in using them.

For one thing, maps slant reality up on its end (unless they are displayed flat or semi-flat), which is hard to get used to. For another, unless they are properly aligned or oriented to the setting, they are virtually impossible to use.

Axonometric (60-degree) views tend to overcome many people's difficulties with maps (they prefer them),[2] as does the use of a photographic base for overhead (90-degree) views. In both cases, the photos are retouched to eliminate unnecessary details and are overlaid with graphics.

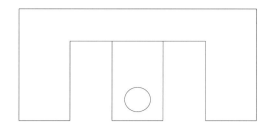

There is a lot less useful information in a direct overhead (90-degree) plan than in an axonometric (60-degree) view.

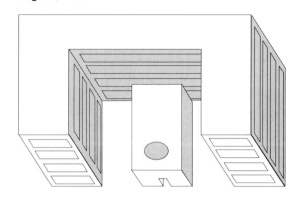

12.2.5 Other

The graphic designer has, of course, other means at his or her disposal – from markings and lines on the walls or ceilings, to signal lights to provide visual information, to bells and buzzers, and color.

12.3 Sign types

12.3.1 By function

Wayfinding signs, whether exterior or interior, have three functions which directly correspond to the functional information types that were the subject of section 12.1 above:

- *Orientation signs:* building directories, maps, hours of service
- *Directional signs:* signs with or without arrows
- *Identification signs:* signs in verbal and/or non-verbal form

12.3.2 By physical characteristics

Although there are several different ways to construct a sign and to create the graphics on it, when we look at signs, we tend to categorize them in one of three ways only:

- *Self-supporting* on a post, a slab, or a plinth
- *Wall mounted*, either flat on a vertical surface or projecting
- *Suspended* from a soffit or ceiling

In addition, of course, self-supporting and suspended signs may be single or double faced. They may be internally illuminated or externally illuminated – or not artificially illuminated at all. They may also be either static or dynamic.

Static signs are the conventional signs that we have always been used to. The messages they display when they are first installed are the messages they will always communicate, whether they are relevant or not to visitor needs at that place and time.

Dynamic signs, by contrast, are designed to respond instantly and electronically to the requirements of the moment. At a given decision or entrance point, for example, it is entirely possible that

1

2

3

4

Signs may be supported (1), suspended (2), mounted on a flat surface (3), or cantilevered off a wall (4).

relevant information in the morning is different from that which should be displayed in the afternoon. Monitors in airports, or large arrival and departure boards, are in a constant state of change throughout the entire day.

Much is made in Chapter 15 of the need to provide wayfinders with the right (i.e., the most up to date) information at the right time (i.e., when they need it), and at the right place (i.e., where they need it). In highly fluid settings such as airports, amusement parks, or sports arenas, for example, dynamic signs provide the obvious answer. In more stable situations, they may still be useful, but on a much more limited basis.

Chapter 13

Forms of graphic information

The purpose of "the graphics" in wayfinding is to assist people first in the decision-making process and then in the decision-executing process, in other words, to help them find their way to their destinations along their chosen routes.

Before we come to the kinds of graphics involved in each process, in two subsequent chapters, we deal here with the forms that graphic information may take.

For purposes of simplicity, we subdivide these forms into two major groups: verbal (or typographic) and non-verbal (or pictographic). Each is discussed in terms of how it is affected by color, layout, and lighting.

13.1 Verbal (or typographic) information

13.1.1 Content and language

In terms of verbal wayfinding information, there are two important points to make about the content of signs:

1. Signs should be plain, not fancy, and to the greatest extent possible in the language of the visitor rather than that of the management or staff.
2. In some cases plain language as the sole content of the sign may be preferable to graphic information.

The challenge of producing good signage is made more difficult by the fact that many people have reading problems that range from just poor reading habits all the way up to not being able to read at all.

Content

All too frequently, the messages contained in signs in a building complex have little – or even nothing – to do with the users and their needs. Instead, all they do is satisfy management's need to inform the public about its organizational structure.

Governments are the worst offenders in this connection – followed closely by health-care facilities (such as hospitals and clinics) and by institutions of learning (such as universities and colleges).

In hospitals, the display of messages in Latin (Otorhinolaryngology, for example, for Ear, Nose, and Throat, or Radiology for X-ray) is sheer elitism, guaranteed to bewilder the already confused wayfinder. Is it any wonder, then, that in a medium-sized hospital up to 8000 hours a year of staff time (or four person-years) are spent explaining the signs and redirecting people?

The sort of highly legible but totally unreadable sign that is still being displayed in hospital environments.

Institutions of learning, particularly community colleges, make it difficult for prospective students (whose sole aim in visiting them is to obtain information on alternative careers) by their practice of displaying only departmental names on their directories. Even worse is the habit of dressing up ordinary skills in fancy names that almost invariably need translation. People wanting to upgrade their clerical skills or to get into social work will have considerable trouble with college calendars or catalogs and with directory boards that identify the information they want under such headings as "records and information manager" or "human services counsellor."

If Canadians who want to travel abroad go to the designated government building for their documentation, they will look in vain for the word "Passports" on the directory board. Instead, they must know the name of the issuing government department (External Affairs) – but only a tiny fraction of them do, and thus they need someone to translate the sign for them.

What all this adds up to is that graphic wayfinding information is more than a physical matter of getting visitors efficiently to their destinations. It also involves helping them to determine what their

Chapter 13
Forms of graphic information
13.1 Verbal (or typographic) information

A plain language alternative to directional signs with arrows placed strategically at vertical circulation areas. It also reduces the number of signs.

Where is information? One level up? Or one down? Or is it, by any chance, straight ahead?

destination is called, because, as we have shown, in many instances they will simply not know.

The simple answer, of course, is to avoid the need for translations. Directory boards should be organized according to the services that people have come in search of – and in the plainest of plain language – not according to the way in which the institution is structured.

Plain language signs

It may seem like the expression of a philosophy of despair to state about anything that we have always considered so "graphic" as signage that these graphic elements, far from being an aid in wayfinding, often contribute to the problem.

As we become more scientific and professional about the nature and purpose of environmental communication, we may come to the conclusion that the answer to many of the more complex problems of providing orientation and directional information in a public building may lie in such non-graphic means as plain language. This may be either spoken (i.e., audible) or typographic (i.e., visual). In Part Six of this book, we deal extensively with the role of the spoken word in wayfinding. In this chapter, we deal with signs.

The point is that there are environments (art galleries and museums come to mind, but there are many others) in which the graphic language of arrows can effectively give way to words by providing answers to questions the visitor has in mind.

For example, the answer to "How do I get to the washrooms?" can be very simply worded on a sign: "Down the stairs, then turn left," with a pictograph of a washroom. Such a sign at the top of the stairs would naturally be expected to provide other information in a similar way. However, its great merit lies in the fact that no further directional information or signs are required – other than proper identification of the washrooms themselves.

There are several reasons why such plain language signs are preferable to those relying upon graphic devices. For one thing, much graphic "language" is not readily understood by the public. It confuses them, and this is the least desirable characteristic that any sign can have.

For example, whereas arrows pointing left or right are reasonably clear, there is nothing clear about those pointing up or down. In some places an arrow pointing down means "downstairs," while in the UK it means "straight ahead." On the other hand, an arrow pointing up never means "upstairs," and in North America it is supposed to indicate "straight ahead."

Symbols or pictographs may be acceptable to many people, but only a few are universally understandable to everyone. By themselves, most of them tend to confuse and therefore to irritate people.

But just as importantly, the use of plain language signs vastly reduces the overall number of signs needed in a complex, particularly those intended to provide directions. For example, providing an easy-to-follow route for visitors to a given department or office in a large building complex is no easy task. Part of the solution is spatial planning that visitors can understand and that actually helps them. But there is still the need for signs.

Directional signs with arrows at each and every decision point is one possibility (see p. 176). However, as any single office is unlikely to be the only destination in so large a building, there would be the need for signs at every one of these decision points for all of the other destinations as well.

The result is not only costly and unsightly, it is also non-assimilable. The average person, confronted with this sort of information overload, whether it be too many typographic messages, too many pictographs, or too many colors, is hopelessly confused and stops trying to use the signs.

By contrast, the number of signs needed can be enormously reduced if signs are in plain language and placed in strategic locations, or if mini-information centers capable of being interrogated are available to visitors. Such an information centre, in answer to the question "How do I get to such and such?" will reply plainly, in the language of the visitor's choice, "Take the elevator at the end of the corridor to the 4th floor, Room 432."

On the other hand, we are far from being unaware that more (not less) language in signs is not going to help people with literacy or reading problems. Obviously, then, this technique can be used only selectively. The universal adoption of a solution to the current ambiguity of arrows would be a help, but the fact remains that directional signs constitute the group that is most responsible for "sign pollution" and some way must be found to reduce the number of signs required to get a visitor to a given destination. The verbal (non-graphic) approach does this – but only, of course, if the visitor can read.

It is also worthy of note that it is not enough for the language to be plain and clear, it must also be consistent: the words used for providing directional information must be identical to those used in other information types. There is no sense in directing visitors to a destination if it is going to be called one thing in the directions and another when they arrive there.

Chapter 13:
Forms of graphic information
13.1 Verbal (or typographic) information

Rail Alphabet black letters and white letters. Designed by Jock Kinneir of British Rail.

A rare case of concern for the fact that when positive and negative letters are used in a sign, some compensation must be made for the fact that there is a 10 to 12 percent difference in weight between the two.

In this alphabet, the two are in perfect balance.

Helvetica regular
Helvetica medium

Helvetica letterforms in light and medium versions. Both are equally legible, despite differences in stem thickness.

13.1.2 Letterforms: what constitutes a good one?

No one knows what constitutes a good signage letter. Not for certain, anyway. The only people with the apparently unlimited funds necessary to find out are in the Department of Transportation (DOT) in the United States. After years of research, they ended

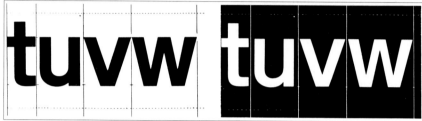

up with a decidedly ugly letterform. At any rate, graphic designers find it ugly, and to our knowledge it has never been used for anything *but* highway signs.

In Great Britain, they do things differently. The designer Jock Kinneir was asked to develop a letterform for signage. His solution, "Rail Alphabet," would not be regarded as ugly by anyone and has, moreover, the enormous advantage of being available in two weights, so it can be used in positive or negative form and can compensate for the effects of halation or irradiation (see section 13.1.7).

The conventional wisdom on the subject is that a "good" letterform for signage is an "efficient" one and that efficiency resides in stem thickness – in other words, the ratio established between the stroke width and the height of the capital letters (cap-height).[1] There is ample evidence to demonstrate this is an irrelevancy. For example, both sighted and partially sighted persons find Helvetica medium and Helvetica light to be equally legible – and yet they are at opposite ends of the scale: the medium has a stroke width to cap-height ratio of 1:5 while the light is 1:8.

The matter of stroke width does become important, however, when letters become excessively bold. This increase in weight is exclusively at the expense of the interstices between such elements as the horizontal bars of a capital E or F or in the counters of letters like O or P. When these spaces become substantially less than is desirable by virtue of the fattening of the letterform, legibility suffers and a less acceptable letterform is the result.

Of far greater importance than stroke width is whether a one inch (25 mm) capital letter will be legible at 50 feet (15 m) under "ideal" conditions (see section 13.1.4).[2] One of the major compo-

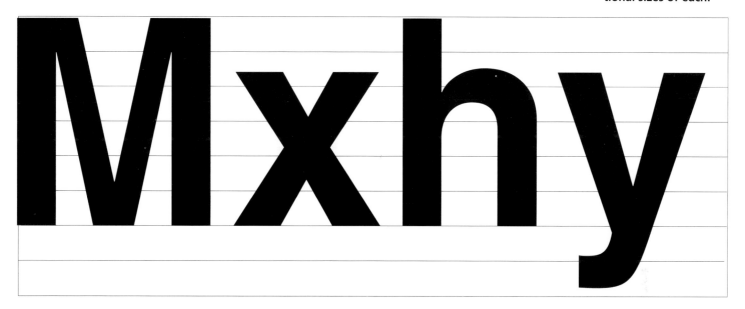

nents in such legibility (or efficiency) is, in our view, not stem thickness but the ratio of the x-height to the cap-height.

We contend that the best letters for signage purposes have a ratio between x-height and cap-height of at least 3:4. We regard letters having smaller x-height to cap-height ratios as inappropriate for signage purposes.

Not everyone agrees. The very talented type designer Erik Spiekermann, when queried recently on this subject, said that the issue of the ratio of x-height to cap-height was a ridiculous irrelevancy (or words to this effect). He contended that any letterform that is legible in print will be equally so in signage.

While Mr Spiekermann always speaks charmingly, and with the benefit of an encyclopedic knowledge of letterforms, we must disagree radically with him on this. On an empirical basis (and, admittedly, this is all we have to go on), we *know* that typefaces such as Bodoni, Walbaum, Times, Garamond, Bembo, and a whole host of others, which may all be perfect for print, make terrible signage faces (although not always for reasons having to do with x-height to cap-height ratios).

Good signage letters have an "x-height" to cap-height ratio of at least 3:4.

The letter "x" is the measure of lower-case letters that are neither ascenders nor descenders and from which comes the term "x-height." In signage letters, the x-height should be not less than 75 percent of the cap-height.

The anatomy of a message and its component parts.

cap ascender ascender ascender ascender

The quick brown fox

descender the letter "x"

Chapter 13
Forms of graphic information
13.1 Verbal (or typographic) information

Stem thickness does, however, play an important role in legibility – but only in terms of its consistency. Because sans serif typefaces like Helvetica enjoy a high degree of such consistency, they may be more efficient than serif typefaces which tend to have greater differences between thick and thin strokes within the same letter. On the other hand, all the typefaces shown on the following pages would seem to be equally legible.[3]

This, of course, is yet another reason for discarding stroke thickness ratio as a factor in determining acceptability of serif letterforms. Moreover, it is impossible to make any statement of any kind about this subject in terms of serif letters.

One might be forgiven for asking why we do not then stick with Helvetica, which gained such wide acceptance in signage in the late 60s and throughout the 70s. The answer is that the esthetic component in signage design, although it may quite properly be disparaged, will not go away. And given the preferences for alternative faces expressed by architects, graphic designers, and building owners, it is unlikely that the current trend towards the use of other sans serif and serif letters will be reversed. The fact, however, remains that there is need for serious research to determine what really constitutes a good signage letter.

A brief selection of suitable signage letterforms.[4]

Century Schoolbook.

ABCDEFGHI
JKL MNOP QR
STUVWX YZ

abcdefghijk
lmnopqrstu
vwxyz

1234567890

A B C D E F G H I
J K L M N O P Q R
S T U V W X Y Z

---

a b c d e f g h i j k
l m n o p q r s t u
v w x y z

---

1 2 3 4 5 6 7 8 9 0

Palatino bold.

A B C D E F G H I
J K L M N O P Q R
S T U V W X Y Z

---

a b c d e f g h i j k
l m n o p q r s t u
v w x y z

---

1 2 3 4 5 6 7 8 9 0

Palatino bold italic.

Chapter 13
Forms of graphic information
13.1 Verbal (or typographic) information

A brief selection of suitable signage letterforms.

Frutiger Roman.

ABCDEFGHI
JKLMNOPQR
STUVWXYZ

abcdefghijk
lmnopqrstu
vwxyz

1234567890

Helvetica regular.

ABCDEFGHI
JKLMNOPQR
STUVWXYZ

abcdefghijk
lmnopqrstu
vwxyz

1234567890

Frutiger bold.

ABCDEFGHI
JKLMNOPQR
STUVWXYZ

abcdefghijk
lmnopqrstu
vwxyz

1234567890

Helvetica medium.

ABCDEFGHI
JKLMNOPQR
STUVWXYZ

abcdefghijk
lmnopqrstu
vwxyz

1234567890

Chapter 13
Forms of graphic information
13.1 Verbal (or typographic) information

A brief selection of
suitable signage
letterforms.

Helvetica bold con-
densed.

ABCDEFGHI
JKLMNOPQR
STUVWXYZ

abcdefghijk
lmnopqrstu
vwxyz

1234567890

Glypha bold.

ABCDEFGHI
JKLMNOPQR
STUVWXYZ

abcdefghijk
lmnopqrstu
vwxyz

1234567890

A B C D E F G H I
J K L M N O P Q R
S T U V W X Y Z

a b c d e f g h i j k
l m n o p q r s t u
v w x y z

1 2 3 4 5 6 7 8 9 0

Eras medium.

A B C D E F G H I
J K L M N O P Q R
S T U V W X Y Z

a b c d e f g h i j k
l m n o p q r s t u
v w x y z

1 2 3 4 5 6 7 8 9 0

Eras demi.

Chapter 13
Forms of graphic information
13.1 Verbal (or typographic) information

Burlington
NEXT RIGHT

An interesting use of
caps and upper- and
lower-case letters in
the structuring of a
message in a highway
sign.[5]

stopped

STOPPED

Miles Tinker in his
Legibility in Print used
this example to
demonstrate his
theory of "word
forms" which he
claims were so much
more distinctive in

upper- and lower-case
letters than they were
in caps. He also
pointed out that caps
require 35 percent
more area than
lower-case letters.

accuse   **pant**

answer   **punt**

While true as far as it
goes, Tinker's state-
ment about the
"distinctiveness" of
shapes of individual

words is not borne
out by the illustra-
tions. *Many* words
have identical shapes.

13.1.3 CAPS vs. lower case: do we really know?

Time was, say in the mid-60s, when the messages in signs were all in caps. Many still are, of course. Corporate logotypes such as IBM, AT&T, store names such as SEARS and EATON'S, and most safety signs (DANGER) perpetuate this practice. But for the majority of signs, the contemporary orthodoxy is to display messages in upper- and lower-case letters because these are "more easy to read."

Highway signs, which used to be exclusively in capital letters, now make use of both alphabets – as in signs with directions (Burlington NEXT RIGHT).

The argument in favor of upper- and lower-case letters is that we don't decode a message letter by letter the way cryptographers do; we recognize whole words and phrases by their shape or "word forms." This, the argument continues, is much easier to do in upper and lower case than when messages are all in caps. A distinctive shape is created (formed by the configuration of caps, ascenders, descenders, etc.) rather than a simple rectangle that is always the same shape.

As a result, it is safe to say that today (and for some time past) professional graphic designers wouldn't dream of using capital letters exclusively in a sign system – although they are having second thoughts about this in advertising and packaging, as we shall see.

Designers regard this as a hard-won victory for common sense over reactionary forces and are always quick to point out, whenever they see a sign anywhere in capital letters, that it would have been "much better" had it only been done properly, that is to say, in upper- and lower-case letters.

Pity the poor Romans who had no lower-case alphabet! The invention of miniscule letters (which came about much later) was a way to increase the speed of writing manuscripts and had, originally, nothing to do with reading them.

Thus when I (Paul Arthur) learned that researchers at Georgia Tech were coming out with the unwholesome theory that blind persons (most of whom don't read braille) found tactile caps much easier to read than combinations of tactile upper- and lower-case letters, my immediate reaction was that this was just too bad. Hard-won victories for the benefit of the majority could not be sacrificed to benefit a relatively insignificant minority.

Now, where did this theory of shape recognition which has so many enthusiastic adherents come from? Our first encounter with it was on reading Miles Tinker's *Legibility in Print*, published in 1963.[6]

Admittedly Tinker was only peripherally referring to signs. His findings were based on reading habits in books. Many of us remember being disappointed that he could not claim that upper- and lower-case letters were more than 12 percent "more efficient" (i.e., quicker to read) than caps. We were hoping for something more dramatic, but these were the only statistics available to us and we made them our own.

More recently, however, we have learned that our reading habits with respect to signs are *not* the same as those with print. Sighted people do not read signs the way they read a book or a newspaper, that is to say, in a highly structured manner, in a series of "takes" from left to right (or even vertically, if the column is narrow enough, as in a newspaper), from top to bottom of the column or the page. As has already been noted (section 5.3.1), people don't "read" signs at all. They "scan" them in a series of unstructured, random glances – in much the same unsystematic way that we search for "meaning" in a non-objective work of art.

Dare we think the unthinkable? Is it possible that, because our reading habits with print and with signs are so radically different, the argument in favor of shape recognition and word forms as a major criterion for legibility in signs may be questioned?

May we even doubt the efficacy of shape recognition? The average English word is five or six characters long and to think that each of these tens of thousands of five- or six-letter words has its own distinctive shape is nonsense. In fact the overall number of different shapes is extremely limited. To start with, all words of five or six characters composed solely of x-height letters have the same shape; so do words of the same length beginning with an ascender and terminating in a descender. And so on.

But having begun to think the unthinkable, let us now introduce the evidence of reading therapists. These specialists have a single function: to help people read properly.[7]

We all have sloppy reading habits, even those of us who do not think of ourselves as having "reading problems" and certainly aren't illiterate. Yet how many of us have read a sign (or a message) for what we thought it *should* say rather than what it *does* say? Or for what we *hoped* or *expected* it to say?

Reading therapists have few good words to say about lower-case letters. They regard them as "treacherous." Fully 70 percent of such letters can be confused with another letter (b and d, p and q, u and n, and so on for eighteen of the twenty-six lower-case letters). Talk about treacherous! By contrast, the use of capital letters reduces the incidence of confusion of one letter with another.

Reading therapists are mainly involved with helping illiterate persons within the context of print. What they have to say to perfectly literate people in the context of signs is that the combination of inadequate lighting conditions, glare, angular distortion, and halation can cause all of us to misread messages in upper- and lower-case letters.

Given that our methods of reading print on a page do not necessarily apply to the way we read signs, and that a large percentage of us (five million Canadians and fifty million Americans) have reading problems, the issue of whether all messages in signs should really be in upper- and lower-case letters needs to be reexamined.

Once we permit ourselves to think the unthinkable, it is disturbing where our thoughts lead us.

Fasten Seat Belts

fasten seat belts

FASTEN SEAT BELTS

Which is easier to read?

b d	B D
c o	C O
h b	H B
l 1	L 1
m n	M N
p q	P Q
u v	U V

Many of the letters in the lower-case alphabet are easily confused with other letters.

This increases the problems of persons who have reading difficulties in their attempts to understand what signs are saying to them.

Note how very much easier it is to distinguish the differences between capital letters.

What does this say to those who always insist that signs must be exclusively in upper and lower case?

Chapter 13
Forms of graphic information
13.1 Verbal (or typographic) information

THE
the
The
the
The
THE
Six ways of saying the same thing.

Roman Roman
Italic *Italic*

Palatino bold with its distinctive italic.

Frutiger bold whose italic is merely a sloping Roman.

Two examples of packaging design that effectively depart from conventional use of upper- and lower-case typography. Loblaws Ltd., 1978, 1983, Don Watt.

In actual fact, what we misleadingly call Roman orthography comprises no less than three methods of conveying messages:

- in CAPITAL LETTERS only
- in lower-case letters only
- in a mixture of the two, using caps for proper nouns and at the beginnings of sentences

Compounding this we have yet another variant: italics, which can apply to each of the other three. Not all italic letters, however, are just sloping Romans. A true italic may be very different in form from the Roman version of the same letter; Palatino is an example.

Whether we like it or not, this issue of caps vs. lower case is already under review. Advertising and packaging in the food industry are both areas of current experimentation. The motivation may be nothing more than novelty. But it may be a genuine attempt to eliminate some of the reading problems of consumers, particularly those problems involving the use of upper- and lower-case letters in combination. Two current and notable trends in this connection are 1) the use of all CAPS and 2) the use of all lower-case letters.

The well-known Bauhaus designer Herbert Bayer made valiant efforts in the 30s, 40s, and 50s to dispense with capitals altogether and to popularize the use of lower case alone.[8] The idea, however, never caught on – until recently. It was considered by most people to be affected or, worse, cute (like the cockroach in Don Marquis' poem who typed letters to his love in lower case because he hadn't the strength to depress the shift key).

Now when we see the exclusive use of lower-case Helvetica medium in Don Watt's packaging, signs, and advertising promotions for Loblaws (a Canadian food chain), we don't find it the least bit cute or self-conscious. It is used in the context of "no-name," generic products, and it somehow symbolically fulfils the "no frills" criterion, which is complemented by the extensive use of yellow as a background color.

More recently, the same designer developed packaging for the same food chain for a newer up-scale version of the chain's own label (called "President's Choice"), which makes use of Futura caps exclusively. Not a lower-case letter in sight anywhere.

Both of these product lines, their signs, and their promotional literature are very attractive *and* very legible, so where does this leave us in a discussion of shape and word form recognition? The answer (if we are honest about it, and if we can just forget about our "hard-won victories") is, nowhere.

The fact that lower-case letters are indeed very treacherous can no longer be totally ignored. Nor can the fact that, in emergency situations, messages that are all in caps seem to be preferred.

Research (when it is done) will probably demonstrate that in hospitals, particularly those with a majority of elderly patients, messages in all-caps will be preferred over those in upper and lower case combined. Building directories, however, which are probably "read" more like print than other signs are (i.e., more systematically), should probably not be in capital letters.

The bottom line is that so much in environmental communication is not known. We just don't know. How long we shall be satisfied with such an unsatisfactory situation is not known either.

13.1.4 Legibility distance

Every letterform or distinctive alphabet has its own legibility distance factor, depending upon its design characteristics. The term "legibility distance" really defines the "efficiency" of the letter (or other graphic element) in terms of use. It dictates the size that letters in a sign must be if they are to be perceived and recognized from a given distance.

If, for example, a sign is going to be seen (and therefore also comprehended) at, say, 200 feet (60 m) away, how large should the letter be? This is not a subjective matter, dependent upon esthetic judgement or the wish not to "spoil" a building by having signs that are "too big." The size the letter must be (to be perceived and comprehended from 200 feet away) will also influence the size that the sign must be.

The classic yardstick for determining these things is the Helvetica letterform, which, under ideal conditions, yields 50 feet (15 m) per inch (25 mm) of cap-height. Thus, theoretically, a one-inch (25 mm) letter can be seen from 50 feet (15 m) away and consequently a 4-inch (100 mm) letter will be required if the sign is to be seen from a distance of 200 feet (60 m).[9]

Of course, this is under ideal circumstances involving little or no angular distortion of the letters, perfectly adequate lighting conditions, no glare off the sign surface – and perfect 20/20 vision by the viewer.[10]

When such ideal circumstances cannot be counted upon, allowances must be made to ensure legibility. When, for example, a sign will be seen in a corridor under less than ideal lighting conditions by persons whose eyesight cannot be counted upon to be perfect, the 50-feet-per-inch rule will be reduced substantially.

Most electronic variable-message displays use capital letters (and digits) exclusively and we don't find them particularly illegible. We don't even object to the fact that contrary to all the rules of legibility, letters are made up from a dot matrix of 35 points of light.

Liquid crystal displays (LCDs) used in digital watches, for example, are also restricted to capital letters and digits. But we don't object to them as being illegible either.

The fact is that we are exposed to both of these in contexts very different from that of reading print. Looking at signs and trying to get information from them has more in common with glancing at our watches than it has with reading a book.

Any letter that is not legible at 50 feet per inch (or 15 m/25 mm) of cap-height is unacceptable.

Chart illustrating legibility-distance data based on cap-heights in Helvetica – under perfect conditions. Campus Graphics, State University Construction Fund, Albany, NY, 1970, Paul Arthur.

Chapter 13
Forms of graphic information
13.1 Verbal (or typographic) information

It is frequently argued that letter sizes in signs need *not* be uniform but that their size should be a function of importance. Some messages, the argument goes, may be more important than others and should therefore be composed of bigger letters.

We disagree strongly. While there may be occasions when it is desirable to structure information in this way, surely the use of bold and regular letters of the same size is superior – particularly in view of the criterion that all of a sign should be capable of being read and understood from the distance at which it is seen.

Collections
American
Canadian
European

Services
Pay phones
Cafeteria
Washrooms

Letter sizes

Given all of the conditions that go into downgrading the ideal situation where a Helvetica letter yields 50 feet (15 m) of distance per inch (25 mm) of cap-height, it is our contention that the minimum lettersize for orientation, general information, and identification purposes is approximately one inch (25 mm) cap-height. Lettering for directional purposes should, for the same reasons, be approximately 1.75 inches (45 mm) cap-height.[11] In very large complexes or wherever such sizes may be considered inadequate (as, for example, when the use of suspended signs is indicated), the letter size will need to be increased.

The reasoning behind the recommendation for these minimum letter sizes is influenced by the following:

- Angular distortion will reduce legibility distance by as much as 30 to 50 percent.
- Less than optimal lighting conditions will reduce it still further.
- The fact that everybody's vision is not perfect must be taken into account.

All of this refers equally to graphic symbols such as arrows and also to pictographics. The design of these elements is discussed in this chapter and it will be noted that the rules of legibility distance affect these elements as well.

13.1.5 Spacing systems

Inter-line

All line-spacing systems are based on units, of which a fixed number are allocated to determine the space above the capital

A hierarchically structured message, providing emphasis by the use of varying weights of letter rather than by size.

In principle, at least, all letters in a sign should be the same size, even if there is a need for a particular emphasis. The assumption has to be that all parts of the sign should be equally legible at all times.

The two most useful sizes of letter for interior signs, measured on the cap-height, are 1 inch and 1.75 inches.

The smaller applies to identification signs to be viewed beside doors or entrances and should be regarded as the minimum size for such letters. The larger is the minimum size for those in wall-mounted directional signs.

1 in. **25 mm**

letter, a further number for the cap itself, and the balance for be-low the x-line. The assumption is made that a signface is divided vertically into the number of message modules required to accom-modate the whole message. (If the sign is to have four lines, it has four such message modules.)

Each of these message modules is subdivided into a number of units. Although we have worked satisfactorily with a 12-unit sys-tem we developed many years ago, we now much prefer the 10-unit system illustrated here. It is easier to work with and accords well with metric measurements which are reasonably well established within the sign industry.[12] The principle, illustrated in the diagram, is that any given message module contains 10 units, as explained at right.

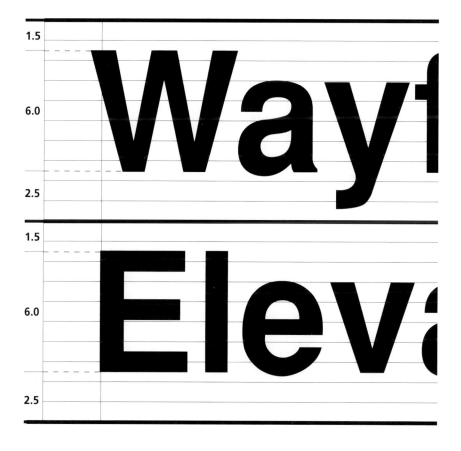

The VisuCom 10-unit inter-line spacing system is extremely easy to use and guarantees consistent vertical spacing of all lines on a sign.

Note that the line or "message module" is 10 units high and that the cap-height is 6. Cap-height is 1.5 units from the top of the "message module" and x-line is 2.5 units from the bottom. The space between the x-line of one message and the top of the message below is 4 units.

On a 1000 mm deep (39-inch) signface with five lines (all same size), each message module is 1000 mm ÷ 5 = 200 mm. Each unit is therefore 20 mm.

The space above the cap	= 1.5 x 20 =	30
The cap itself	= 6.0 x 20 =	120
The space below x-line	= 2.5 x 20 =	50
Height of message module		= 200 mm

1.75 in.   **45** mm

Chapter 13
Forms of graphic information
13.1 Verbal (or typographic) information

Inter word spacing

	fjstvwxz 147)	acdegoq 2356890	mnpru 7&	bhikl
TVWY	0	0	0	2
fkrstvwxyz AKLPQXZ (	1	2	3	3
abceop BCDEFORS 247	2	3	4	4
dghijlmmnqu GHIJMNU 135689&	3	4	5	5

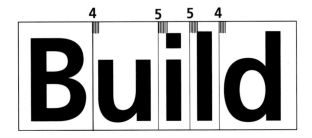

The old-fashioned way of determining inter-letter spacing was done on "tiles," each comprising a letter, and used a 5-unit system.

Today inter-letter spacing is a function of the computer-driven cutters and plotters which produce the graphic images on signs. This equipment uses a similar system automatically.

Inter-word

Because there is never any need to justify the lines of messages in a sign, the typographer's ideal of equal word spacing is easy to achieve and has the advantages of making the sign look better and increasing legibility. The space between words should, in our opinion, be equal to the space occupied by a lower-case "r."

Inter-letter

Good practice in signage, as in print, is to vary the amount of spacing between letters to compensate for their shapes and thus to produce the illusion that the spacing is equal. (In fact, if one did not do this, and inserted identical amounts of space between all letters, the line would appear to be *un*equally spaced.)

The determination of how much space to put between letters (between two o's, for example, as distinct from between two l's) used to be done by eye, and craftsmen became very skilled at doing it just so. Manufacturers of individual letters (or "tiles") for sale would also imprint on the masking tape a series of units of space. An accompanying table indicated how many units to place between individual letters depending on their juxtaposition, cap to lower case, lower case to lower case, lower case to digits, etc. All of this is now done on the computer – and frequently not very well. The principle is, however, the same.[13]

13.1.6 Angular distortion and legibility

Whenever a signface is not perceived by the viewer straight-on, angular distortion occurs, reducing the legibility of the letters. A successful signage letterform will retain at least 75 percent of its legibility when distorted 45 degrees. Under such conditions, a one-inch (25 mm) letter is legible at 35 feet (10.7 m).

13.1.7 Halation and its effects

Two identically sized images, side by side, one in positive (black on white) form, the other in reversed or negative (white on black) form will seem to be different in size. The reversed image will appear to be up to 10 to 12 percent bigger, bolder, or fatter than the other.

Recent research at Georgia Institute of Technology's College of Architecture has confirmed what designers have known from experience for some time: that good "target value" is one of a sign's most valuable characteristics.

A light-colored sign on a white wall is more difficult for anyone to spot than is a dark sign on the same white wall. This being so, the effects of having light-colored letters and symbols on darker fields must be taken into account. The phenomenon involved is called halation or irradiation because a light image located on a dark field will seem to radiate and as a result appears to be considerably larger.

British Rail in the UK has gone to the trouble of developing its standard alphabet in two different weights to compensate for one being displayed in positive, and the other in negative, form. The result is that they appear to be of identical weight (see p. 154).

13.2 Non-verbal (or pictographic) information

13.2.1 Is a picture really worth 10,000 words?

Ivan Turgenev, the 19th-century Russian writer, elaborating on an old Chinese proverb, which is the title of this section, said in one of his novels that "a picture shows me at a glance what it takes dozens of pages of a book to expound."

The wisdom of this may be sound enough in respect to technical manuals and until recently was accorded *de facto* recognition in its application to wayfinding as well. But we are now beginning to doubt this very much.

In the period that Marshall McLuhan chose to call (in order to distinguish it from our own, but with dubious accuracy) "preliterate,"[14] life was on a simpler, smaller scale, and much slower. A boot on a sign (or a sign in the form of a boot) outside a shop was a perfectly adequate identifier of the cobbler's business. But it wasn't of any real importance because everyone in town knew where his shop was anyway. So the sign was really an advertisement – or it was meant for strangers.

Other establishments advertised themselves to visitors in the same way: a mortar and pestle for the apothecary, a glove for the glovemaker, and so on. Or something a little more abstract: a helicoidally striped red and white pole with gold knobs on the top and bottom for the local surgeon and barber.

In this preliterate period, symbols might also be used effectively to represent a name, for example, names of pubs traditionally went in for exotic names such as the "Elephant and Castle" or the "Wheatsheaf."

Life in our so-called literate society is much more complex. Cities are bigger and may contain several hundred shoe stores. Besides, a boot or shoe on a sign is not adequate identification for the owner of a chain of shoe stores who will insist on the importance of the company name or the brand name of the merchandise to distinguish the chain from the competition.

Pictographs, glyphs, and symbols (all of which are names for more or less the same thing) are used today to fulfil more complex functions: to prohibit or deem obligatory certain actions; to warn people of potential or imminent hazards; to identify things; and so on. But no one can claim that, by themselves, all pictographs perform their functions effectively. This is because people in general don't (except perhaps when smoking and parking are involved) readily recognize more than a handful of glyphs. As a result they don't know what they are being prohibited from doing, obliged to do, or warned against.

In the mid-70s, the American Institute of Graphic Arts (AIGA) developed for the US Department of Transportation what came to be known as the DOT symbols. They comprise some thirty-odd individual glyphs more or less equally divided into "common-service symbols" (washrooms, telephones, and smoking) and

Which set of letters looks larger? Both are identical. Halation causes the reversed letters to appear about 12 percent larger than their positive counterparts.

"So-called" because 20 to 25 per cent of adults are functionally illiterate.

Chapter 13
Forms of graphic information
13.2 Non-verbal (or pictographic) information

others that are much more specialized, identifying customs, immigration, and so on. They were ostensibly designed for use in US transportation facilities.

Largely because they are free of copyright restrictions, however, the DOT glyphs have also been widely displayed in all sorts of commercial and retail environments that have nothing at all to do with transportation.

Invariably they are displayed without verbal accompaniment and the question arises: How successful (i.e., effective) are they after such a prolonged exposure? On this, as on so much that affects environmental communication, little research has been done. It would probably not be far wrong to guess that insofar as the fifteen or so common-service symbols are concerned, there is a reasonably widespread recognition of their meanings.

Also in the mid-70s, the Canadian Standards Association (CSA) embarked on the development of a national Canadian standard for signs and symbols in the work environment. This was a more sophisticated and useful document than the one for DOT because it focused much less on the design of the glyphs and more on the contexts in which the glyphs would be used – thereby giving this new language of vision the benefits of grammar and syntax.[15]

The problem of recognition, however, remained identical. There are some fifty-odd glyphs identified in CSA'S Z321 and most have a broader base in everyday use than do the DOT symbols. Nonetheless, only the same fifteen or so of them could be said to be readily recognizable by the public at large.

One of the reasons for this is that the use of symbols in signage is based on the assumption that the language of vision is the only language in the world that no one needs to learn. We have been conditioned to believe that it just comes to us naturally, without effort. This is claptrap. Of course symbols have to be learned, although admittedly some require more effort than others.

There are three categories of glyphs or symbols, not just one:

• Object related
• Concept related
• Abstract[16]

Object-related glyphs such as a telephone handset symbol (which looks like a side view of what it represents), or a smoking cigarette are the easiest to recognize. But in spite of all the efforts of graphic designers who try to make the glyphs resemble the objects, a learning process is still required. (The better the symbols are, however, the easier they are to learn and to retain.)

But even these symbols have a built-in limitation: a symbol of a respirator (used to signify "Breathing protection must be worn") may not contain all of the information the user needs. What *sort* of breathing protection (against CO, $COCl_2$, or what)? There is no benefit to be derived from having visually different designs for each respirator type because so frequently the essential differences between them are internal. In any case, would these many different designs all be recognizable to all employees? The answer is, certainly not. The solution is to have a single recognizable glyph to

NATIONAL STANDARD OF CANADA   CAN3-Z321-77

Signs and Symbols for the Occupational Environment

CSA

Canadian Standards Association

Canada's national standard on signs and symbols in the occupational environment.

represent breathing protection and then to identify the type required in any given situation by words.

The remaining two types of glyph present further learning difficulties. A *concept-related* glyph, an arrow, for example, does not represent an arrow in the way that a telephone handset represents a "pay phone." It conveys, instead, the concept of movement and direction.

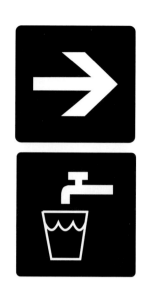

A further example of this relatively small category is the symbol for water. Actual water in a glass does not have waves on the surface. But wavy lines are used in the glyph (as in the symbol sign for "Potable water" or "Do not drink the water") to convey the *concept* of water. This is a rule, or convention, that must be learned.

Similarly, there are conceptual approaches to portraying explosions, or the idea of "hot" as distinct from "cold." These are all concepts and are not to be taken literally – and the symbols for all of them must be learned. Once learned, however, they are easily retained. When next we see symbol signs for swimming and wading pools or for no swimming, for example, the symbols will make contextual sense to us.

And finally, the third type, the *abstract* glyph, has little or no apparent relationship to its referent. What did people make of the red disc with the white bar across it when it first appeared on North American roadways? The answer would have been nothing at all if the words "No Entry" had not been prominently displayed below. The fact that some twenty years later these words are no longer considered necessary does not disprove our point. Rather, it confirms the fact that a lengthy learning period is required. Mathematical signs and letters of the alphabet (particularly "P" and "H") are also abstractions that must be learned.

The three distinctive shapes that enclose the CSA glyphs have each been assigned meanings which have little or nothing to do with them as shapes.

The circle is helped by the diagonal slash to convey the idea of prohibition. (Earlier attempts to convey this idea were squares or rectangles with diagonal slashes in them so there was nothing inevitable about the selection of the circle to convey this idea.)[17]

The triangle, with its spiky, attention-getting shape, is used to convey the idea of warning. (It is considered more distinctive than the North American diamond, which is not a distinctive shape but merely a square on its corner.)

The square shape, used to convey the idea of general information and permission, is the most arbitrary and abstract of all – but it was the only distinctive shape still available after regulation and warning had claimed the other two.

These, then, are the reasons why we should not expect all pictographs to explain themselves and not complain if they do not. Their effective use does imply some effort by the users to learn their meanings, and, we maintain, they also need to be complemented by words. Words should be an integral element in all symbol signs. If this were to happen (and there is increasing support for it among designers), it would represent a real advance

Chapter 13
Forms of graphic information
13.2 Non-verbal (or pictographic) information

REGULATION

Prohibition.

Obligation.

WARNING

Caution!

Danger!

INFORMATION

Identification.

Emergency.

Color code for pictographs above:
B = black
BL = blue
Y = yellow
G = green
R = red

over the use of words alone or of symbols alone. In terms of effective visual environmental communication, it would represent a breakthrough because the combination of pictorial and verbal elements would permit each to do what it does best:

1. The color and the shape are seen first and establish the context of the message (prohibition, obligation, warning, etc.).
2. The glyph is perceived next and immediately tells us *what* is being prohibited, etc.
3. Finally, the verbal message provides repetition which, far from being a mistake or unnecessary, is a necessity in any forgiving system and is essential in signs for the elderly; words may also provide a further level of meaning for the sign.

13.2.2 A grammar for symbol signs

There is no need to invent a grammar for symbol signs because one already exists. It depends upon the combination of three elements:

- Shapes
- Colors
- Glyphs

Inasmuch as there *are* only three simple shapes known to us, it is fortunate that this language of vision has only three aims: to regulate behavior, to warn of hazards, and to identify objects and services. The three simple shapes are circles (used for regulation), triangles (used for warning), and squares (used for identification).

There are two subsets for each of the three "aims":

- *Regulation* is both prohibition (what one must not do, such as "do not smoke") and obligation (what one must do, such as "wear protective goggles").
- *Warning* is both for potential hazards (such as for a "Wet floor" that may be slippery) and for imminent hazards (such as the danger of explosion).
- *Identification* conveniently also divides into two categories: one for emergency and life-protection equipment or facilities, and one for everything else from washrooms to mechanical rooms, and includes the concept of "permission" for identifying areas where something that is otherwise forbidden (like smoking) may be done.

Colors are used as a means of coding the differences between the two subsets in each case. Regulation utilizes on the one hand a red circle with a slash through it to prohibit the action represented by the glyph. On the other hand, it utilizes a black disc in which is located a white glyph representing an action that is mandatory. Warning utilizes a yellow triangle for potential hazards ("Caution!") and a red one for imminent hazards ("Danger!"). Finally, a green square identifies life-protection equipment or facilities while a blue square identifies everything else, including the concept of permission.

Thus glyphs can be used in several contexts to depict the different modes or contexts for given actions or the use to be made of certain objects.

A glyph of a walking figure inside a red circle and slash, for example, makes the statement that no pedestrians should be here, while the same glyph located inside a yellow triangle indicates a caution: that pedestrians are in the vicinity. The very same glyph in a blue square identifies a pedestrian crosswalk and it may also indicate that it is permissible (in a restricted area, for example) for a pedestrian to be here.

Alternatively, with objects, a white respirator in a black disc signifies that breathing protection must be worn, while the same glyph in a blue square identifies the locker where respirators are kept. This is a splendid communications system conferring on those who put up signs (management) and those who use them (employees) the benefits to be derived from universality of meaning. One may wonder why it is not universally adopted.

13.2.3 The symbol of accessibility

The form of the symbol for accessibility to disabled persons has achieved a large degree of recognition. Its meaning, however, is still far from clear, and its use is often at variance with the sponsors' intentions. As a symbol for persons with non-mobility-related disabilities, it is wholly inadequate.

In his book *Designing for the Disabled*, Selwyn Goldsmith writes: "During 1969, the International Society for Rehabilitation of the Disabled subcommittee on technical aids, housing, and transportation conducted an enquiry to find a device suitable for international use. . . . Six symbols were selected for an international opinion poll."[18]

The most successful, according to the jury, was the symbol submitted by a Danish design student, Susanne Kofoed.

However, the chairman of the jury committee found the lack of a head on the symbol "inconvenient" and inasmuch as "two members of the jury, independent of each other, have suggested to equip the symbol with such a 'head,' we have had this done."

The result was not only the addition of a head. The symbol shown has been properly described by Goldsmith as "a weak and ineptly modified version of the original."

Largely as a result of the efforts of the chairman, the design in general use today is the revised version. It will be noted, however, that as finally approved for general use, the symbol may appear in several versions – which does nothing to protect its integrity.

First, it may appear in negative (i.e., white glyph on a dark field) or positive form. In its negative form, it has no border, while in its positive form it does, this border being the same thickness as the stem thickness of the glyph itself.

Second, the symbol may be reversed to indicate direction, thus it may be "looking" left or right, with appropriately left- or right-pointing arrows.

We have been unable to discover a proper specification for the colors in which the symbol may be displayed – other than that it

In a true visual language, the same glyph can de displayed in different "moods" to convey different things.

Very substantial improvements have been made in the past dozen years in eliminating architectural barriers from buildings. In 1969 the world focused on the problems of the physically disabled, with the 11th World Congress on Rehabilitation of the Disabled. The symbol of accessibility was designed and promulgated in that year.

Although its colors, form, and use have never been truly standardized, as a means of identifying facilities (and entrances thereto) that are accessible to the mobility impaired, the symbol of access has been a success.

As a symbol for "The Disabled" (the original intention was that it would be this), it is a failure. It is constantly misused and, worse, by focusing attention on the mobility disabled, it diverts public attention from the far greater numbers of persons who are also disabled, but not in terms of their mobility.

1. The original design by the competition winner.

2. The "weak and ineptly modified version" (S. Goldsmith) that emerged from the committee.

Chapter 13
Forms of graphic information
13.2 Non-verbal (or pictographic) information

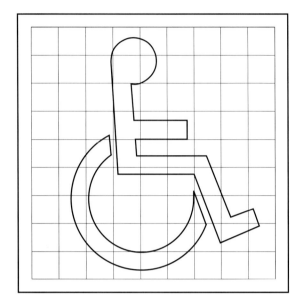

1. The grid for the superior version of the symbol for accessibility, as revised by the Department of the Environment (DOE) in the UK.

2. The superior version, revised by the DOE, in the UK.

The symbol of access should always be framed in. The frame is integral to the design.

should be blue (generally the instructions are as vague as "the blue used in this booklet").[19] As manufactured, however, the color used is generally PMS 293C in the Pantone Matching System.

It is our recommendation that the symbol in its negative form with a white border should be the only approved version. There is no advantage in having to stock two directional versions; the original right-pointing version should be adequate under all circumstances. The matter of the symbol's meaning is far more disputatious.

The statement is made that "The symbol tells a handicapped person, *particularly one using a wheelchair,* that a building or facility is accessible and can be entered and used without fear of being blocked by architectural barriers."[20] The italics are ours but they strongly imply universality of application to *all* disabled persons which the symbol patently does not have.

Apart from this, however, and leaving for the moment the question of what would be acceptable and appropriate as symbols of accessibility for other types of disabilities (assuming that such are necessary) what, precisely, does this particular symbol mean?

Doubtless, it was hoped, in the days prior to 1969 when there was no such symbol, that, to quote Mr Goldsmith again, a principal objective would be "to make an impression on normal able-bodied people. The intention is that normal people should, by being confronted by unambiguous signs, be encouraged to think about the nature and implications of disablement, and should develop a more realistic appreciation of the circumstances of disabled people."[21]

In other words, it was hoped that such a symbol would help to change attitudes and that was one of the chief objectives. In this, its success has been limited.

As a symbol of access *per se,* it tells a mobility-disabled person in a wheelchair that these facilities are barrier free. Alternatively, it also clearly directs such a person to an appropriate entrance if the main entrance is *not* barrier free.

This being so, what is the "symbol of access" doing on an automobile licence plate, as is now so common? And particularly when, in the first place, it by no means guarantees that the driver is handicapped, and in the second, it is not being used as a "symbol of access" to anything. What is it doing in advertisements, as an attention-getter for travel and other services for the mobility impaired?

On a toilet or other door, does it indicate that these facilities (or this door) are for the exclusive use of the handicapped? (In actual fact, it sometimes does, thereby making the matter constantly one of doubt.)

In a recreational facility, as likely as not one of its functions is to advertise the availability of wheelchairs for those needing them.

All of which only serves to confirm what has been known for some time: that the "symbol of access" is frequently misused, and that its integrity (in terms of its original intention of guaranteeing accessibility) has been seriously impugned.

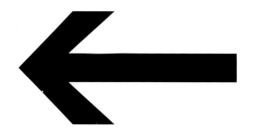

There are probably as many forms of arrows as there are letterforms. Some are better than others – "better" in the sense that they more effectively communicate direction than do others. Most, however, are just fanciful.

When it comes down to making a statement about which is the "best" arrow, we just do not know. During the preparation of work for Expo 67, I (Paul Arthur) did some research with focus groups and came to the conclusion that an arrow in which the proportion of wings to shaft was 1:2 was best. Furthermore, the proportion of stem thickness to shaft, I was sure, had to be 1:8.

Nobody agreed with me and the Expo arrow was never seen again. Instead, designers favored for a long time an arrow with a wing-to-shaft relationship of 1:1, mainly because it fitted so neatly in a square and could, as the Expo arrow could not, be rotated easily through 360 degrees.

The processing of environmental graphic communication can, however, produce the most bizarre results on occasion. Many people tended to perceive the "square" arrow (under certain circumstances) as a chicken footprint moving in the *opposite* direction to that which was intended.

The chamfering of the ends of the wings (to reinforce direction), the slight lengthening of the shaft (to an approximate 7:9 relationship), and the groining of the area where shaft meets wings (which had been a feature of the Expo arrow) all came later, and by the mid-80s many of us were reasonably sure that *this* was the best arrow.

Designers, however, with their eyes so firmly fixed on form, are frequently blind to content. The form of the arrow is one thing and whether there will ever be agreement on a "best" form is unlikely. It may not even matter very much. What does matter a great deal is what designers do with these arrows.

As we have already observed earlier in this chapter, the arrow is a concept-related glyph representing movement of some sort, but we frequently are not sure what kind of movement is indicated. If the only movements we ever needed to make were either to the left or to the right, there would be no problem at all. However, we often want to indicate movement up and down – or straight ahead – and here many real wayfinding problems arise. If the whole world were perfectly literate we would advocate dropping arrows altogether and just using words.

Under such circumstances of universal literacy, the words "straight ahead" would be much clearer than arrows that point indiscriminately up *and* down to mean the same things. (Even worse, such arrows *may* actually mean upstairs or downstairs. We never know for sure.)

Sometimes, a simple square is used to convey the concept of "straight ahead," indicating that the arrow holds no solution whatsoever. Is this really true? Is it really to be believed that while man can actually walk on the moon, he cannot design a "straight ahead" sign? Or a non-verbal "push" or "pull" plate on a door that everybody can understand? (Of course, best of all is no sign at all and,

The Expo 67 arrow was diligently researched and specially designed for the Fair. When it was done, we thought there would never be a need for another . . .

This particular arrow enjoyed a terrific vogue in the decades just after the Second World War, because it looked "modern" and because it could be so easily rotated through 360 degrees.

We always thought it looked like chicken tracks in the snow – going in the reverse direction to that intended. Several people have made this same comment.

It also seems excessively thick at the **juncture of the stem and the wings. Although there is no question that the arrow points in a given direction, the fact that the wings are shaped as they are causes it to have a static look.**

The VisuCom arrow, which has a wing-to-shaft ratio of 7:9, grew out of the chicken-foot arrow crossed with that for Expo. Note that the wings are not constant in thickness. This results in the juncture with the stem not appearing as thick as it does in the chicken-foot arrow.

Cutting the ends off the wings parallel to

the direction of flight also helps.

The stem thickness is 20 percent of the distance across the wings.

Chapter 13
Forms of graphic information
13.2 Non-verbal (or pictographic) information

Below: When located over a fire exit, this is what passes for an arrow pointing to safety – even when the route is obviously straight ahead!

A perspective arrow is a possible answer. Some concepts for a uniform means of expressing left and right, and up and down – as well as straight ahead directions are shown here.

Sometimes, however, this sign (without the arrow) is accompanied by a hollow square when the direction to be followed lies straight ahead.

Below: Although more often than not this is what one sees as a layout for directional signs, it is not acceptable for wayfinding

for several reasons:
• There are too many listings in a clump.
• There is no valid reason for repeating the arrows.

Directory
← Information
← Elevators
← Washrooms
→ Pay phones
→ Cafeteria
→ Security
↑ Admin
↑ Cashier

instead, hardware on the door that unequivocally tells us whether to pull or to push.)

A contribution to this universal dilemma is shown in the accompanying illustrations in which efforts are made to use perspective to reinforce the meaning of the straight-ahead arrow.

"Upstairs" and "downstairs" are indicated by oblique-pointing arrows located at the tops or bottoms of stairwells. "Up to" and "down to" arrows in elevator lobbies are similarly unequivocal.

A system of this sort would, at long last, introduce a measure of unambiguous meaning to the business of providing directions in interior spaces. Each arrow would thus have only a single meaning.

On a less exotic level, how many arrows are enough? Take a directional sign with, say, seven or more destinations on it (more than there should be, but, nonetheless, there it is). Does each one get an arrow pointing in some direction? The answer, generally, is yes. But is this an effective solution? We do not think so, particularly if many of them are pointing in the same direction.

Such mindless and gratuitous repetition does more to puzzle people than to help them. It is our contention that interior signs should never contain more than two directions – and two arrows. If there is a third or fourth direction involved, a separate sign should be used. (see page 182).

We also hold that the arrows, when space permits, should be displayed as "headings," so to speak, for the messages that follow, and should be differentiated from them in some way.

That clever Cretan princess, Ariadne, who preceded Kevin Lynch and the articulation of concepts of wayfinding by several thousand years, showed the Athenian warrior Theseus how to find his way *out of* the Minotaur's labyrinth. It was her much-celebrated idea that Theseus would, on his way through the labyrinth to the Minotaur, pay out a thread. This he would subsequently follow back to the entrance after he had killed the Minotaur.

Lines on walls, ceilings, and floors in hospitals, universities and colleges, and other buildings do precisely the same thing – although, when well planned and executed, they can lead one *to*, as well as *from*, one's destination. The color coding and the planning of the use of colored lines are all discussed in detail in section 13.3.1.

Markings of another type, mainly through striping of columns, curbs, and overhead or vertical potential hazards are more the subject of public safety than of wayfinding as such – although it is better not to separate them because public safety must *always* be the wayfinding designer's concern.

A building designed with wayfinding in mind would probably not include free-standing staircases rising in the middle of plazalike areas, because they represent potential hazards to everyone – the able-bodied and the handicapped alike. However, they do exist, and although striped markings on them may substantially reduce their attractiveness, such markings – or an alternative – are considered necessary today. (The preferable alternative, when it is feasible, is to place a low wall or a planter at the point where it is necessary to prevent people's heads from colliding with the staircase.)

Because we all have relatively poor depth perception, the marking of treads on stairs is now mandatory in many jurisdictions. Such markings are generally required in building codes on every tread on a flight of stairs even though in most cases only the top and bottom treads really demand this treatment.

In either case, it is essential that the markings provide good contrast with the tread and that they be highly visible to people ascending as well as to people descending the stairs.

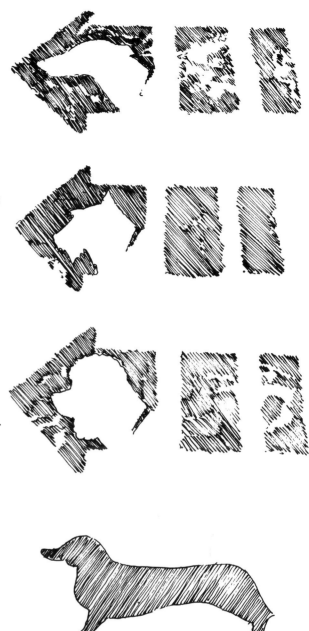

Pavement markings in Paris to tell pet owners to curb their dogs.

13.3 Color

Color coding is the first thing that staff are likely to suggest as a solution to settings where wayfinding is acknowledged as a problem. To most people, however, color coding means something that is rarely practical and can considerably increase initial as well as maintenance costs. In a community college, for instance, it means color coding departments: graphic design would be one color, fashion another, meat cutting yet another, and so on.

One serious impediment to color coding by function is that the requirement is probably for a large number of colors when, in fact, no more than nine hues, plus black, white, and grey, are available

Colors available for color coding:
- Red, yellow, and blue
- Orange, green, and purple (or violet)
- Brown and beige
- Pink
- Black, white, and grey

Turquoise is the sort of ambiguous hue that is not available for this purpose because for the many people who call it "blue," there is an equal number who call it "green" which, of course, defeats the whole purpose of color coding.

for color coding purposes. The *only* colors available for color coding purposes are those to which a generally agreed-upon name can be put – like red or yellow or blue. While there may be a large number of tints and shades of these colors, they would still be called red, yellow, blue, etc., and because there cannot be two of anything in a color code (like dark blue and light blue, for example), there are still only nine individual colors. There just aren't enough colors – and if there were, the memory load extends to no more than five at most, after which people can neither remember nor distinguish between the colors used.

Another problem is the impracticality of color coding anything transient. If graphic design is yellow, and fashion is blue, for example, what happens when they move to another area? If the color code manifested itself in painted doors, the problem is insurmountable. Even if it is only the signs that are colored, the problems of stocking so many signs in different colors could be one sort of nightmare while switching the signs about could well be another.

A way around this problem, however, is to color code by areas, not by function. Thus a complex, large, square building might be subdivided into quadrants, each of which had a color assigned to it permanently, irrespective of which departments or functions occupied each. Graphic design could move from the yellow to the blue quadrant with no need to change anything. If one is going to apply a color code in this way, then it should always be on a geographic, and never on a functional, basis.

But then there is still the matter of fading. Say five years later one has to match colors of new signs to those of the originals. It is most unlikely that this can be done. The old signs will have faded and, as a result, one will have two blues, two greens, and so on.

A far more practical approach is to consider the colored lines which are briefly discussed in section 13.2.5. Tapes in individual colors should be thought of as so many highways routed through the complex. One color might, for example, link together entrances, elevators, stairs, and perhaps washrooms. Small signs in verbal and non-verbal form along the route could indicate the direction of the closest stair, elevator, or washroom.

Another color could lead to inter-connected buildings while two others could pick up designated departments or facilities. As long as people always knew which facilities were on each of the colored routes, with small directional signs along the way to help, wayfinding could be much simplified and the number of signs reduced.

The question of where the lines should be placed is always raised. Everyone prefers the floor – like Hansel and Gretel in the forest. But this is rarely a practical solution. The lines wear out or are obscured by objects placed afterwards in the corridors – or just by people. The ceiling is better and, when it can be accomplished, eye level on the wall is best of all.

13.3.2 Color selection

The severe restriction on the numbers of colors that may be used in color codes does not necessarily apply to signs. Turquoise (or teal) backgrounds, for example, may certainly be used in signs where color coding is not involved.

But here another restriction takes its place. And it concerns contrast. Any color may be used on a sign provided there is adequate contrast when it is combined with a second color to create a message. The question is, how to ascertain this adequacy of contrast?

Something tells us – or it should – that red letters on a green background or pink letters on a grey background (or the reverse of both of them) are somehow not a good idea if legibility matters at all. But how do we determine this?

There is a reliable formula based on the light reflectancy (LR) readings in percentages for each of the two colors involved. (Many paint suppliers provide this information as LRS for each of their colors.) By subtracting the darker reading from the lighter, dividing the difference by the lighter, and multiplying by 100, we get the "brightness differential" between the colors.[22]

When the brightness differential is 70 percent or higher, adequate legibility is pretty well assured. When it is less, and particularly when it is a lot less, the two colors should not be used in combination.

The target value of a sign is its ability to be seen easily on a wall. This is always greater when the background of the sign is the darker color. However, the brightness differential will be the same regardless of which color (the lighter or the darker) is used for the background.

	beige	white	grey	black	brown	pink	purple	green	orange	blue	yellow	red
red	78	84	32	38	7	57	28	24	62	13	82	0
yellow	14	16	73	89	80	58	75	76	52	79	0	
blue	75	82	21	47	7	50	17	12	56	0		
orange	44	60	44	76	59	12	47	50	0			
green	72	80	11	53	18	43	6	0				
purple	70	79	5	56	22	40	0					
pink	51	65	37	73	53	0						
brown	77	84	26	43	0							
black	89	91	58	0								
grey	69	78	0									
white	28	0										
beige	0											

☐ do not use

▨ acceptable

Hues	LR(%)
red	13
yellow	71
blue	15
orange	34
green	17
purple	18
pink	30
brown	14
black	8
grey	19
white	85
beige	61

A table for calculating brightness differentials between the two colors that normally constitute the letters and the background of a wayfinding sign.

By subtracting the darker value (B2) from the lighter (B1), dividing by the lighter, and multiplying by 100, we get the brightness differential which should be 70 percent or higher.

The formula is:
$$\frac{B1 - B2}{B1} \times 100 = LR$$

The light reflectancies of the twelve hues identified are for the purposes of illustration only. Those for actual colors being used should, of course, be substituted in practice.

Mainly, when one sees it, this sign is red. In certain enlightened jurisdictions in North America, the color is being changed to green for a very good reason: the safe assumption that in case of fire, the red sign would not be legible, but would be reduced to a red glow or a blur.

With which color of blur would people associate the concept of safety: red or green?

A final point on the selection of colors for signs, one which makes the task even more restrictive, is that there are certain colors that should be reserved for public safety uses only. These are red, yellow, and green.

13.4 Layout

13.4.1 Information groupings

There is a rule of thumb to the effect that no signs should ever contain more than five or six messages or "bits" of information, of which the sign itself is one. There is, however, some latitude in the meaning of "bits."

On a highway sign, bits are single lines. Thus a sign for motorists' use should contain no more than three lines of copy. The kind of information intended for pedestrian use, however, may be more extensive. There would be little value, for example, to the average building directory if it could only display three or four lines of information. The information required at decision points, in the form of directional signs, will frequently also run to much more than three or four bits.

It is important to remember in this connection how we "read" signs. We don't read signs the way we read print. There our habits are very structured: we read consistently and sequentially left to right (in Roman orthography) and top to bottom. Signs, however, in an unfamiliar environment, are read in the same way we read the rest of the setting: using a scanning and glancing process that is akin to a person looking for "meaning" in a non-objective work of art. (See section 6.2.2 for a description of this process of scanning and glancing.)

Thus we read signs in a relatively unstructured way, as a series of glances. (This is at the root of why people so frequently "read" signs for what they think they should say, rather than what they do say, as we saw in section 13.1.3.)

This glancing process requires that information on directional signs be somehow grouped into smaller units of, say, three lines each when large amounts of information need to be displayed.

As the illustrations on the following page show, three columns of three messages side by side are easier to assimilate than a single column of nine. Alternatively, if space requirements demand a vertical sign, the information is equally acceptable as three groups, of three messages each, arranged vertically.

Even better, when space permits in directional signs, is the separation of the groups into two signs – with those that lie on the viewer's left in one sign and those on his or her right in another.

It is still, however, desirable that information be displayed in groupings of no more than three or four messages each.

1

Administration
Cafeteria
Cashier
Elevators
Information
Maintenance
Pay phones
Security
Washrooms

2

Administration
Cafeteria
Cashier
Elevators
Information
Maintenance
Pay phones
Security
Washrooms

3

Administration
Cafeteria
Cashier
Elevators
Information
Maintenance
Pay phones
Security
Washrooms

4

Administration
Cafeteria
Cashier

Elevators
Information
Maintenance

Pay phones
Security
Washrooms

5

Administration	Elevators	Pay phones
Cafeteria	Information	Security
Cashier	Maintenance	Washrooms

Three different ways to display typographic information: 1) flush left (preferred), 2) flush right, and 3) centered.

However, figures 1–3 break the "rule of 3," which states that information needs to be grouped in threes as shown in figures 4 and 5 in order to make it readable in a sign.

A preferred method for displaying directional information is to restrict the number of arrows (see page 176 for an example of the alternative method) and, when feasible, to split the signs into two, as shown on the right. This reinforces direction and enables all the information to be displayed in InfoBand 1 (see page 201).

This subject of the layout of directional signs is also dealt with in section 13.2.4.

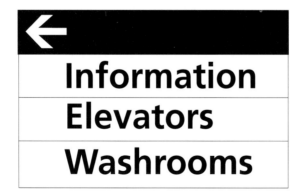

13.4.2 Flush left, centered, or flush right

Messages in signs can be arranged flush left, centered, or flush right, and while there will be occasions where there are esthetic arguments for each of them, is any one of them actually "best" from a communications viewpoint?

As we have seen in the previous section, people do not read signs as they read print. Nonetheless, and despite the "glancing" process, the eye does crave organization such as a consistent starting point when more than one message must be displayed. The only way that this can be achieved is through flush left, ragged right arrangements.

At the same time, there is an exception in directional signs. Signs with arrows should still be organized with the text of the whole sign being flush left. The arrows, however, should be on the left or right of the sign, depending on which way they point, as shown in the illustrations. Straight-ahead arrows, assuming we can arrive at a consensus on this subject, should be on the left side of the sign. Where space permits, we also strongly advocate dedicating complete blades of a sign to the directional function, particularly when several messages are involved.

In other words, the arrows should be on lines by themselves and should be differentiated in some way from the rest of the text.

13.5 Illumination of signs

13.5.1 Methods of illumination

All signs, no matter where they are located, require illumination of some sort. In most basic terms, this can take one of two forms: signs may rely upon ambient lighting, or they may have their own artificial illumination.

Inside a building, ambient light is generally considered adequate, particularly for the needs of smaller-scale signs in corridors, hallways, and reception or office areas.

On the other hand, this form of lighting is not generally considered adequate in large-scale spaces such as concourses in airports or railway or bus stations. There, signs generally have their own artificial illumination.

In exterior settings, the same rules apply. If the spill from existing light sources is considered adequate, signs will not be provided with any other illumination. But if ambient light is inadequate, signs will need artificial illumination.

There are two categories of artificial illumination for signs: interior, and exterior. In the case of interior illumination, the sign contains its own light source which, as likely as not, will be fluorescent; the graphics will be on either the first or the second surface. In other words, they will be either in front of or behind the signface.

There are arguments in favor of both, although from an esthetic viewpoint, it is prefereable to have the graphics on the first surface and thus to reduce specular (or veiling) glare.

In addition, when plastic faces are fabricated from material that has come off a roll, they tend to retain some of the "memory" of the roll and not to be perfectly flat. This effect, called "oil-canning," is very much accentuated when the graphics are on the second surface – and very much reduced when they are on the first.

A point to keep in mind, however, is that plastic faces sometimes contain ultra-violet inhibitors intended to prolong the colors and the life of the graphics. Placing the graphics on, rather than behind, the signface will of course nullify the effect of the inhibitors.

The exterior illumination of signs – lighting them from the outside – is becoming increasingly popular. It is more energy efficient and truer colors are achievable. Transmitted light (from interior illumination) affects the colors on a signface, frequently adversely, whereas in reflected light (from exterior illumination) the true colors can be better maintained.

13.5.2 Veiling glare

Light reflected off a signface into a viewer's eyes will cause a sign to "white-out" partially or completely, thereby rendering it illegible – if not invisible. The illustration demonstrates the principle.

Thus, while it is practical to use ambient light for illuminating signs inside a building, the positions of the light sources in relation to the sign are important as well.

Some signage materials have a shiny surface while others have a matte or non-lustrous finish. The manufacturers of coatings and of other signage materials such as vinyl films, have established five degrees of gloss, tabled below:

Description	Degrees of gloss
flat or wall	<15
satin (in UK: silk)	15–20
eggshell	20–35
semi-gloss	35–70
full-gloss	>70

Chapter 13
Forms of graphic information
13.5 Illumination of signs

It must be noted that some gloss on signs is unavoidable. Even a surface that appears flat or totally lacking in sheen when illuminated and viewed at an angle near to the perpendicular will actually appear somewhat glossy when the angle of view shifts to near the grazing angle of 85 degrees off the perpendicular. In other words, angular distortion creates the appearance of gloss on coatings or materials that are inherently flat.

Thus a satin finish will appear to be eggshell or even semi-gloss when viewed at a grazing angle, and semi-gloss finish will appear to be full-gloss under the same conditions.

On the other hand, there is the complication of vandalism. Glossy surfaces, which decrease legibility, also discourage vandalism and are easy to clean; matte surfaces, which enhance legibility, may encourage vandalism and are difficult to clean. So it is a tradeoff, but concern for vandalism is not a valid argument in favor of shiny signfaces.

From a purely practical standpoint, signs are the cause of many of the problems that beset people trying to find their way in unfamiliar settings. They affect able-bodied and disabled people alike – but consider the extent to which faulty signage exacerbates the problems of the disabled.

13.5.3 Why people have trouble with signs

1. Ambiguity
Although a message might be quite clear to the person who originally put the sign up, it may be wholly unclear to the observer.

2. Conflict
Bits of conflicting information in a sign (or in two signs close together) create difficulties. This happens particularly when new signs are installed and the old ones are not removed. Or it may be the result of two signs that complemented each other at one time, but that conflict in new circumstances.

3. Deficiency
Too little information is just as bad as too much. A sign must contain all the information that a person needs at that particular place.

4. Excess
Confusion generally results when more data than a person needs is provided at a given decision point.

5. Glare
Signs are much more efficient when they are well illuminated. Sometimes a sign can be well illuminated from some standpoints but obscured by reflected light from others. Signs placed opposite windows, for instance, can end up reflecting the outside, cars moving on the street, passersby, and so on.

6. Illegibility
Messages that are illegible are those that are too small to be seen (or recognized) from the reading distance of the sign, even though there may be nothing wrong with the message. Readability and legibility are not the same.

7. Inaccuracy

It is essential to provide all the information that people need, when they need it. But it must be the right information – up-to-date, and accurate.

8. Obstructions

There is a constant jockeying for position in the environment and things end up obscuring or blocking the view of other things. Some things don't matter, but when a planter or light fixture or piece of HVAC equipment is placed in front of a sign, it does matter.

9. Unreliability

Most people are prepared to depend on signs in an unfamiliar setting, but only for as long as they are dependable and do not, for no apparent reason, suddenly let them down.

10. Us

Finally, we are not always able to give our full attention to the wayfinding task. We are easily distracted. As a result, we may miss a crucial piece of information, a sign, a landmark, an architectural feature we were told to turn left at, or whatever. A carefully planned wayfinding system is forgiving in the sense that we are not hopelessly and forever lost because we missed that last cue, sign, or signal.

Chapter 14

Graphic information for decision making

People need graphic information in order to formulate an action plan with respect to wayfinding in an unfamiliar setting, in other words, for decision making. The graphic information they need involves orientation and general information about the setting. The type of information needed once an action plan has been developed and is in the process of execution is the subject of Chapter 15.

14.1 Orientation

For most of us, under most circumstances, the only "good" map is a three-dimensional, colored model which reduces the complexities of the real world to a scale that permits us to get a bird's-eye view of it, and, therefore, to understand it, where we are in it, in what direction our destination lies, and how best we may get there.

For such a model to be most effective, however, it should be displayed lying flat, like the real world, rather than tipped up on its end.

Finally, in order to assure perfection, this model should be oriented or aligned with the setting it portrays so that as a person stands and looks at it, buildings and natural features that are located on the left in the model will also be on the left in the setting itself.

All this, however desirable, is utopian and in many cases impractical – except for the matter of proper alignment, which is absolutely basic to our ability to use maps efficiently, that is, assuming we can use them at all. Many people cannot, as recent wayfinding research has demonstrated. That consideration aside, however, any map will be made more useful if it is properly aligned. The converse, of course, is just as true: even the best-drawn map will be less than useful if it is not properly aligned.

While acknowledging that three-dimensional maps are "best," what else is "good"? It depends on the purpose of the map.

A map as a simple two-dimensional object represents a high degree of abstraction. In other words, in its smallness, in its verticality, and in its two-dimensionality, it is many stages removed from the real world it purports to represent. Furthermore, it would seem that people are willing to accept higher levels of abstraction (or stylization) in maps of interior spaces than they are in those for the out-of-doors.

From the very beginning of their existence (in the mid-19th century), subway route maps have been effective because of, and not despite, the way in which they have sacrificed reality for simplicity. All we care about when consulting such a map is to be able to select the correct line (or train) and have it deliver us to our intended destination. The convolutions it goes through to get us there are not our concern. This is not always the case when it comes to our finding our own way to our intended destination, particularly on foot. Here we should make a distinction between maps of exterior and maps of interior settings.

Exterior settings

For exterior settings, we have always favored map bases that display an aerial photo of the setting, either from 90 degrees (directly overhead) or from an oblique view of 60 degrees. Extraneous information, such as deep shadows from trees and buildings on roads or pathways, or HVAC equipment on roof-tops, is not included and a system of graphic information is superimposed.

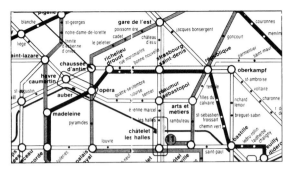

1

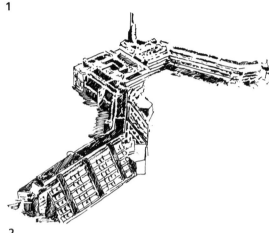

2

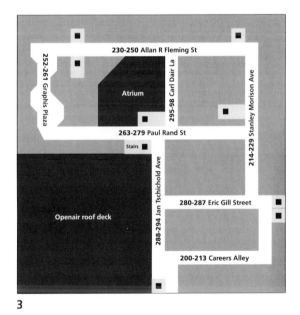

3

Three different approaches to maps on signs.

1. A subway route map in which the process of travel is less important than the identification of destinations.

2. The preferred method of depicting three-dimensional space for general orientation purposes.

3. A good example of a simplified floor map or plan of a complex setting.

Experience demonstrates that the 60-degree oblique view is preferred by most people because it is regarded as more realistic. However, such views introduce the problems of perspective and cannot be used to measure distances (or even to indicate them on any sort of scale).

Whether this preference for maps which include photographic information (even though modified) is soundly based or merely subjective must be determined by others. However, it is safe to say that the more "realistic" a map of an exterior setting is, the more efficient it will be.

And, of course, it must be remembered that orientation or alignment to the setting is crucial. This will help to compensate for the map's shortcomings which, as we have already noted, are its verticality and its two dimensionality, irrespective of what sort of map it is.

Interior settings
Rather different rules apply for interior settings. Axonometric and perspective views are rarely as helpful as they are outside. A higher degree of stylization (than is desirable in exterior maps) is not only acceptable but is likely to be helpful as well.

At the same time, paradoxically, it must be noted that people have more difficulty finding their way about in interior spaces, where they are deprived of the kinds of cues they find so useful in the outdoors. In section 15.1, we present the reader with some concepts in floor and room numbering systems that are helpful to wayfinders.

Wayfinders often have a very difficult time when they are confronted with too much information (or, of course, too little). Almost any map tends by its very nature to contain large amounts of information. To digest or sort through this can be a problem in itself and it is only compounded when the visitor is presented with several maps in one location (each of a different floor or level in the building).

When faced with such a "choice of maps," visitors may become confused and ignore the maps altogether. A far better practice is not to try to do everything at once, but to take things a step at a time:

- Provide visitors with level numbers for all the tenants in the complex, listed alphabetically.
- Get visitors to the correct level for the tenant they have come to see.
- Provide, on each level, a map (of that level) to show where the tenants are actually located, with their addresses.
- Ensure that this map is properly aligned with the floor itself. Such a map can be very stylized and simplified. Wherever possible, landmarks or building features should be identified on the map as a means of helping the visitor.

Legibility
Legibility in map design for wayfinding has two aspects. First, as an abstraction, the map should be developed in a manner that

facilitates understanding of it as a representation of reality: it should be simple enough (as we have observed above) not to contain unnecessary information, but at the same time realistic enough to compensate for the fact that it *is* an abstraction.

The second is its size or scale, particularly that of its lettering. The insistence on a minimum cap-height of one inch (25 mm) is a virtual impossibility in most maps. Nevertheless, the problems of legibility do not necessarily go away just because a person is looking at a map and not a sign. The smallest letters on a wayfinding map should never have a cap-height of less than .625 inches (10 to 15 mm).

14.1.2 Panoramic views

Panoramic views are not much used for wayfinding (except at places like Niagara Falls or on the tops of tall buildings, where they are used to identify other buildings or geographical features on the horizon). This is a pity, because they represent, in the right conditions and setting, a very useful alternative to conventional maps. They also share few of the limitations of maps:

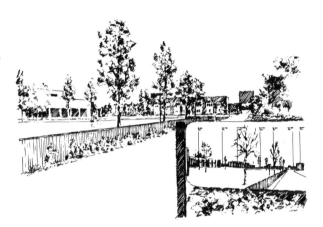

- They are vertically positioned.
- They are reasonably realistic in that they display an outline drawing of the setting a person is looking at.
- They are perfectly aligned to the setting itself.
- They provide verbal (typographic) identification for all major landscape elements and building names.
- If they are transparent, the setting is viewed through them and the typographic labels are superimposed on landscape elements or buildings.
- If they are opaque, the setting is seen from an aerial viewpoint (this is a less effective, but generally more practical, solution).

Thus identified, the buildings and the landscape elements become the visitors' own signs and there may be no further need to identify them or to provide directions to them en route.

14.1.3 Building directories

When building directories form part of a particular wayfinding system, they are generally, and properly, associated with maps. Too often, however, they compound wayfinding difficulties instead of helping to solve them. They may, for example, be constructed as towers with much of their information high above people's heads (and therefore illegible to many of them). Or they may be organized by bureaucratic hierarchy in the structure of departments and not by visitor needs for information. Or they may be tucked tidily out of sight in the security desk. Building directories, despite their misnomer, generally provide visitors exclusively with orientation information concerning the names of tenants and the floor levels where they will be found.

But what if a tenant organization is less well known than the service it offers to the public? Old Age Security cheques, for example, can be picked up at a department office. But what information is required by the person who has come for his or her cheque: the departmental name or the reference to Old Age Security cheques? (Both are, of course, necessary, but pride of place should probably be given to the latter.) Thus it is good wayfinding practice to find some typographic device to structure information in building directories (particularly in government buildings) by giving priority to the major generators of traffic and by using the name by which they are known to the public.

14.2 General information

14.2.1 About the setting

In addition to orientation as an aspect of decision making, wayfinders may need to know what they cannot do (such as smoke) or what they must do (such as wear eye protection). In addition, they need to know the hours when individual facilities are open or closed.

No smoking. **No parking.**

14.2.2 Prohibitions and obligations

A clear identification of prohibited activities is obviously required within the decision-making process. Is smoking permitted in the restaurant? If not, a smoker will decide not to go there. Can one park by the front door? If not, the motorist will have to go somewhere else. These prohibitions are most effectively communicated by means of pictographs in the prohibition mode, with words to identify more precisely what is prohibited within the setting. (On the other hand, signs telling us what we must do are not common in public spaces – no matter how much in evidence they are in the work environment. They are, therefore, relatively unimportant within the decision-making process of most wayfinding situations.)

Hours-of-service signs must make provision for changes to conform with seasonal schedules. Canada Post Corporation, Ottawa. Paul Arthur, Lawrence Burak, 1990.

Open		Ouvert
Monday	09.00-21.00	Lundi
Tuesday	09.00-21.00	Mardi
Wednesday	09.00-21.00	Mercredi
Thursday	09.00-21.00	Jeudi
Friday	09.00-21.00	Vendredi
Saturday	09.00-18.00	Samedi
Sunday		Dimanche

14.2.3 Hours of service

Signs (or decals) providing information on hours of service are required only where certain facilities within a setting or building are open or closed at different times of the day from those of the rest of the building and it is important for visitors to know this.

Graphic information for decision executing

Having successfully formulated their action plans (see Chapter 14), visitors to an unfamiliar setting will need different types of information to assist them in getting efficiently to their chosen destinations. Unfortunately, however, few of these "types of information" have ever been standardized and, as a result, they are called different things in different buildings.

Floor level names are an example of this. Is the floor on which a person enters a building from the street called "main," or "ground," or "lobby," or "1," or something else again? And what if this same building has major entrances not just on one level, but on two? Are each of these also called "ground" or "main," etc? And if not, then how are they distinguished? How are they identified on elevator control buttons? Room numbering is another area where, apparently, anything goes. Is there such a thing as a system? And if so, will it work on open-landscape floors as well as on those with conventional corridors? Where do signs "go"? Is there a point to standardizing this, or is it good enough to continue the practice of putting them wherever they can conveniently be fitted in?

These and other issues dealt with in this chapter are, we feel, very important and, on all of them, we have recommendations to make. On the other hand, there are many ways of doing things, some neither better nor worse than others. It is therefore less important that our recommendations be adopted than that out of them there should emerge an agreement among practitioners and building owners and managers that standardization is desirable.

15.1 Floor and room numbering systems

15.1.1 Floor and level numbers

It is frequently a source of surprise to designers to learn just how many people do not know (without being told) that room (or office) 1115 is on the 11th floor. This is one of those things designers and building managers take for granted without having any reason for doing so.

Another is the identification of floor levels themselves. North Americans have not so far developed a coordinated, universally accepted method of identifying levels, from the parking or other levels below grade, through the ground or main floor (which may or may not be at grade all around the building perimeter), to the other floors above.

The general practice is to start at grade and call it something (M or G or 1 or something else) and then to work *down* through the floors below and *up* through those above. This is all very well for buildings built on level ground but becomes a problem when the building is on the side of a slope or is connected to another building by an above-street pedestrian walkway.

In such cases, there are two levels at which we can gain access, one higher than the other. Thus, in addition to what the owners (and their architects) think of as the "main" entrance, there is another one at level 2 (or even 3).

Now imagine going to a clinic on level 2 in a hospital built into the side of a steep slope. We enter on level 3 (although we are not necessarily conscious of this on entering). Which elevator button do we press? Up, of course, when we should be going down. More frustration. More stress.

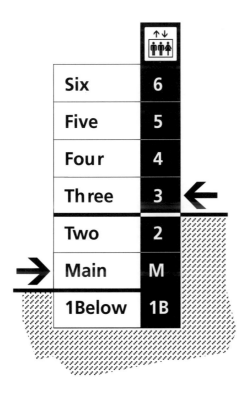

There is a hospital in Montreal that has active entrances on the main and third levels. The result is that visitors entering on the third level and going to the second level generally push the "up" button.

Chapter 15
Graphic information for decision executing
15.1 Floor and room numbering systems

What can be done to help in such situations is to ensure that in every elevator lobby (as part of the floor directory) there is a prominent identification of the floor level, as shown by the stars in the illustrations.

The use of a tactile star is gaining currency and it does unequivocally identify the ground floor. What it does not do, however, is identify *another* ground floor (when there is one, as in the example on the previous page).

Right: Two examples of elevator control panels that at least have the benefit of logic. For this reason alone, they are worth considering as standards.

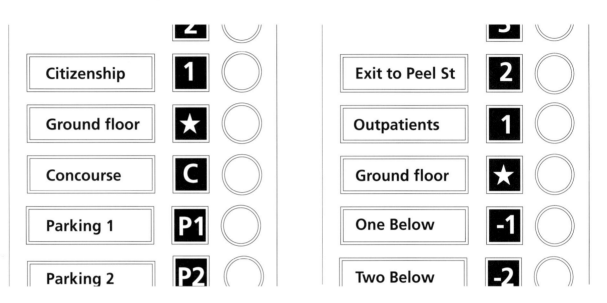

Our own recommendation is shown in the illustration: beside the control button there is a tactile and high-contrast floor number or symbol and beside it an explanatory plaque identifying anomalies such as a second main exit, or other features such as information. The tactile star must also be explained because no one is going to call this level the "Star floor." We feel that it should be standardized as "Ground floor."

Now, what about the level above "Ground"? Is it "1" (as in Europe) or "2" (as in North America)? From a purely logical viewpoint, it should be 1 (particularly if the level below it is –1), as the accompanying illustrations show.

The level below "Ground" in so many commercial buildings is a concourse of shops, restaurants, and other services; it should be identified as "Concourse" and on the elevator control button as "C." The meaning of the word "concourse" may be well enough established in our minds for this to be a workable solution, but it should still be explained on the control panel.

Below the concourse level there are generally several levels of parking which are appropriately identified as P1, P2, P3, and so on, in a downward direction. A different sort of problem arises in parking garages, however, when some of their levels are below grade and some above. Imagine such a garage where the third level is at grade with two more levels above it and, say, three more below. How, under such circumstances, should one label the levels? Reentering the garage at P3 as a pedestrian to retrieve one's vehicle is not helpful.

Above: A parking garage with levels below, as well as above, grade. What would the various levels be called in this case?

The "P" is probably necessary as part of the identification above ground, but what about below?

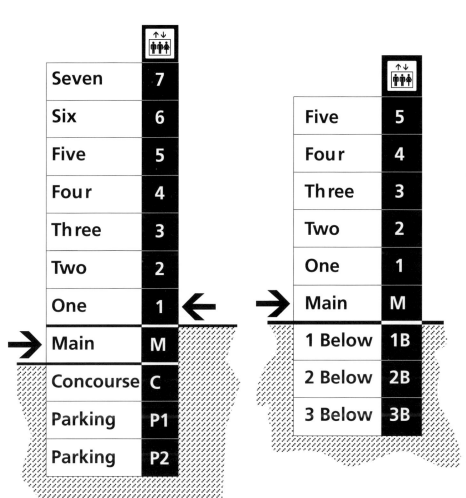

Far left: Section through a mixed-use office building with a concourse and parking levels below grade and entrances on two levels – always a disorienting experience for visitors.

Left: Section through a retail establishment having a main floor with several floors above and three below and with an entrance at grade only.

Remembering that we are accustomed to the idea of numbers dividing at grade and progressing upward toward the roof, and downward to the bottom, we find "P1," "P2," "P3," etc. for the above-grade levels and "–P1," "–P2," "–P3," etc. for those below a useful concept, although it begs the question of what to label the level which is *at* grade. Logically, it should be "★P" "1" or "0."

Finally on this subject, the identification of the floor levels themselves, whether they are used for offices, retail outlets, or parking, should be very clearly identified, particularly at the tops of stairs and escalators and in elevator lobbies.

15.1.2 Room numbering

We have just been discussing how to identify the levels in a building. Let us now focus on what the average visitor finds when emerging from an elevator on one of these levels.

Floors with corridors

We have often speculated on why it is that a person arriving by bus at a small town comprising only a handful of streets will have little or no trouble finding his or her way while that same person, arriving by elevator at, say, the third or fourth level of a hospital or university building, comprising the same number of corridors, may be at a total loss.

Thoughts on control panel nomenclature:

The star has gained wide currency as a tactile symbol for the Ground floor, so why not use it as a substitute for "Main" or "1" or "Ground" – particularly if it is explained in a panel close by, as shown in the illustration on the opposite page.

If the concept of levels below grade being identified as –1, –2, and so on, is accepted, there is still a need to explain the meaning of these symbols. Obviously "One below" is better than "Minus one." If one accepts the logic of the star as a kind of zero, then it follows that there should be a 1 above it and a –1 below it, even though North American custom is generally in favor of the level above Ground being identified as 2.

Some researchers prefer SUB1, SUB2, etc., for these below-grade floor levels.[1] A determination should, however, be made as to which is the best solution and to stay with it.

Note the explanation of the fact that there are two, not one, main entrances to one of these buildings: one on the Ground floor and another on the third level.

Chapter 15
Graphic information for decision executing
15.1 Floor and room numbering systems

We recognize that the two situations are not completely parallel. There are differences. One of these lies in the way the "addresses" in the town and on the floor of the building are organized. One (those in the town) we can relate to easily. The others can be far more difficult.

The town is made up of streets. These streets have names (or numbers) and the addresses on them are sequential and ordered – with even numbers being on one side and odd on the other. It would be very odd to find a number 57 being next door to number 17. But this is not the least uncommon on the floor of a building such as a community college.

Is there not something to be learned here? Why should floors of some buildings present themselves to visitors as incomprehensible labyrinths? There is no valid reason, of course, and if we could only apply the same system used in numbering houses or buildings on streets to rooms in corridors, we would at least have a dependable series of sequential numbers in these corridors – which would be an admirable start.

The problem confronting building managers and those who are responsible for the physical plant is change. Suppose that a room, which may have been a large classroom since 1910, is now to be divided into two rooms, each with an entrance into the corridor. How is this new door to be identified? No one wants to contemplate a whole new numbering system for the floor, so some arbitrary "unused" number is allocated to it. (This is how room 57 came to be next door to room 17.)

A room numbering system that takes account of change by allocating numbers to fixed modules within a corridor, whether they contain a door or not, is one way. This, of course, could result in room 17 being next to 23, which might offend some people. But no one is looking for 19 or 21 in any case, simply because they don't exist yet. The important thing is that as and when the space inside needs to be subdivided, a number can be given to the new door without disturbing the overall sequence.

There is a trend in supermarkets to turn the aisles into streets and even to give them names, either to evoke the neighborhoods they serve or to create "atmosphere." Whether this is truly effective as a wayfinding device in supermarkets or is just another passing fad remains to be seen. However, in university and hospital buildings, just to pick two examples, it is not a fad, and it does work.

This system takes people's well-established manner of getting about the town or city and applies it to a building:

- Get to the right part of town (read "floor level").
- Find the right street (read "corridor").
- Find the right address (read "room number").

For such a system to work, obviously it is essential that the streets be named in some way and that the numbers (or addresses) be sequential. In this system, even numbers would be on the north and west sides of corridors and corresponding odd numbers on the other sides.

Proposal for renumbering the second floor of a community college in a series of sequential numbers by the imposition of a uniform grid. Corridors are treated as "streets" and are renamed: "A" (200–224), "B" (225–249), "C" (250–271), and "D" (275–290).

Open-landscape floors

Not all floors have corridors in the conventional sense. They may, for example, be made up of open space with dividers to create offices. While there are still corridors of a sort, they are not nearly as evident as they are when the walls go from floor to ceiling.

The whole idea of open-landscape interiors is to acknowledge and to facilitate change. This has led us to the conclusion that room numbering in such cases is impossible. Instead, we have found it useful to create a series of clearly identified zones based on the spaces defined by the columns. The complete or partial layout of a floor can change radically from time to time to accommodate changing work habits or the growth of a department that requires relocation of personnel.

By imposing an alpha-numeric grid over all the levels of the building in the normal way (with letters on one axis and numbers on the other), a consistent matrix is created. Thus the spaces (or zones) defined by the columns are identified as A1, B1, C1 (or A2, B2, C2) in one direction and A1, A2, A3 (or B1, B2, B3) in the other. This generally results in three to five persons sharing an "address." If each of them is identified by name at the entrance to their work space, a visitor coming to see one of them will experience no difficulty.

As often as not, floors in modern office buildings are a mixture of offices with regular partitions and work stations with dividers. This zone system works equally well here – even though it is inevitable that some of the columns will be inside offices and, therefore, cannot be used to display the addresses.

15.2 Landmarks

15.2.1 Uses

Designers and architects are making increasing use of landmarks as part of integrated wayfinding systems for a wide variety of new projects, from underground pedestrian walkways to airports, hospitals, and college buildings. Generally speaking, landmarks perform two principal wayfinding functions:

- They help visitors to get their bearings, as the Eiffel Tower does in Paris, for example.
- They help staff to provide directions to visitors, such as, "To get to my office, take the elevator to the third floor, go left, and continue on till you can see the drinking fountain. My office is just opposite."

These two examples help to demonstrate the fact that landmarks have very real and effective uses, and that they can be virtually anything from a distinctive exterior structure to an interior drinking fountain. Their wayfinding usefulness is enhanced in interior spaces particularly when, as is so often the case, the space is relatively bland or uniform. Many college buildings, for example, consist of anonymous undifferentiated spaces connected by similarly anonymous corridors.

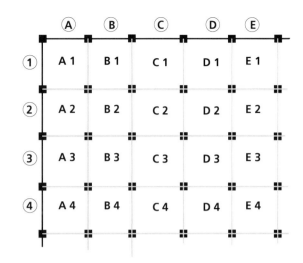

An open floor plan with "addresses" defined by the grid established by the columns in the building. Each address is identified by an alpha-numeric.

Each individual address is thus home to no more than a few people who are identified by name.

This is a useful alternative to attempting to provide each work station with its own number. Turnover on these floors can be so rapid that numbers quickly become out of date anyway.

In this system, no matter how often the configuration of work stations and offices changes, the addresses remain the same.

The theoretical basis for this assertion will be found in section 10.3.2 where landmarks are also referred to as anchor points.

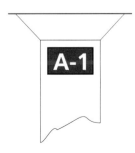

Small "address" sign on column face. (It is, of course, the *spaces* and not the columns that are being so identified. Thus the same "address" will appear on the four faces of columns enclosing this space called A-1.)

197

15.2.2 Content

The placing of physical objects to act as landmarks within buildings creates an invaluable wayfinding tool. The more bizarre and startling the object, the more effective it will be, of course (which is not to discount the usefulness, as we have already observed, of mundane building features). Although there may be initial resistance from staff at the idea of directing visitors in a hospital to "go down the corridor till you see the big red tomato, and it is two doors further along on the left," because they fear they will smile or giggle as they give such directions, is there anything basically wrong with that? Surely in a hospital of all places, anything that makes people smile (or giggle) cannot be all bad.

Because, in many of our cities, we are so used to thinking of everything in terms of the cardinal points of the compass, our sense of *dis*orientation inside big buildings (and particularly in those where we have no views to the outside) is total. We would not, however, be so disoriented if only someone or something would tell us which way is north or south. For this reason, the frequent display (on floors or ceilings) of compass roses is very helpful.

15.3 Location of signs

15.3.1 At decision points

In executing a decision plan, visitors are asked to make many decisions en route to their destinations. The fewer decisions they have to make, the more efficient the route.

It is important that routes to destinations be the same for the able bodied and for persons in wheelchairs.

Decision points manifest themselves mainly as corridor intersections and it is here that visitors must have assistance – frequently in the form of signs.

As the illustrations show, we strongly recommend as good wayfinding practice the use of four signs per intersection, irrespective of its configuration. This ensures maximum visibility of this vital information for visitors coming from all directions. The need to provide "the right information at the right place" (which is what every wayfinding designer attempts to do) is thus fulfilled.

But what of the content? How much information can usefully be provided in these signs? Most cities that permit exterior directional signs to important destinations at all, permit them only within a given radius of the destination itself. Thus the hopeless effort of trying to provide, at every street corner, directions to every destination in the city is avoided. The same discipline must be applied to interior signs. It is a hopeless and self-defeating task to attempt, at every intersection, to provide directions to every location in the building. We have seen this actually done, and the effect is nothing less than chaotic.

What sort of information, then, should be included in signs at intersections? If the concept of destination zones (see section 10.1) has been incorporated into the planning of the building, the answer is obvious and the results will be efficient.

In new construction, we would go so far as to say categorically that it is essential that routes for the able bodied and for wheelchair users be the same. We recognize, however, that in existing structures, this is not always feasible.

"Efficiency," for its own sake, cannot be considered the sole criterion in selecting a route for visitors to take. If the most efficient route to X-ray is via Surgery, for example, it would be preferable to select a less efficient path.

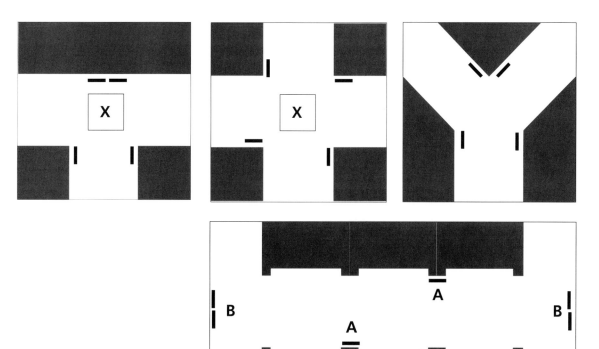

There are three types of corridor intersections, as shown in the illustrations. Each of them requires the same number of signs.

Even when a large chandelier-type sign (X) is mounted overhead for long-distance viewing at these intersections, the information it contains must be repeated in the lower area of InfoBand 1 (see section 15.4).

Typical signs in an elevator lobby. A-type signs are floor directories, identifying the floor by number and directing visitors to the left or right for individual tenants. B-type signs are "splitters" which again direct visitors left or right.

But when destinations of a like type or kind are distributed throughout the complex, like raisins in a cake, the wayfinding designers must resort to a different strategy:

- First, it must be established (through maps or directories or both) that this particular destination is on a certain level or in a certain wing of the building or in some other general area.
- Then, directions to these large areas must be provided.
- Finally, having arrived at the large area, the visitor must be provided with more finely tuned information about the particular destination.

Each of the signs in the illustrations should contain no more than five pieces of information, in letters with a cap-height of not less than 1.75 inches (45 mm).

When it becomes essential to provide more information, this should take the form of additional signs, each displaying different information types. For example, in a hospital, one of these signs might be restricted to administrative information (Admitting, Cafeteria, Cashier, Washrooms) leaving the accompanying sign for medical information (Chest, ENT, Nursery, X-ray).

It is very helpful in complex settings such as hospitals or university buildings to locate properly oriented or aligned maps strategically at decision points. This will also tend to reduce the need for information on signs – particularly if one of the maps displays only "local" information.

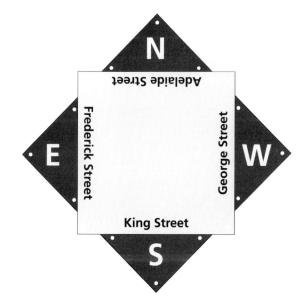

"Compass rose" sign for installation on ceilings at all corridor intersections in an academic building with a highly complex interior setting. The street names and cardinal points provide orientation to the outside world and facilitate instructions on how to get to given destinations. George Brown College, Toronto.

199

Chapter 15
Graphic information for decision executing
15.3 Location of signs

We make a distinction between "locating" and "placing" signs. The former has the sense of location on plan, while the latter term refers to placement in elevation.

A 1.75 inch (45 mm) cap-height message is displayed on a 3 inch (75 mm) "blade" or message module. Five such blades total 15 inches (380 mm).

15.3.2 Reliability

The main problem with directional signs is that if they are to be the least bit effective, they must be totally reliable, in the sense that wayfinders must be able to follow a trail or series of signs, located at reassuring intervals, to their chosen destination. This is why it is so important that planners select with care what destinations they are going to provide directions to.

Once any destination is featured on a directional sign at a given intersection, there is an obligation to include it on every subsequent directional sign until the destination is reached. This is further substantiation for the concept of providing long-distance directions for gross areas or destination zones but strongly restricting the distances at which individual destinations (our "raisins" in a previous metaphor) first appear on directional signs.

15.4 Placement of signs

15.4.1 InfoBand 1

We have long cherished a dream that at some time in the future the entire world will acknowledge the need to enshrine graphic wayfinding information in a horizontal band, exactly 16 inches (400 mm) deep and positioned 47 inches (1200 mm) off the ground (or floor). This is VisuCom's InfoBand 1. It should be restricted exclusively to wayfinding information and therefore should be free of thermostats, light switches, and other distractions (although it is proper that fire alarms should be located within it).

InfoBand 1 has been restricted to the level between 47 to 63 inches above the floor (120 to 160 cm) for two reasons:

1. This level fits more or less comfortably within the cone of vision of pedestrians, both adults and children, and of people in wheelchairs. It is designed to accommodate as many people as possible, including those with low vision who must be able to get very close to a sign in order to read it. It also ensures reliability in terms of where users should expect to find a sign, the absence of which has a devastating effect on wayfinders.

2. This level may extend no more than 16 inches (400 mm) in height, allowing for no more than five lines of type. This is in keeping with the wayfinding principle that no more than five lines or "bits" of information should be displayed on any one sign and with the recommendation that the cap-height of the typeface used should be 1.75 inches (45 mm). Under such restrictions designers must be extremely selective in the wording of the messages.

One can only speculate on what a different world it would be for wayfinders in unfamiliar settings if this principle of a band, sacred to the display of information, were to be established in every building, everywhere.

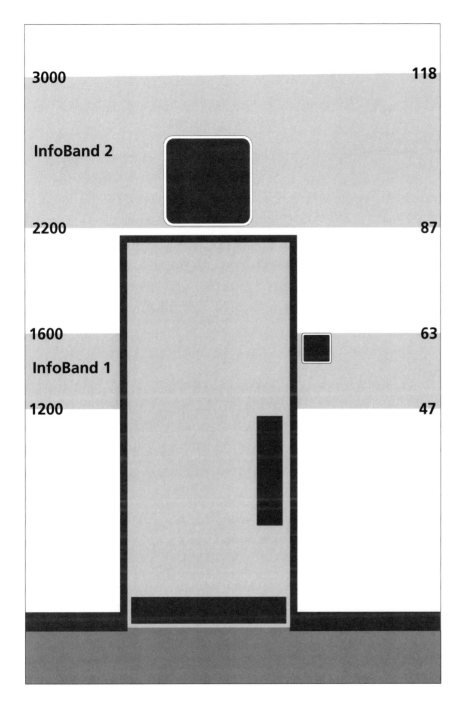

3000 — 118

InfoBand 2

2200 — 87

1600 — 63

InfoBand 1

1200 — 47

InfoBands 1 and 2 are designed to display graphic information in the most efficient way possible.

InfoBand 1 is well within the cone of vision of most people, including those in wheelchairs.

Persons with low vision can get close to signs displayed here. Any information displayed for long-distance viewing in the upper band must be repeated in the lower.

The dimensions are given in millimeters on the left and inches on the right.

15.4.2 InfoBand 2

A larger, broader band, has been established just above door height, at the 87 inch (2200 mm) level and extending to the ceiling, or to a maximum height of 118 inches (3000 mm).

This is InfoBand 2, for the display of large pictographs on walls over doorways to identify their use from a distance. It may also include suspended signs that have a similar (or a directional) function.

There can be no question about the utility of larger signs within this secondary InfoBand. At the same time, such signs are totally illegible, and therefore useless, to persons with low vision. For this reason, any sign placed in InfoBand 2 must be duplicated

Chapter 15
Graphic information for decision executing
15.4 Placement of signs

in a smaller size in InfoBand 1. This repetition is useful for everyone, not just low-vision people. It is an important element in a "forgiving" system.

15.5 Equipment

15.5.1 TDDs

Telecommunications Devices for the Deaf (TDDs) enable hearing- or speech-impaired persons to communicate by translating the sounds they cannot hear or make into visual signals on a screen – or as hard copy on paper.

A TDD keypad is used to type verbal messages (in, say, a person's home) which are transmitted via telephone lines to another TDD terminal (in, say, an office somewhere) providing that the other address, in addition to its regular telephone number, also has a TDD number. It can then receive such a call.

This equipment is, of course, interactive in that it transmits dialog between the parties involved. It is relatively inexpensive and now there are portable versions weighing not much more than a couple of pounds.

The role of TDDs as wayfinding devices to speech- and hearing-impaired persons is obvious. By enabling them to call ahead and thereby obtain the kinds of information they need about a setting or the services it offers, they are much more likely to make the journey than they would be if this information were not so readily available.

15.5.2 Passive video displays

Passive video displays are otherwise known as "electronic posters" despite their relatively small size. They are mentioned here more for the sake of completeness than for their usefulness in helping people find their way about.

15.5.3 Interactive video displays

When automatic teller machines (ATMs) were first introduced on a broad scale, people who were pessimistic about their usefulness to the banking business used to say that they would never work. They gave a variety of reasons, but chief among them was the conviction that people hated to have to deal with a machine.

These Jeremiahs were proven very wrong indeed and the enormous success and popularity of ATMs has encouraged the automation of many other forms of information transfer, including wayfinding information. Interactive systems represent the very last word in information technology because they are so extraordinarily versatile in what they can do and because of the entertaining (perhaps intriguing would be a more accurate word) ways in which they do it.

The genius who grasped the opportunities offered by the combination of computers, television touch screens, and electronics and

put them to use for wayfinding purposes is Edwin Schlossberg, whose Siteguide™ system is now becoming well established in North America and Europe.[2] Schlossberg's system offers visitors to shopping malls and multiuse complexes (but also to hospitals and any other facility that can afford to purchase them, the list of applications is virtually endless) the broadest conceivable range of information types. In commercial settings such as shopping malls, Siteguide™ addresses the two most asked types of questions by first-time visitors: "How do I get where I want to go?" and "What is there here that might interest me?"

The Siteguide™ system provides answers like nothing a visitor has ever experienced before – and does so in a manner that subscribes to every principle of good wayfinding design. Following is a list of some of the types of information it provides:

- A video tour or overview of the settings so that the visitor can form a cognitive map of it
- The visitor's location within the setting at that particular moment
- The location of places of interest or potential interest
- Directions on the screen to a selected destination
- A dot-matrix print-out summarizing the route, with a map
- Alphabetical listings of all the tenants in the building
- Categorized listings of these tenants, if the visitor prefers
- Announcement spots by the tenants (a form of advertising)
- A calendar of current and up-coming events

Typical Siteguide™ dot-matrix print-out of instructions on how to get to a given store in a large shopping mall. First is a map, then the words:
1. "Go up escalator to the upper level."
2. "Turn left and follow the hallway to the American Express entrance."
3. "Cross the lobby to the Winter Garden balcony."
4. "Turn left and follow the curve to…" and so on through several more instructions until, on the last line, these words appear: "Your destination is to the left."

In principle, interactive video displays could provide these wayfinding instructions in the language of the visitor's choice, thereby satisfying yet another wayfinding problem discussed in this book: some visitors, while perfectly fluent in their own language, cannot read instructions in a "foreign" language.

203

Most of the time when we talk about wayfinding, we are discussing answers to well-defined questions such as, "How do I, in this particular location within this overall setting, get to my destination, namely the such-and-such?" But what if the location of the destination is *not* well defined? Or what if it is not defined at all? In other words, what if a significant part of the wayfinding equation is missing?

For example, what happens when a person arrives for the first time at, say, a community college campus comprising some four or five buildings to attend a course of lectures – but has no idea whatsoever where the lecture that evening will be held? Imagine, too, that several hundred courses are offered every day by this institution.

Assuming the person has been lucky enough to ascertain from someone who knows that the class is in room 420 in "A" Building at 7 o'clock, we return to the relatively simple business of providing directions to Building A, then to the fourth floor, and finally to room 20 on that floor.

But what if the student had not had the good fortune to meet someone who knew where the class would be held? Trusting to luck is not good enough and this is where touch-screen interactive equipment of some kind can provide all the information a person could want in these or similar circumstances.

The often used argument that only one person at a time can use such equipment, whereas many people can look at sign simultaneously, is perfectly valid. However, the type of information we are discussing here could not be displayed on a sign for a wide variety of reasons. The room in which a class is held may well vary from week to week. Several hundred different classes are offered every day of the week and any sign displaying them all would be impossibly huge and also impossible to read.

The alternative to the obvious impossibility and impracticality of billboard-sized signs is an information desk with a knowledgeable attendant in charge. However, the same objection applies: the attendant can deal with only one person at a time. Besides, the chance of there being more than one staffed information desk is extremely remote, whereas small info-kiosks of the type we are recommending can be strategically located throughout the setting.

What Schlossberg and others have made possible is the realization of a dream that one day accurate up-to-date information could be made available to people on a highly personal, tailor-made basis, specific to their particular needs at a particular time.

15.5.4 Electronic directories

Although the manufacturers of electronic directories are apt to make extravagant claims for what their products will do, there is no question that this equipment solves the age-old problem of containing vast amounts of information while displaying only as much as a viewer can absorb at any given time.

By means of a touch screen or keypad, users may scroll through the directory, which provides names and room numbers of the building's tenants and sometimes other information as well.

Moreover, and even better, these directories display this information at eye level and not high above our heads. The degree of contrast (between the type, usually orange, and the background, generally black) may be inadequate for low-vision people, but the size of letters (at about one-half inch (15 mm) is quite adequate.

Only one person at a time can make use of such a directory, a serious limitation, but one that is shared with all other types of interactive equipment, and, as we have observed before, only one person can talk to an attendant at an information desk.

The most interesting of these directories make use of flat, not curved, plasma TV screens that require, to all intents, no depth at all as they can be accommodated within the thickness (4 inches or 100 mm) of the average wall.

15.5.5 Signal lights

The most typical signal light is the one that goes on (usually red or green or white) over the elevator door to signal the car's arrival and, in the case of green or red lights, to indicate to those waiting the direction of its travel: green for up, red for down.

Another valuable but rare use for signal lights is to alert the deaf that an alarm has rung. Visual fire alarms used to consist of a pulsing strobe light which was guaranteed to get everybody's attention. Recent research, however, has demonstrated that while a pulsing low-wattage light could be useful, strobes tend to be frightening and may cause temporary blindness in some people.

Part Six:
Audible and tactile components of wayfinding design

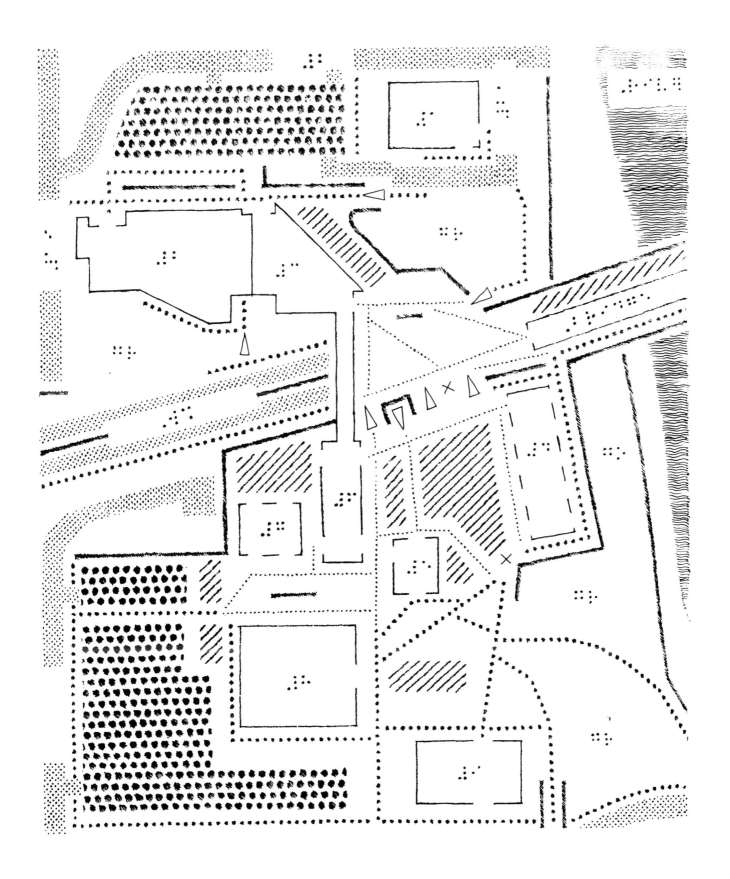

Chapter 16
Audible information for decision making and executing

The ear is the main source of information for the sightless and the visually impaired. Literacy-impaired and developmentally and situationally impaired persons also may find that obtaining information by ear is preferable to trying to obtain it visually.

The application of audible forms of communication is, however, by no means limited to these categories of users. Most, if not all, of the means discussed in this chapter have a broad application to wayfinding generally to the extent that sighted persons, under certain circumstances, will actually prefer to have information imparted audibly rather than visually. This is particularly true of directional information.

16.1 Information desks

16.1.1 Desk design

It is a sign of the times that the old-fashioned information desk has been transformed into a security bunker, all too frequently staffed by rather officious people whose function is not giving out information – as though security and information were mutually exclusive terms.

Paradoxically, building directories are frequently built into these security desks – irrespective of whether this is the right place for them or whether they should be completely separate units.

If the security desk actually does have the additional function of providing wayfinding information, then placing the directory on or closely linked to the desk is appropriate. However, in such cases, the desk needs to be clearly identified with a large sign with the word "Information" on it. (This is rarely, if ever, the case.)

When providing information is not a function of the security staff or when the desk is dedicated exclusively to security and surveillance matters, then the directory should be a separate unit elsewhere – either on a wall or as a free-standing unit. (People cannot be deterred from asking questions if they are having difficulties with – or cannot read – the directory, and there is no point subjecting the security staff to questions they can't answer anyway.)

A desk intended to provide audible communication should have the following characteristics:

- It should be highly visible immediately on entering the building.
- It should be clearly identified by the word "Information," preferably above the desk.
- There should be directions to it, if there is more than one entrance to the building.
- Its work surface should be of a height that is comfortable for the attendant and for visitors, both those who are standing and those in wheelchairs.
- It requires a recess to accommodate the knees and feet of a person in a wheelchair to enable them to get as close to the desk as a standing person can.
- It must have adequate storage space within it for maps of various floor levels onto which the attendant will trace the route visitors should take to get where they want to go.
- It should have whatever electronic or other equipment is required to enable the attendant to do an effective job of providing information other than simple directions; there is in many situations a need to determine what office or room persons should go to, in addition to telling them how to get there.
- It should be accompanied by a building directory located so that both attendant and visitor can view it at the same time. If the directory (with or without a map) is placed on a horizontal surface, it should not be flat but inclined 15 degrees or so to favor the angle of view of the visitor (who may be seated or standing) and to avoid picking up reflections from light sources overhead.

Different circumstances having to do with the particular functions of the building in which the information desk is located will dictate other requirements, but these are the most basic.

16.1.2 Attendant training

With the advent of electronic directories (see section 15.5.4), the information desk and its attendant have in most types of buildings gone the way of tellers in banks with the widespread introduction some years ago of automatic teller machines (ATMs).

Visitors looking for a human source of information now find, as we observed in the preceding section, security guards who may, or very well may not, be prepared to provide wayfinding information.

In any case, because the prime responsibility of these personnel is security, it is extremely unlikely that they will have been exposed to any sort of training in dealing with visitors' questions, much less in helping people with impaired speech, hearing, or sight.

In wayfinding terms, this is regrettable because, as we have so frequently stated throughout this book, wayfinding information is not limited to architecture and signs. It is also verbal and aural. We know that speech is actually the preferred medium for most perfectly able-bodied people to receive certain types of information – particularly that type which used to be the main purpose for having an information desk in the first place, namely, to provide directions to destinations. If given the choice, most of us would much prefer to be *told* how to get there, rather than having to figure it out from a directory, a sign, or even a map.

For one thing, when you ask directions of people, you can get an idea of whether or not they know what they're talking about (and therefore whether or not their information is reliable). This you cannot do with signs and maps which, you may have learned from experience, may or may not be trustworthy sources of information. A person can explain to you in detail (and more than once, if necessary) how to get to a given destination and can trace a route on a map which you can take with you. These are things no static sign could ever be expected to do.

All of these things are, admittedly, precisely what sophisticated interactive video systems are designed to do – right up to and including providing the visitor with a printed map. The point is that this form of interaction, whether with a live human being or with a machine, is a desirable part of obtaining directional information.

If information is to be imparted in the old-fashioned way, person to person, it should be done in such a way as to take into account that visitors may have articulation, hearing, seeing, or understanding problems. In other words, attendants should be trained to deal with these disabilities in an understanding manner. They should, for example, enunciate each word clearly, look visitors squarely in the face while talking, and never put their hands to their mouths (or fiddle with their moustaches) while they are talking. They never know when they may be talking to someone who is lip-reading or hard of hearing or blind. (Giving information to the blind requires special training, referred to in section 8.3.1.)

Attendants should be trained in the use of touch-screen electronic video equipment to obtain information about activities, events, courses of study, or other details visitors may ask about. They should know how to trace a path on a pre-printed map, explaining the route while they are doing it, and particularly pointing out, and highlighting, anchor-points or landmarks visitors will encounter en route.

For persons with speech disorders, attendants should be able, in the most natural way possible, to switch from speech to writing, providing the visitor with a pencil and pad and communicating with him or her in this manner.

Above all things, however, the attendant should be understanding and like people, prerequisites for which no amount of training can substitute.

16.2 Audible systems

16.2.1 Telephones

The next best thing to an information desk staffed by trained attendants is the telephone – and while there is likely to be only one information desk in a building, inexpensive telephones can be strategically located throughout it.

A telephone with a human being at the other end has essentially all the versatility that that particular human being is able to bring to the task of conveying audible information. If sight- or literacy-impaired users could count on finding either an information desk or a telephone with a direct line to an operator or receptionist near the entrance of any public building, this would go a very long way towards true accessibility.

A telephone service, available to users before they even come to the building, would be particularly useful for blind people and for people who are confined to wheelchairs, both of whom may need to know whether the building is accessible to them. The number should be listed in the telephone book, and calls should be answered by someone with communication skills, knowledge of the building and of the needs of users, and common sense.

If the provision of telephones involving operators is considered extravagantly expensive, it should be remembered that this versatile device can operate very well indeed without an operator. It can be equipped with a series of taped messages (in several languages) which, upon commands actuated through a tactual keypad, can provide orientation and directional information cheaply and efficiently.

This system of self-help telephones can also be programmed to provide general information to satisfy (as no conventional sign can) visitor needs of a more specific nature, also through taped messages.

In general, telephones should all have receivers that contain a magnetic fluxcoil in order to be accessible to the hearing impaired.

These are not more expensive than other telephones. Telephones should also not be situated near a fluorescent light – one closer than 15 feet (4.5 m) may interfere with reception. At least one public telephone in each area should have a volume control in the handset. The telephone company will convert public telephones in this way on request. The volume control also boosts the strength of the magnetic field and therefore makes the telephone more accessible for users with hearing aids as well.

16.2.2 Audible maps

Telephones provide an excellent means of conveying orientation and wayfinding information. The audible map is an example. While its origins lie in attempts to provide a richer form of mapping information for the blind than tactual maps can give, many persons who are not blind prefer to obtain this sort of information in this way, rather than in visual form. Typically, upon lifting the handset from its cradle, visitors are provided with a verbal description of the building's chief characteristics, where they are within the setting, where certain facilities are in relation to their position, and so on.

On a more exotic level, there are, actually, signs that talk upon command, activated by a hand-held infrared control mechanism and received through either earphones or the hand-held device itself, acting as a speaker.

16.2.3 Public address systems

Conventional public-address systems are usually of such poor quality and so badly installed as to be more of a nuisance than a help. It may also be argued that they have no place in environmental communications in public buildings.

However, a properly designed and installed PA system of reasonable quality is an effective medium for informing visitors of particular conditions (such as emergencies) and for imparting general information, as is successfully done in the airport in Atlanta, Georgia. There, as one proceeds from one major zone of the building to another, a voice identifies this fact and provides helpful information which *is* useful to everyone, but which is particularly valuable to the sight impaired.

A good PA system should have a broad frequency range, equalized to suit the environment and set at a medium volume with several speakers (rather than a high volume with few). Its usefulness can be augmented by some sort of visual display, such as an electronic sign.

16.3 Mechanical sounds
16.3.1 Bells, buzzers, alarms

In the past, bells, buzzers, and other audible alarms had an almost exclusively emergency-related role to play in environmental communications. We recommend that audible alarms be keyed to visual signs (such as pulsing, but not strobe, or colored lights) to provide visual reinforcement to the alarm.

An imaginative and helpful use has been given to the bell in elevator lobbies: it is sounded twice to indicate that the arriving elevator is going down and once to indicate up. Another method for achieving the same result would be the use of differentiated tones: a higher one for up, a lower one for down. Blind persons otherwise have no way of knowing, particularly if they are alone, which way the elevator is going to take them.

It would be unfortunate if we were to consider this and other such devices of value to sight-impaired persons only. In Salt Lake City, in Stockholm, and in most Japanese cities, downtown intersections are equipped with two different birdlike sounds which indicate the direction in which it is safe for pedestrians to cross the road. A robinlike sound, for instance, indicates it is safe to cross north-south, while a cuckoo, say, performs the same function east-west.

The original intention probably was to help blind or sight-impaired persons. But able-bodied visitors to the city report that the sounds act as a means of reinforcing (in an insistent manner) the evidence of their eyes. This repetition of cues or prompts is helpful to everyone and probably results in more efficient traffic management.

Mention has already been made in the previous section of the cost effectiveness of telephones for providing information to blind or illiterate persons. The problems the blind experience in this regard begin with the fact they cannot know precisely where such a telephone would be located. "Just inside the front door" is open to much interpretation, given the fact that not all public buildings are identical in plan.

A high-pitched, low-volume pulsing whistle that identified such a telephone just inside the door and that could be activated by blind persons would be irritating to no one and would ensure that blind visitors could find this telephone.

16.3.2 Voice synthesizers

The idea of an artificial larynx producing humanoid sounds from a variety of inputs is one of the wonders of the age. This device, however, is not of the same rank or order in the scale of environmental communications devices as, say, telephones or video displays. Rather, it is a component that can be built into them whenever there is a suitable application, as in the case of interactive computers with handsets.

The most suitable application at this stage in the built environment is in elevator cars where a synthetic voice announces floor levels.

Chapter 17

Tactile information for decision making and executing

At the end of Chapter 8, we expressed our preference for the macro- (as distinct from the micro-) approach to planning. Everything in this book to this point has been predicated exclusively on the macro-approach.

Nothing in the previous chapter on audible wayfinding components, for example, could possibly be described as specifically related to any particular user group: information desks, audible maps, public address systems, even bells and buzzers – all have application in one way or another to the entire population.

Having said all that, this book would have been decidedly incomplete without reference to the area of tactual information, which has a more tenuous relationship to the wayfinding practices of the population as a whole, but is nevertheless significant.

Tactile spatial maps would be meaningless to the congenitally blind if they were unable to conceptualize space. These comments refer exclusively to hand-held maps.

Blind people can incorporate information from different maps and figure out routes that involve movements in three dimensions.

17.1 Maps

Tactile maps are only one of the means of communicating wayfinding information to the blind and visually impaired users. (Information contained in maps may also be provided in spoken form. These are referred to as audible maps and are potentially useful for everyone, but are generally devised for people who have difficulties reading tactually. They are also useful in situations when tactile maps are not available – such as in telephone and other oral communications environments. Audible maps work best for single, simple routes. They are sequential by nature, describing how to get from point A to point B.)

Tactile maps usually contain a description in braille of a route to be taken to reach a given destination. In other words, they provide the braille-reading users with a decision plan.

Like visual maps, tactile maps have two functions: to give information on how to reach a destination, and to provide generalized information about the spacial layout of the setting.

Tactile maps are generally hand held, although in some urban transit systems, they are free-standing units located on station platforms. The problem that free-standing units pose, of course, is that before they can be used, they have to be found, and this severely limits their usefulness. Another limitation is the extent of the information they can contain if they are to be legible in tactile terms.

A tactile map is not simply a translation of visual into tactile phenomena. Visual and tactile perception are quite different in character. The visual perception of a map is immediate, providing the viewer with a global impression of spatial relationships. A spatial form (Gestalt), or a spatial system like a grid is understood at a glance. The tactile perception of a map is sequential. The user has to build up a total impression from a series of details. While the cues can be quite small and dense for visual perception, they have to be much larger and more spaced out for tactile perception.

While tactile maps have the potential of providing blind users with spatial information that is not easily communicated to them through other means, these maps are often useless because they are too cluttered to be legible or because they contain insufficient information for wayfinding.

The design challenge in composing tactile maps is to provide sufficient information in a small enough area to be conveniently scanned without being cluttered. Research literature seems to agree that raised (i.e., relief) lines and points are far easier to perceive on a tactile basis than are those which are engraved (i.e., intaglio). Information content can be increased without clutter by three means:

- The use of differently scaled maps
- The use of overlays
- The use of different heights for the raised symbols

The scale of a map can be chosen as a function of the information to be communicated. A large-scale map may be suited to give

Tactile spatial maps would be meaningless to the congenitally blind if they were unable to conceptualize space.

215

These comments refer exclusively to hand-held maps.

the general form of a layout, while a small-scale map may be needed to provide users with detailed information of a route.

Interlocking overlays can be used to increase information content. A map may, for example, give the spatial disposition of a layout, while the overlay gives a braille description of the facilities contained. Small tactile maps have been designed in which the description is underneath the map in reversed braille. Although the map is handy to use, reading braille in reverse is not easy.

The third option for increasing information on a tactile map is to differentiate between the heights of the raised symbols. Environmental features are represented by three types of symbols. Single locations are represented by points, links between places and barriers by lines, and spaces by surfaces. By using different heights for each type, as well as the braille legend, comprehension has been shown to increase.[1]

The content and form of an international symbol vocabulary for tactile maps is still being debated. While a standard set of symbols has been adopted by organizations such as the First European Symposium on Tactual Town Maps for the Blind (Brussels, 1983), it has been rejected by others who consider that more research is needed on the cartographic content, the symbol design, the quality of reproduction, and the effect of standardization on map quality.[2]

Various materials have been used to make tactile maps. These range from sandpaper glued to surfaces, to vinyl, to paper. While vinyl maps tend to be more intelligible, paper maps tend to produce less fatigue. Recent innovations in paper production such as capsule paper, however, have made it possible to easily produce inexpensive maps of excellent quality.[3]

17.2 Signs

17.2.1 Tactile signs

The practical realization of an audible (or "talking" sign) that is effective (you touch it, it provides information) and inexpensive (low cost to purchase and low maintenance also) is about to come on the market.

When it does, it will be an exciting development – not only for the blind where it will effectively do away with the need for tactile letters, but for the entire population as well. Such a device not only cuts across literacy problems, it also renders the "verbal signs" approach even more efficacious.

At a time when the number of sightless people able to read braille comfortably is shrinking, there is nonetheless an increase in the use of braille cells in signs connected with elevators (on elevator door jambs and in the cars themselves). At the same time, these braille cells are generally accompanied by tactual (or raised) digits. There is good reason to believe that many blind people have difficulty interpreting the raised numbers also, but those who can use them outnumber those who can use braille.

None of this is an argument against displaying braille or tactual signs, because if such signs were more in evidence in environmental communications, there could be no question that blind and sight-impaired persons would learn how to use them and would find them very helpful.

Nonetheless it must be remembered that while braille cells can be interpreted by a skilled reader relatively speedily, the haptic exploration of Roman letterforms that are raised 1 mm above the surface of a signface is a relatively slow process.

A study conducted some years ago at Georgia Institute of Technology's College of Architecture for the Architectural and Transportation Barriers Compliance Board (ATBCB) in Washington, DC,

216

demonstrated that teaching blind people how to read tactile letters seems to be on the same level as the teaching of braille. Many of the volunteers had had no experience with tactile letters, while the remainder had been instructed in the reading of CAPITAL letters only. It is, then, not surprising that they all had very real problems in interpreting lower-case letters.

None of these, as we have said, are convincing arguments either for not providing tactual letters in signs for the use of the blind – or for reverting to the idea that all signs for sighted as well as sight-impaired persons should necessarily be in upper case.

Pro and con

What should or should not be done to assist the sight impaired in getting about with greater facility?

Tactile signs are very rarely installed anywhere. Why is this? Is it because of ignorance? Is it the difficulty (and added expense) involved in their manufacture? Or is it because blind people don't want, or need, them?

See section 13.1.3 for a counter-argument in favor of the use of caps in signs.

There is no agreement on the desirability of tactile signs, which is a major reason why we see them so infrequently – except, of course, in elevators where their presence is now standard. If there, however, why not every-where?

Tactile signs are more expensive to manufacture than engraved or screen-printed signs (and considerably more than computer-cut vinyl legends), and yes, blind and low-vision people can and do use them when they are available (although, as noted elsewhere, they find capital letters much easier to read than lower case letters). Well, what about the other issues? Is there any objection to their use? The Canadian National Institute for the Blind (CNIB) takes the rationalist view that anything that helps is good, and it is good because it is helpful. In the United States, on the other hand, opinion is sharply divided with one side (represented by the American Foundation for the Blind and the National Council of the Blind) being of a view similar to that of the CNIB, whereas the other side (represented by the National Federation of the Blind) is violently opposed, maintaining that "enriching" environmental communication especially for blind people (the micro-approach) is a clear signal that they cannot get about (or earn a living) without these devices. And inasmuch as very few environments are already furnished with special signs and signals for the blind, employers have an obvious "excuse" not to hire them.

This may well prove to be a dispute for which there is no satisfactory solution but the evidence that blind persons perform well in orientation and even directional situations (see section 8.3.1) is not, it seems to us, an argument against having tactual identification signs and directional signs.

Content

Verbal content for tactile signs is the same as for non-tactile signs, although in the upper left-hand corner of the sign raised dots restate the message in braille cells.

Capital letters are easier to read tactually than are lower-case letters, and in locations where tactile letters are particularly appropriate, signs in capital letters (instead of upper- and lower-case letters) might be more appropriate also.

Glyphs or pictographs are not appropriate subjects for tactile signs – with the sole exception of the arrow in the case of tactile directional signs. The problems blind persons experience in interpreting lower-case letters are magnified several times with pictographs.

The ideal tactile letters for the sight impaired have a cap-height of between 1 inch (25 mm) and 1.75 inches (45 mm). Larger tactile letters begin to cause problems in interpretation. Braille cells are standardized at just over a quarter of an inch high (7 mm). Sans serif letters are preferable to serif letters in tactile signs.

Pictographs in interior situations are probably a minimum of 5 inches (or 125 mm) high; because they are so much larger and more complex than letterforms, the blind find them difficult to interpret.

17.3 Clues

17.3.1 Tactile markings

Markings in paint or tape have the functions of drawing attention to potential hazards and of defining walkways, safety lanes, parking spaces, and other designated areas.

Such markings can, at some cost, be made tactual. The black and yellow tactile marking that separates the floor from the edge on many subway platforms is a case in point. And if it is made from a rubberized compound, its sound and resiliency, when struck by a cane, will be quite different from that of the other flooring materials.

17.3.2 Shorelines, trails

The curb of the sidewalk is an example of a shoreline followed by a blind person using a cane to negotiate streets.

Leaving the relative security of such a shoreline for the potential dangers of the open streets requires great determination – and the blind person experiences considerable relief when the farther shore is eventually reached.

Buildings do not, as a general rule, have anything similar to such well-defined paths as sidewalks. They do, however, frequently have large open spaces that may or may not be filled with potential hazards for the sightless, although the sighted person can usually negotiate them without any problems.

It is desirable that architects, as they become more aware of the problems of the sightless, who are literally adrift in these open spaces, will introduce into floor surfaces the necessary trails or shorelines that will at least allow a blind person to cross the lobby from the front door to the information desk, and to find the elevators. However, this differentiation of flooring materials and surfaces must be an integral aspect of the architectural design from the very beginning, because it cannot easily be done on a catch-up basis afterwards, once the flooring is installed.

One could hope for more, of course. For example, a change in floor surface could be used to alert all visitors to the fact that a step or a stair or an escalator is just ahead. This is done in the Eaton Centre, in Toronto, with great style, and most of the sighted visitors think it is just an esthetic device, a part of the floor pattern. It consists of a high degree of textural contrast between a black-pebbled textured area and the smooth white quarry tile of the floor that abuts it. This noticeable granular contrast is present wherever there is a flight of steps or an escalator.

17.3.3 Textures, resiliency

Resiliency is the more easily detected than texture, from both an aural and a tactile standpoint. It used to be the practice to introduce differences of texture, in sidewalks, for example, to alert the blind that they were coming to an intersection – even in some cities, such as Montreal, to attempt a guidance system for the blind.

It was, however, one of the findings of the Georgia Tech research in the early 80s that blind people were less sensitive to changes of texture than was originally thought and that most textures introduced into sidewalks or floors, intended to assist the blind, were either undetectable or indistinguishable from one another. Resiliency, on the other hand is highly detectable and distinguishable (provided one can hear), and has the added advantage of manifesting itself both aurally (see section 16.3.3) and tactilely. A rubberized area at the edge of a subway platform, for example, will not only *sound* different from the masonry floor, it will also *feel* different, and of course, it should *look* different as well.

Postscript

On the emergence of a new kind of professional

What did the first signs look like? Broken branches on the hunting paths of prehistoric man? Piles of rocks guiding nomadic tribes to their next camp? Maybe even earlier than that – claw marks on tree bark, or scent messages, the keys for which have been lost long ago.

We know a little bit more than this about architecture and wayfinding. Already in antiquity, wayfinding design was practised for some settings: labyrinthine spatial layouts were specifically designed to disorient people. The purpose was twofold: to protect some treasured or sacred objects from thieves, or to protect a place or even a city from invaders.

The power of the labyrinth was physical – to disorient people and get them lost. It was also psychological – to induce a feeling of danger and fear.

Today we are rediscovering wayfinding and wayfinding design, not to bury sacred crocodiles as the old Egyptians did in the labyrinthine pathways within their pyramids, nor to confuse invaders of our cities as was done in some urban centers of antiquity, but to assist the wayfinding person in the built environment, an environment that has become more complex and often more confusing than anything the Greek historian Herodotus wrote about in his descriptions of the ancient world.

Assisting people in this context means making the built environment accessible, wayfinding efficient, and safe for all – including people with temporary and permanent disabilities.

Throughout this book, we have made it clear that wayfinding design is not the antithesis of interesting design. Quite the reverse. It provides the designer and planner with excellent reasons to develop interesting spatial organizations, to articulate settings, and to communicate interest to the user.

Because wayfinding design comprises basic issues such as accessibility and safety, it covers large areas of concern, some of which pose difficult questions involving societal choices.

Wayfinding design is based on wayfinding behavior. This implies that designers need to know the basics about environmental perception and cognition; they need to know about decision making and spatial problem solving.

In addition, it is necessary to understand and to know about wayfinding behavior in specific situations such as emergencies, in specific settings such as underground facilities, and for particular groups such as the visually impaired.

Wayfinding design is also a skill – some might call it an art. It involves landscape design, urban design, architectural, interior, industrial, and graphic design.

Wayfinding design is now recognized as a major issue and one may well ponder the best policy for its practice. It is quite clear that architects, urban designers, landscape designers, and environmental graphic designers should know the rudiments of wayfinding design. This can only be assured if it is incorporated into educational curricula. Professional training, in the long term, is our best guarantee. This book has been partly conceived with this use in mind.

It must be remembered that architects have many issues to consider when planning a project. Although they ought to know about wayfinding design, they may not themselves be able to do it justice in the development of complex settings. They use structural and mechanical engineers. Why should they not use wayfinding specialists as well?

The time has come to start thinking along those lines.

ROMEDI PASSINI

Appendix 1

Glossary of wayfinding terms

Ambient light: spill from existing light sources

Anchor point: a reference point used to retain and mentally structure environmental information; landmarks can be anchor-points

Angular distortion: deleterious effect (on a letterform or image) caused by viewing obliquely or at a high angle of incidence

Arrow: concept-related symbol representing movement

Ascender: part of a letterform rising above the x-height or middle area, as in b, d, f, or h

Audible communication: information that is perceived through one's sense of hearing

Audible map: oral description of a building layout or complex space provided in the interests of orientation

Blade: modular component of a signface

Blind: descriptive of persons having no useful vision

Block letters: popular term for capital letters

Braille cells: the original (1829) definition was a "method of writing words . . . by means of dots, for use of the blind"; each cell is an arrangement of dots within a six-dot matrix and represents a word or a sound

Brightness differential: means whereby the suitability of the two colors comprising a sign (one for the back-ground, the other for the message) may be determined

Building directory: information, usually typographic in nature, that provides the names and locations of tenants in a building

Cap-height: vertical distance occupied by a capital or upper-case letter

Capital letters: upper-case letters (as distinct from lower-case)

Cartography: abstract representation of a physical space; mapmaking

Center: to position a word or image in the lateral middle of the viewing area, as distinct from either flush left or flush right

Character: a symbol or mark used in a writing system, such as a letter of the alphabet

Circulation system: the overall horizontal and vertical pedestrian paths of a setting; circulation systems can be organized on a linear, central, composite, or network basis

Cognition: understanding; a generic term that includes retaining, structuring and manipulating information

Cognitive map: an overall mental representation of a setting that cannot be grasped from a single viewpoint but that has to be integrated from different vistas

Cognitive mapping: the mental structuring process leading to a cognitive map

Color coding: the use of a limited number of nameable colors for the purposes of visual orientation or direction

Color deficiency: inability to distinguish between certain colors

Counter: the negative portion of a letter that is wholly enclosed by positive parts – as in O or B; counters constitute an essential aspect of the legibility of a typeface

Deaf: descriptive of persons with a profound hearing loss

Decision diagram: a diagram of a decision plan, used for design or research purposes

Decision execution: transforming a plan of action (or decision plan) into action and behavior

Decision making: developing a plan of action to go somewhere

Decision plan: a mental solution to a wayfinding problem as it is developed by the user

Descender: the part of a letterform below the x-line, as in g, j, or p

Destination zone: a group of destinations in an area to which people can be directed; the grouping can be on a functional basis (e.g., shopping) or on a spatial basis (e.g., a given part of a building such as the concourse)

Developmentally/situationally impaired: persons who are learning disabled, mentally retarded, or mentally disturbed; persons who are angry, apprehensive, confused, or distraught

Direction: one of the three basic information types in environmental communications

Disability: in the context of physical health, a disability is any restriction or lack (resulting from an impairment) of ability to perform an activity in the manner or within the range considered normal for a human being

Distinctiveness: that which gives an object or a place its unique identity

Dynamic signage system: interactive signage system, as distinct from a passive signage system

Environmental communication: a combination of three forms of information transfer: architectural, graphic, and audible

Equivalence: (see *identity*)

Flush (left or right): a typesetting term to indicate no indentation from the margin; when type is flush (left or right) it aligns at the margin

Functionally illiterate: descriptive of a person, sixteen years of age or older, who has received fewer than nine years of formal schooling and who is not attending school full time. (official UN definition); in the context of wayfinding, descriptive of a person who is incapable of reading the language in which a message contained in a sign is expressed

General information: one of the three basic information types in environmental communications; concerns, obligations and prohibitions, hours of service, and other things a visitor needs (or wishes) to know in a public building

Gestalt: organization of visual stimuli into figure and ground

Gestalt pattern: organization of space according to a simple geometric form such as an I, an L, or a T

Glancing: looking at an item for a very short duration

Glare: undesirable degree of sheen reflected off the surface (of a sign) causing deterioration of legibility

Glyph: symbol; pictograph; pictorial representation of an object or a concept; may also be an abstraction representing an instruction

Glyph Content Description (GCD): verbal description of the graphic elements constituting a glyph

Halation: irradiation; the visual effect resulting when a light image (or letter) is set in a darker field, causing an apparent increase in its size

Handicap: in the context of health experience, a handicap is a

disadvantage for a given individual, resulting from an impairment or a disability that limits or prevents the fulfilment of a role that is normal (depending on age, sex, and social and cultural factors) for that individual

Haptic: pertaining to the sense of touch

Hearing impaired: descriptive of persons who have a moderate to severe hearing loss

Helvetica light, Helvetica medium: popular typefaces with application to signage

HVAC: heating, ventilating, and air-conditioning equipment

Identification: one of the three main information types in environmental communications; concerns means whereby people know that they have arrived at their destination

Identity and equivalence: complementary rules by which all environmental information can be classified; identifying that which is distinct (identity) and that which is similar (equivalence)

Image: a physical or mental representation; as a mental representation it can refer to a particular view of an object or an overall view of a large setting (cognitive map)

Imageability: the ease with which the spatial layout of a setting can be understood and mapped

Impairment: in the context of health experience, an impairment is any *loss* or *abnormality* of psychological, physiological, or anatomical structure or function

Inductive loop: specialized sound system in which insulated wire placed in a room transmits an electrical current, which sets up a magnetic field, which is in turn reconverted into sound by a receiver; the receiver can consist of a hearing aid with a "T" switch

InfoBands: horizontal zones cut through a setting and reserved for the display of wayfinding information

Information types: all environmental communications consist of one of the three basic visual information types (orientation and general information, direction, and identification)

Information processing: generic term comprising environmental perception and cognition

Infrared system: specialized sound system that converts sound into infrared light; the light is reconverted into sound by a portable receiver

Interactive: capable of being interrogated

Interactive display: device used in environmental communication that can, on demand, produce information specific to a user's needs, generally through a presentation on a video screen and/ or through a telephone connection

Inter-letter spacing: correct lateral space between letters, determined optically

Inter-line spacing: correct vertical space between lines, determined mechanically

Inter-word spacing: correct lateral space

between words, equivalent to a lower-case "r"

Justify: adjust a graphic message with word spacing and letter spacing so that all of its lines are of equal length

Layout: result of the design process that determines the spatial relationships between the various elements in the viewing area of a sign

LED: acronym for light-emitting diodes, used in the smaller versions of electronic signs

Legend: verbal message on a signface; specifically relates also to cut-out vinyl letters or images

Legibility: the ease with which a displayed message can be seen or discerned; see also *readability*

Legibility distance : distance at which a given letterform in a given size can be discerned and understood

Letterform: form that a letter (or alphabet of letters) takes in a given design as identified by such names as Helvetica, Century; letterforms are also classified as serif or sans serif

Literacy impaired: descriptive of persons who are functionally illiterate in any given language, with respect to that language

Lower case: descriptive of letters that are not capitals; see *upper case*

Mobility: ability to move about or travel safely, comfortably, gracefully, and independently

Mobility impaired in wheelchairs: persons who are permanently or temporarily restricted to wheelchairs

Mobility impaired who can walk: persons who have impaired strength, endurance, dexterity, balance, or coordination; those using crutches or other walking aids; persons with strollers, carts, or other encumbrances

Mood: the form or shape a sign takes to communicate regulation, warning, or general information, e.g., circle, square, triangle

Nameable colors: colors to which commonly understood names (e.g., blue, red) can be given without fear of confusion

Network pattern: organization of space according to a repetitive geometric law such as the orthogonal grid or the hierarchical network

Non-verbal communication: those types of communication that rely upon symbols, glyphs, or pictures rather than words for their meanings

Oral: spoken

Organization pattern of the circulation: the underlying geometric form or law of a circulation system; distinction between four patterns: the shoe-string or random pattern, the Gestalt or form pattern, the systematized pattern, and the repetitive or network pattern

Orientation: one of the three basic information types in environmental communications; concerns a person's ability to perceive an overview of a given environment and recognize where he or she is at any given time within it

Overload: a state of general confusion resulting from excessive information

Perception: the obtaining of information through the senses

Pictograph: glyph or symbol incorporated into a sign

Plain language: language without jargon

Program: verbal and descriptive plan for a subsequent series of events and activities, with recommendations

Public address system: audible system consisting of microphone, amplifier, and loudspeaker

Ragged: see *justify*

Readability: the ease with which a message can be understood; see also *legibility*

Recall: to remember something in its absence

Recognize: to remember something in its presence

Redundancy: repetition, reiteration; ". . .introduce redundancy into messages, thereby making their correct reception more certain" (Colin Cherry); ". . .only by repetition can I get my message across" (Marshall McLuhan)

Resiliency: ability of material or object to return to its original form after being depressed; can be perceived aurally or tactually; see also *texture*

Sans serif: descriptive of letterforms without serifs

Scanning: visual sweeping intended to get an overall idea of a setting; see also *glancing*

Schemata: basic mental image or concept which allows features of the environment to be recognized

Serif: short cross-lines at terminals of letters classified in this way (as distinct from sans serif)

Shoestring pattern: random or quasi-random distribution

Shorelining: maintaining of meaningful contact, by a blind person using a cane, of a continuous and recognizable environmental component, such as a curb

Sight impaired: persons with poor eyesight, partial vision, or anomalies of vision such as color deficiency and reduced fields

Signface: reading area of a sign on which are displayed its legends

Spatial cognition: retaining, understanding, structuring, and manipulating information of a spatial nature

Spatial organization: the relationship among spaces of a setting; the typology of spatial organizations is equivalent to that of circulation systems, that is: linear, central, composite, and repetitive (networks)

Spatial orientation: having an adequate cognitive map of a setting and being able to situate oneself therein

Spatial planning: design phase to determine the layout of the setting at an urban, landscape, and architectural scale

Specular gloss: sheen reflected off a surface, measured from matte (lacking in gloss) to super-gloss

Speech impaired: persons who have articulation or voice disorders, or who have a developmental disorder that adversely affects their speech

Standard: measure(s) or rule(s) to which the performance, accuracy, and quality of a product, service, or fabrication method must conform; there are two main standards-writing organizations in Canada: the Canadian Standards Association (CSA), and the Canadian Government Standards Board (CGSB); in the US, the National Bureau of Standards (NBS) and the American National Standards Institute (ANSI) fulfil this function

Stem thickness: the width or thickness of vertical letter strokes; plays an important role in legibility and is more consistent (therefore more legible) in sans serif letters than in most serif letters

Stroke width: width of letter stroke; with respect to a cap-height ratio stroke width varies according to whether the letterform in question is *light, medium,* or *bold*

Symbol of access: symbol that represents *specifically* that the access (entrance) next to which it is displayed is accessible to persons in wheelchairs, and *generally,* that the facilities of buildings on which it is displayed are as a whole similarly accessible

Symbol: glyph or pictograph; pictorial representation; used in signs, symbols constitute a non-verbal means of conveying information; such signs are called symbol signs

Systematized pattern: organization of space according to a geometric law, such as axial symmetry or central symmetry

Tactile signs: signs having raised letters which are interpreted or read by tracing with fingers over the surfaces; letters are raised 1 mm

Tactual communication: information perceived through the sense of touch

Target value: the effectiveness with which the message displayed on a sign separates from or contrasts with its background – either by color or by tone – and hence its value to the viewer as a target to be perceived from a distance

Telecommunications Device for the Deaf (TDDs): device that enables visual typographic messages to be transmitted and received over telephone lines between one user and another

Texture: extent to which essential differences in the constituent parts of a material, or object can be discerned visually, audibly, or tactually; in cues for the sight impaired, texture and resiliency are both used

"T" switch: switch in a hearing aid which allows a deaf person to use a telephone

Typographic communication: written or verbal communication set in type

Unimpaired: adults without serious perceptual or physical disabilities; persons with normal perceptual and physical abilities

Upper case: descriptive of capital letters; a term derived from the days of hand composition of letters which were organized in a case or drawer, comprising majuscule (capital) and miniscule (cursive) letters

Verbal: concerned with words; distinct from non-verbal (concerned with pictures); not to be confused with oral

Vinyl: very thin plastic film, opaque or translucent, used for creating graphic messages or backgrounds in signs

Visual communication: information perceived through the sense of sight

Voice synthesizer: artificial larynx which from a basic phonic vocabulary can put together oral statements upon demand

Wayfinding: finding one's way to a destination; spatial problem solving comprising three interdependent processes: decision making, decision executing, and information processing

X-height: the middle zone of lower-case alphabets occupied by such letters as a, c, e, or x

X-line: a horizontal line running through the bottom extremity of the x-height

Anatomy of a public building complex

Just as wayfinding information can be broken down into its component parts (see Chapter 12), it is useful to think of building complexes as comprising a number of components as well. This makes everything more manageable.

We have found it useful to divide the average building complex into five zones (or component parts) and three circulation systems, as follows:

The five zones:
- parking lots or garages
- entrance(s) to the building
- main lobby
- communal facilities
- departments, offices, tenants

The three circulation systems:
- vertical circulation
- horizontal circulation
- egress throughout the building

The five zones

Building zones	Building component	Information needs
1 **Parking lot or garage**	**Approaches to the parking lot**	Clear and unencumbered view of the entrance; failing this, directions are necessary.
	Vehicular entrance to the parking lot or underground garage	Prominent identification of the entrance; information on buildings served, if applicable; cost for parking, if applicable; directions to reserved visitor parking spaces for the mobility impaired.
	General visitor parking spaces	Identification of these spaces; prohibition information to prevent parking by others.
	Reserve parking spaces	Identification of these spaces; prohibition information to prevent parking by others.
		This also includes identification of parking spaces for handicapped visitors.
	Pedestrian exit from the garage	Reminder information prominently identifying parking level.
	Pedestrian corridor to the building from the parking lot	Identification of walkway and delineation thereof; directions for the mobility impaired to nearest accessible entranceway.
	Pedestrian corridors to elevators in the garage	Identification of and/or directions to elevators.

Building zones	Building component	Information needs
2 **Entrance(s) to the building**	**Approaches to the building**	Clear and unencumbered view of the entranceway and of the sign(s) identifying it.
	Immediate environs to the main entrance	Identification of the building by name and of the federal preference therein; identification of major departments or tenants; identification of accessibility for the mobility impaired or directions to nearest accessible entranceway.
	Main entranceway (door to side lights)	Repeat of building name; hours-of-service information.
	Immediate environs of the secondary entrance (if used by the public)	Identification of the building by name and of the federal preference therein; identification of accessibility for the mobility impaired or directions to nearest accessible entranceway.
	Secondary entranceway (if used by the public)	Repeat of building name; hours-of-service information.
	Non-accessible entrance doors to mobility impaired	Directions to nearest accessible entranceway.
3 **Main lobby**	**Inside main entrance door**	Information, reliably located, for the blind and for low-vision visitors. Immediate apparent availability of reliable visual information.
	Manned reception or information desk	General information, orientation, and directions; directions to elevators, if they are not visible from the desk.
	Info center	General information, orientation, and directions; directions to elevators, if they are not visible from the info center.
4 **Communal facilities**	**Toilet doors or adjacent wall areas**	Identification of gender; identification of accessibility; directions thereto if doors to these facilities are not visible from the corridors.
	Cafeteria, entrance	Identification of facility; hours-of-service information; menus and prices information; identification of availability; special reserved seating areas, if any.
	Cafeteria, foodline	Menus and prices information.
	Cafeteria, cashier	Total-cost-of-meal information visible to customer on the cash register.
	Cafeteria, reserved seating areas	Identification of "No smoking" or other reserved seating areas, if applicable.
	Other communal facilities	Identification of entranceways; hours-of-service information.

Building zones	Building component	Information needs
5 **Departments,** **offices, tenants** **in the building**	**Entranceways,** **generally**	Identification of departmental/tenant name and suite number; hours-of-service information.
	Manned reception **areas or counters**	Identification of departmental/tenant name; identification of service(s) offered; general information, as necessary.
	Unmanned recep- **tion areas**	Identification of departmental/tenant name; telephone link with the reception; general information, directions, and orientation.
	Office doors or **adjacent wall areas**	Identification of office and/or function and/or occupant(s); identification of suite number.
	Individual work **stations within an** **open-plan area**	Directions thereto, as feasible; identification thereof; unobstructed views of identification of other work stations in the same area.
	Doors to restricted **areas or walls** **adjacent thereto**	If door is locked, no information is required other than the suite number; if door is unlocked, identification of the potential hazard involved is necessary; identification of suite number.

The three circulation systems

Building zone circulation system	Building component	Information needs
A **Vertical** **circulation** **system**	**Underground** **garage** **elevator lobbies**	Identification of the level as a reminder of where visitor has left vehicle; hours-of-service information about the garage.
	Main elevator lobby	Identification of levels of the building served by individual elevator banks; ability to summon elevator and to determine direction of travel by departing car; level identification on both door jambs of each elevator. *Level identification on door jambs is important because severely sight-impaired and blind users may not have any other way of knowing whether the elevator has stopped at the right floor, unless the elevators has a voice annunciator.*
	Elevator lobbies, **other floors**	Ability to summon elevator and to determine direction of travel of arriving car; level identification on both door jambs of each elevator; directional information to offices/tenants with identification of their suite number; emergency information with directions to nearest stairwell. *Level identification on door jambs is important because severely sight-impaired and blind users may not have any other way of knowing wether the elevator has stopped at the right floor, unless the elevator has a voice annunciator.*

Building zone circulation system	Building component	Information needs
	Elevator cars	Identification of car positions; identification of level reached as car slows to a stop; accessible car controls and other instructions clearly identified.
		Severely sight-impaired and blind users may have difficulty with standard elevator controls, such as heat-sensitive floor buttons which are triggered by the touch. Level identification is also particularly important to these users. Users who have restricted reach ability (such as those in wheelchairs or very short people) may not be able to reach standard elevator controls.
	Stairwell doors in corridors or walls adjacent thereto	Identification of level; emergency information about cross-over floors.
		Most users have difficulty with level identification, particularly in knowing which floor must be used for emergency egress. This is especially a problem for sight-impaired and blind users.
	Doors to adjacent walls on stairwell landings inside stairwells	Identification of stairs with assigned number, if any; emergency information about cross-over floors.
		Most users have difficulty with level identification, particularly in knowing which floor must be used for emergency egress. This is especially a problem for sight-impaired and blind users.
	Stairs, treads, and handrails	Identification of top and bottom treads; identification of handrail.
		The theory is that sight-impaired and blind users in particular need this, but the fact is that we all do.
	Ramps	Identification of accessibility for the mobility impaired.
B Horizontal circulation system	**Corridor intersections**	Directional information.
	Corridors	Reinforcement of the above in extra-long corridors.
	Entrances to restricted areas or the wall areas adjacent thereto	If door is locked, no information is required other than the suite number; if door is unlocked, identification of the potential hazard involved is necessary; identification of the suite number.
C Egress	**Throughout the building as necessary**	Emergency information; exit identification.
		Emergency alarms in particular must be understandable by virtually all users, including the deaf and hearing impaired. Exits must also be identified in such a way that during an emergency alarm blind users can find them quickly.

Notes

Introduction
Who will help me find my way?

1. Lynch 1960.

2. Kaplan 1976.

3. Downs and Stea 1973, 1977.

4. Passini 1984b.

Chapter 2
The impact of wayfinding difficulties

1. Carpman, Grant, and Simmons 1986.

Chapter 3
Standing in the way of wayfinding solutions

1. Dragun 1983.

2. Giovannini 1989.

Chapter 4
What are spatial orientation and wayfinding?

1. Carpenter 1989 summarizes succinctly the recent popularity of wayfinding in professional circles and suggests that the concept be taken seriously. He also warns of the inevitable fuzziness of meaning that comes with indiscriminate application of the term.

2. Early articles describing case studies of disorientation due to brain lesions are Förster 1890, Meyer 1900, and Holmes 1918.

3. For a description of spatial amnesia and spatial agnosia and the effect on spatial orientation, see De Renzi 1982 and Benton 1969. For a vulgarized literature review on the subject, see Passini 1987.

4. Fine et al.1980.

5. Lynch 1960.

6. For two excellent reviews of the contribution and the limits of cognitive mapping research, see Moore 1979 and Evans 1980.

7. Evans 1980, for example, notes that for many, the knowledge of even familiar settings is incomplete and uneven.

8. Proulx 1987, in a study of wayfinding behavior in a complex underground subway station in Montreal, found that a majority of people have difficulties in mapping the station, but at the same time, they do not have a sensation of being disoriented. One of the major problems for the subjects was to relate the underground space to the cityscape. The study explored the strategies that were used to solve the required wayfinding problems and followed the evolution of strategies after having provided the subjects with additional information about the spatial organization of the setting.

9. Gladwin 1970; Lewis 1975.

10. For descriptions and definitions of wayfinding, see Gärling, Böök, and Lindberg 1986; Passini 1977, 1984b; Downs and Stea 1977; and Kaplan 1976.

Chapter 5
How the wayfinding process works

1. The need to form subordinate plans is described in Gärling, Böök, and Lindberg 1986. The authors also propose a model of information-processing stages and the formulation of travel plans which are conceptualized in terms of decision plans.

2. Passini and Proulx 1988b.

3. In this context, it might be interesting to note the effect of superficial familiarity with a setting on wayfinding. Researchers have found that wayfinding tasks did not seem to be facilitated for subjects who had gained a superficial knowledge of a public building through a few previous visits (Beaumont et al. 1984).

4. Simon 1957, 1979; Downs and Stea 1973.

5. Svenson 1979; Adelbratt and Montgomery 1980.

6. Wright 1985; Driver 1974.

7. These results were reported in Passini 1977, 1984b.

8. For the structure of goal-directed behaviors, see Lichtenstein and Brewer 1980; Hayes-Roth and Hayes-Roth 1979; and Miller, Galanter, and Pribram 1960.

9. The conceptualization is based on Miller, Galanter, and Pribram's TOTE system, described in Miller, Galante,r and Pribram 1960.

10. Pallis 1955.

11. Gärling, Böök, and Lindberg 1984; Passini 1984a.

12. Ittelson 1973.

13. For a description of pre-attentive and attentive perception, see Neisser 1967. The author argues for similar processes in perception and the thinking process.

14. The fixation time can vary according to the situation and the context of viewing and also according to population characteristics. Japanese researchers found that the most frequent value of fixation time for simple compositions of points on a screen was around 0.2 seconds; small but systematic variations were observed for senile elderly and also for schizophrenic subjects. See Adachi and Araki 1989.

15. See Richesin et al. 1987; see also Transportation Research Board, National Research Council of Canada.

16. Andreason 1980.

17. Süskind 1986.

18. Duplessis 1984; Passini and Rainville 1990.

19. Appleyard 1979; Evans, Smith, and Pezdek 1982.

20. See Appleyard 1970a; Downs and Stea 1977; and Siegle and White 1975.

21. For references to the landmark theory, see Hart and Moore 1973; and Siegle and White 1975.

22. For references to the path theory, see Lynch 1960 and Appleyard 1970b.

23. For a review introducing the propositional and analogue representations, see Evans 1980; and Gärling and Golledge 1989.

24. Studies exploring the differences between the two representations include Gärling, Böök, and Lindberg 1984; and Thorndyke and Hayes-Roth 1982.

25. Passini, Proulx, and Rainville 1990. The study was actually done to measure the spatio-cognitive abilities of the visually impaired and the blind population. Some conclusions of the study are given in Chapter 6.

Chapter 6
What is wayfinding design:

1. Researchers have suggested that if a setting is too simple, or too easily understood, it might be boring. If it is too complex, it might be confusing (Evans 1980). Our position is that the critical issue in complex settings is the presence of a clear spatial organization principle and the communication of the essential wayfinding information.

Chapter 7
Who is involved in wayfinding design?

1. Carpenter 1989.

Chapter 8
For whom do we plan?

1. Passini, Dupré, and Langlois 1986.

2. Two excellent reviews that summarize the needs of people with visual impairment are Jansson 1988; and Templer and Zimring 1981.

3. Passini and Proulx 1988b. A group of fifteen congenitally totally blind subjects and a matched control group of fifteen sighted subjects were guided through a complex architectural setting. After two guided tours, all subjects had to make the journey on their own. All subjects were asked to 1) describe the journey in as much detail as possible before making it, which provided data about the planning of the trip; 2) verbalize all decisions, behaviors, and information used to make the trip; and 3) reproduce the configuration of the route with the help of a tactile model.

4. See Hollyfield and Foulke 1983; Dodds, Howarth, and Carter 1982; and Fletcher 1980.

5. Passini, Proulx, and Rainville 1990. The tests in this experiment consisted of eight basic wayfinding tasks, each representing a specific spatio-cognitive operation. The tasks were executed in a labyrinthine layout allowing for the control of the difficulty level of the tasks and limiting extraneous perceptual factors, which tend to interfere with the measure of spatio-cognitive abilities. The experimental groups were composed of congenitally totally blind, adventitiously totally blind, and subjects with a weak visual residue; the control was established with a sighted and a sighted blindfolded group. The sample's eighteen subjects per group were matched in terms of age, education, and sex.

6. Henri 1969. Pierre Henri has written a marvelous book about the world of the blind person in which he explores the nature of the senses. It is appreciated by the blind for touching on the essentials of their world.

7. De Forges de Parny 1981.

8. For a review of dementia and the design of supportive environments, see Rand et al. 1987 and Gilleard 1984.

9. Cohen and Weisman 1988.

10. Newton Frank Arthur Inc. 1984. The finding was further confirmed by wayfinding assessment studies done in hospitals, settings, one would think, that are barrier free in the full sense of having all routes accessible for all users, regardless of their temporary or permanent handicaps.

11. Goldsmith 1976.

Chapter 9
Planning for wayfinding conditions

1. Sime 1980, 1985; Bryan 1983; Abe 1976.

2. Tache and Selye 1978.

3. Some authors have suggested a circular effect whereby inefficiency in performance increases anxiety, and anxiety increases inefficiency in performance (Schönpflug 1983). It would seem to be important not to get people into that incapacitating circle.

4. For assisted escape guidelines addressed to designers and building managers, see Gartshore and Sime 1987.

Chapter 10
Spatial Planning

1. Two studies, Passini and Proulx 1988a, and Passini and Shiels 1986, are suggested to illustrate this point. The first was done for the Royal Victoria Hospital, Montreal, and the second for Complex Guy Favreau, Montreal.

2. In order to explore other typologies, the reader is referred to Ching 1979, Cousin 1980a, and von Meiss 1986.

3. In a mathematical sense, rotations, screws, and repetitions of identical figures are all forms of symmetry. For example, the reflection of a figure on a first axis, a, and then on a second axis, b, is equivalent to the rotation of the figure around the point where the two axes, a and b, intersect. In this book we shall use the popular meaning of symmetry, which limits itself to axial and central symmetry. For references, see Shubnikov and Koptsik 1974 and Weyl 1952.

4. Passini 1984a.

5. Narumi 1989. The spatial organization reflects social customs. Participation in the life of the neighborhood community is automatic. According to the author, it requires an act of will to avoid participation.

Chapter 11
Architectural wayfinding communication

1. Entrances to buildings have a great variety of forms and expressions. For references, see Ching 1979, Cousin 1980b, and von Meiss 1986.

2. Symmetries have been associated with order, formality, and rest, asymmetry with play, freedom, and life (Weyl 1952).

3. Passini, Rainville, and Paiement 1990.

4. Passini and Proulx 1988a.

Chapter 12
Classification of graphic information

1. There is no "scientific" basis for this statement apart from our own practical observations. When, in the mid-70s, however, the Canadian Standards Association was preparing CAN3-Z321-77, *Signs and Symbols for the Occupational Environment*, and AIGA was working on its transportation symbols, the assumption was in both cases that the glyphs needed no verbal amplification.

2. Carpman, Grant, and Simmons 1986.

Chapter 13
Forms of graphic information

1. The literature is full of references to stem thicknesses, for example, ANSI A117.1 1980, specifications for making buildings and facilities accessible to physically handicapped people. Building codes, national and local, make constant references to the importance of stem thicknesses.

2. This statement is based on tests done with the help of the Department of Optometry at Guelph University (Arthur 1970).

3. This statement is based on tests conducted by Paul Arthur at George Brown College, Toronto, over a period in the mid-80s.

4. The letterforms have been selected more to demonstrate diversity and characteristics of suitable signage faces than for any other reason.

5. Originally, all highway signs were exclusively in capital letters.

6. Tinker 1963.

7. Dolch 1986; Bellan 1948.

8. Herbert Bayer's "universal alphabet" was an attempt to do two things simultaneously. Bayer wanted to reduce letterforms to simple geometry as part of a broader vision. He also wanted to bring written (or typographic) and spoken (or audible) communication more in line with one another. See Lupton and Miller 1989.

9. Arthur 1970.

10. Normal, or 20/20, vision is defined as "describing a person who sees at 20 feet what other people with normal vision see at the same distance." By contrast, a person with 20/200 vision must stand only 20 feet away from an object (or message) that people with 20/20 vision can perceive 200 feet away. Source: *Columbia University College of Physicians and Surgeons Complete Home Medical Guide,* rev. ed., p. 698. New York: Crown Publishers, 1989.

11. Arthur and Passini 1990.

12. This statement, admittedly, applies more to the sign industry in Canada than that in the United States.

13. The system is based on one developed by Paul Arthur for the Steel Company of Canada in 1970.

14. McLuhan 1962.

15. Canadian Standards Association 1977.

16. We are indebted to conversations with the late Rudolph Modley (author of the *Handbook of Pictorial Symbols,* Dover Publications Inc., New York, 1976) and the late Henry Dreyfuss (compiler of *The Symbol Sourcebook,* McGraw Hill Book Company, New York, 1972) for the development of these concepts.

17. Dewar 1976.

18. Goldsmith 1976.

19. Quoted from *People Are Asking About . . . Displaying the Symbol of Access,* a joint publication of The President's Committee on Employment of the Handicapped, Washington, DC, and The National Easter Seal Society for Crippled Children and Adults, Chicago. [no date]

20. Arthur 1970; Newton Frank Arthur Inc. 1984.

21. Goldsmith 1976.

22. Arthur 1970.

Chapter 15
Graphic information for decision executing

1. Carpman, Grant, and Simmons 1986.

2. Siteguide™ by Edwin Schlossberg Incorporated, New York, is an interactive directory system which serves the World Financial Center, New York.

Chapter 17
Tactile information for decision making and executing

1. Schiff 1967 suggested using the following elevations: 0.02 inches for braille, 0.04 inches for line and areal symbols, and 0.06 inches for point symbols.

2. Karentz (Andrews) 1988; Armstrong 1978; Grahame 1982.

3. Karentz (Andrews) 1985.

Bibliography

Abe, K.

1976 "The behavior of survivors and victims in a Japanese nightclub fire: A descriptive research note." *Mass Emergencies* 1:119–124.

Adachi, K.; and Araki, H.

1989 "Eye fixation behavior in senile elderly." Paper presented at The World Congress of Gerontology. Osaka, Kansai University. 13 pp.

Adelbratt, T.; and Montgomery, H.

1980 "Attractiveness of decision rules." *Acta Psychologica* 45(3):177–185.

Andreason, M. E. K.

1980 "Colour vision defects in elderly." *Journal of Gerontological Nursing* 6(7):382–384.

Appleyard, D.

1970a "Why buildings are known." *Environment and Behavior* 1:131–156.

1970b "Styles and methods of structuring a city." *Environment and Behavior* 2:100–116.

1979 *Planning a Pluralistic City*. Cambridge, Mass.: Massachusetts Institute of Technology Press.

Armstrong, J. D.

1978 "The development of tactual maps for the visually handicapped." In *Acute Touch*, edited by G. Gordon, pp. 249–261. London: Pergamon Press.

Arthur, Paul

1970 *Campus Signage, Criteria/State of the Art*. Albany, N.Y.: State University Construction Fund.

Arthur, Paul; and Passini, Romedi

1990 *The 1, 2, 3 Design Guide*. Ottawa: Public Works Canada.

Beaumont, P. B.; Gray, J.; Moore, G. T.; and Robinson, B.

1984 "Orientation and wayfinding in the Taurang department building: A focused pos-occupancy evaluation." In *The Challenge of Diversity*, edited by D. Duerk and D. Campbell, pp. 77–90. Washington, DC: Environmental Design and Research Association.

Bellan, Ruth

1948 "The integrated method of reading therapy." *Journal of Learning Disabilities*.

Benton, A. L.

1969 "Disorders of spatial orientation." In *Disorders of Higher Nervous Activities: Handbook of Clinical Neurology*, edited by P. J. Winkel and G. W. Bruyn, pp. 212–228. Amsterdam: North-Holland.

Bryan, L. J.

1983 "An examination and analysis of the dynamics of the human behavior in the Westchase Hilton fire, Houston, Texas." National Fire Protection Association, USA.

Canadian Standards Association

1977 *Signs and Symbols for the Occupational Environment*. Publication no. CAN 3–Z321–77. Toronto: Canadian Standards Association.

Carpenter, Edward

1989 "Wayfinding: Design breakthrough or trendy buzzword?" *Print* 43(1):92–163.

Carpman, Janet Reizenstein; Grant, Myron A.; and Simmons, Deborah A.

1986 *Design that Cares*. Chicago: American Hospital Publishing.

Ching, F.

1979 *Architecture, Form, Space and Order*. New York: Van Nostrand Reinhold.

Cohen, U.; and Weisman, G. D.

1988 *Environments for People with Dementia: Design Guide*. Milwaukee: University of Wisconsin, The School of Architecture and Urban Planning.

Cousin, J.

1980a *L' espace vivant*. Montreal: Les Presses de l'Université de Montréal.

1980b *Topological Organization of Architectural Spaces*. Montreal: Les Presses du l'Université de Montréal.

De Forges de Parny, I.

1981 "La perception de l'espace urbain par les déficients auditifs." M.A. thesis. Université de Paris.

De Renzi, E.

1982 *Disorders of Space Exploration and Cognition*. New York: Wiley.

Dewar, Robert E.

1976   "The slash obscures the symbol on prohibitive traffic signs." *Human Factors* 18(3):253–258.

Dodds, A. G.; Howarth, C. I.; and Carter, D. C.

1982   "The mental maps of the blind: The role of previous visual experience." *Journal of Visual Impairment and Blindness* 76(1):5–12.

Dolch, E. W.

1986   *Problems in Reading.* Champaign, Illinois: Garrard Press.

Downs, Roger; and Stea, David, eds

1973   *Image and the Environment: Cognitive Mapping and Spatial Behavior.* Chicago: Aldine.

1977   *Maps in Minds.* New York: Harper and Row.

Dragun, Richard

1983   "Where you are, where you've been and where you're going." *Journal of the Society of Typographic Designers*, December, pp. 4–9.

Dreyfuss, Henry

1972   *The Symbol Sourcebook.* New York: McGraw Hill Book Company.

Driver, M. J.

1974   *Decision Style and Its Measurement.* Los Angeles: Graduate School of Business Administration, University of Southern California.

Duplessis, Y.

1984   *Les couleurs visibles et non visibles.* Monaco: Editions du Rocher.

Evans, G. W.

1980   "Environmental cognition." *Psychological Bulletin* 88:259–287.

Evans, G. W.; Smith, C.; and Pezdek, K.

1982   "Cognitive maps and urban form." *Journal of the American Planning Association* 48:232–244.

Fine, E. J.; Mellstrom, M.; and Timmins, M.; and Timmins, J.

1980   "Spatial disorientation and the Dyke-Daidoff-Masson syndrome." *Cortex* 16:493–499.

Fletcher, J. F.

1980   "Spatial representations in blind children I: Development compared to sighted children." *Journal of Visual Impairment and Blindness* 74(12):381–385.

Förster, R.

1890   "Über Rindenblindheit." Albrecht von *Gräfes Archiv für Ophthalmologie* 36:94–108.

Gärling, T.; Böök, A.; and Lindberg, E.

1984   "Cognitive mapping of a large-scale environments: The interrelationships of action plans, acquisition, and orientation." *Environment and Behavior* 16:3–34.

1986   "Spatial orientation and wayfinding in the designed environment: A conceptual analysis and some suggestions for postoccupancy evaluation." *Journal of Architectural and Planning Research* 3:55–64.

Gärling, T.; and Golledge, R.

1989   "Environmental perception and cognition." In *Advances in Environment, Behavior, and Design*, vol. 2. edited by E. H. Zube and G. T. Moore. New York: Plenum Press.

Gartshore, P. J.; and Sime, J.

1987   "Assisted escape: Some guidelines for designers, building managers, and the mobility impaired." *Design for Special Needs* 42:6–9.

Gilleard, C. J.

1984   *Living with Dementia: Community Care of the Elderly Mentally Infirm.* Philadelphia: The Charles Press.

Giovannini, Joseph

1989   "A zero degree of graphics." In *Graphic Design in America: A Visual Language History,* pp. 201–213. New York: Walker Art Center and Harry N. Abrams.

Gladwin, T.

1970   *East is a Big Bird: Navigation and Logic on Puluwat Atoll.* Cambridge, Mass.: Harvard University Press.

Goldsmith, Selwyn

1976   *Designing for the Disabled.* 3rd. ed. London: RIBA Publications Limited.

Grahame, A. J.

1982   "Mobility Maps." In *Tactual Perception: A Source Book*, edited by W. Schiff and E. Foulke, pp. 334–363. Cambridge, Mass.: Cambridge University Press.

Hart, R.; and Moore, G.

1973   "The development of spatial cognition: A review." In *Image and Environment: Cognitive Mapping and Spatial Behavior*, edited by R. Downs and D. Stea, pp. 246–288. Chicago: Aldine.

Hayes-Roth, B.; and Hayes-Roth, F.

1979   "A cognitive model of planning." *Cognitive Science* 3:275–310.

Henri, Pierre

1969   *La vie des aveugles.* Paris: Presses Universitaires de France.

Hollyfield, R. L.: and Foulke, E.

1983 "The spatial cognition of blind pedestrians." *Journal of Visual Impairment and Blindness* 77(5):204–209.

Holmes, G.

1918 "Disturbances of visual orientation." *British Journal of Ophthalmology* 2:449–516.

Ittelson, W. H.

1973 "Environmental perception and contemporary perceptual theory." In *Environmental Cognition*, edited by W. H. Ittelson, pp. 1–19. New York: Seminar Press.

Jansson, G.

1988 "Non-visual guidance of walking." In *Perception and Control of Self-Motion*, edited by R. Warren and A. Wertheim, pp. 507–522. Hillsdale, N. J.: Erlbaum.

Kaplan, Steven

1976 "Adaptation, structure and knowledge." In *Environmental Knowing*, edited by G. Moore and R. Golledge, pp. 32–46. Stroudsburg, Penn.: Dowden, Hutchinson and Ross.

Karentz (Andrews), S.

1985 "The use of capsule paper in producing tactile maps." *Journal of Visual Impairment and Blindness* 79:396–399.

1988 "Applications of a cartographic communication model to tactual map design." *The American Geographer* 15(2): 183–195.

Lewis, D.

1975 *We, the Navigators: The Ancient Art of Landfinding in the Pacific.* Honolulu: The University Press of Hawaii.

Lichtenstein, E. H.; and Brewer, W. F.

1980 "Memory for goal directed events." *Cognitive Psychology* 12(3):412–445.

Lupton, Ellen; and Miller, J. Abbott

1989 "A timeline of American graphic design, 1929–1999." In *Graphic Design in America: A Visual Language History.* New York: Walker Art Center and Harry N. Abrams.

Lynch, Kevin

1960 *The Image of the City.* Cambridge, Mass.: Massachusetts Institute of Technology Press.

McLuhan, Marshall

1962 *The Gutenberg Galaxy: The Making of Typographic Man.* Toronto: University of Toronto Press.

Meyer, O.

1900 "Ein- und doppelseitige homonyme Hemianopsie mit Orienterungsstörungen." *Monatsschrift der Psychiatrischen Neurologie* 8:440–456.

Miller, G. A.; Galanter, E.; and Pribram, K.

1960 *Plans and the Structure of Behavior.* New York: Holt, Rinehart and Winston.

Modley, Rudolph

1976 *Handbook of Pictorial Symbols.* New York: Dover Publications.

Moore, G. T.

1979 "Knowing about environmental knowing: The current state of theory and research on environmental cognition." *Environment and Behavior* 11:33–70.

Narumi, K.

1989 Space and Community. Comparative Studies Series. Osaka: University of Osaka.

National Research Council, Transportation Research Board

1988 *Transportation in an Aging Society: Improving Mobility and Safety for Older Persons,* vol. 1. National Research Council, Transportation Research Board, Washington, DC. *Special Report* 218, 1988 Washington, DC : The Board

Neisser, U.

1967 *Cognitive Psychology.* Englewood Cliffs, N.J.: Prentice Hall.

Newton Frank Arthur Inc.

1984 *Orientation and Wayfinding in Public Buildings.* Ottawa: Public Works Canada, National Research Council of Canada.

Pallis, D. A.

1955 "Impaired identification of faces and places with agnosia for colours." *Journal of Neurology, Neurosurgery and Psychiatry* 18:218–224.

Passini, Romedi

1977 "Wayfinding: A Study of Spatial Problem Solving." Ph. D. dissertation. Pennsylvania State University.

1984a "Spatial representation: A wayfinding perspective." *Journal of Environmental Psychology* 4:153–164.

1984b *Wayfinding in Architecture.* New York: Van Nostrand Reinhold.

1987 "Brain lesions and their effects on wayfinding: A review." *Proceedings of the Environmental Design Research Association. EDRA* 18: 61–67.

Passini, Romedi; Dupré, A.; and Langlois, C.

1986 "Spatial mobility of the visually handicapped active person: A descriptive study." *Journal of Visual Impairment and Blindness* 80 (8):904–909.

Passini, Romedi; and Proulx, G.

1988a "Étude pour l'élaboration d'un système de communication environnementale." Research Report. Montreal: Royal Victoria Hospital, University of Montreal.

235

1988b "Wayfinding without vision: An experiment with congenitally totally blind people." *Environment and Behavior* 20(2):227–252.

Passini, Romedi; Proulx, G.; and Rainville, C.

1990 "The spatio-cognitive abilities of the visually impaired polulation." *Environment and Behavior* 22(1):91–118.

Passini, Romedi; and Rainville, C.

1990 "La perception dermo-optique dans l'orientation spatiale chez les handicapés visuels." Research Report. Ottawa: National Research Council of Canada.

Passini, Romedi; Rainville, C.; and Paiement, L.

1990 "Orientation spatiale des handicapés visuels et l'information environnementale." Research Report. Quebec: Conseil Québécois de la Recherche Sociale.

Passini, Romedi; and Shiels, G.

1986 "Wayfinding Performance Evaluation of Four Public Buildings." Internal Report. Ottawa: Public Works Canada, Architectural and Engineering Services.

Proulx, G.

1987 "Orientation spatiale dans un espace souterrain." *Proceedings of the Environmental Design Research Association, EDRA* 18:68–73.

Rand, J.; Steiner, V. L.; Toyne, R.; Cohen, U.; and Weisman, G. D.

1987 *Environments for People with Dementia: Annotated Bibliography.* Washington, DC: Health Facility Research Program.

Richesin, Ch.; Grace, G.; Lautkow, M.; and Gillies, K.

1987 "Access needs of blind and visually impaired travellers in transportation terminals." Report. Toronto: Canadian National Institute for the Blind.

Schiff, W.

1967 *Using Raised Line Drawings as Tactual Supplements to Recorded Books for the Blind.* Recordings for the Blind, final Report, Project No. RD 1571-S. Washington, DC: Vocational Rehabilitation Administration.

Schönpflug, W.

1983 "Coping efficiency and situational demands." In *Stress and Fatigue in Human Performance*, edited by G. R. J. Hockey, pp. 299–330. Chichester: Wiley.

Shubnikov, A. V.; and Koptsik, V. A.

1974 *Symmetry in Science and Art.* New York: Plenum Press.

Siegle, A. W.; and White, S. H.

1975 "The development of spatial representations of large scale environments." In *Advances in Child Development and Behavior*, vol. 10, edited by H. W. Reese, pp. 9–55. New York: Academic Press.

Sime, Jonathan

1980 "The concept of panic." In *Fires and Human Behavior*, edited by D. Canter, pp. 63–81. Chichester: John Wiley.

1985 "Movement towards the familiar: Person and place affiliation in a fire entrapment setting." *Environment and Behavior* 17(6):697–724.

Simon, H. A.

1957 *Model of Man.* New York: Wiley and Sons.

1979 *Models of Thought.* New Haven: Yale University Press.

Süskind, Patrick

1986 *Perfume: The Story of a Murderer.* New York: Alfred A. Knopf.

Svenson, O.

1979 "Process description of decision making." *Organizational Behavior and Human Performance* 23:86–112.

Tache, J; and Selye, H.

1978 "On stress and coping mechanisms." In *Stress and Anxiety*, vol. 5, edited by C. D. Speilberger and I. G. Sarason, pp. 3–24. New York: John Wiley.

Templer, J.; and Zimring, C.

1981 "Accessibility for persons with visual impairments." *Access Information Bulletin*, pp. 1–8

Thorndyke, P. W.; and Hayes-Roth, B.

1982 "Differences in spatial knowledge acquired from maps and navigation." *Cognitive Psychology* 14:560–589.

Tinker, Miles

1963 *Legibility in Print.* Ames, Iowa: Iowa State University Press.

Von Meiss, P.

1986 *De la forme au lieu.* Lausanne: Presses Polytechniques Romandes.

Weyl, H.

1952 *Symmetry.* Princeton, N.J.: Princeton University Press.

Wright, P.

1985 "Decision variance." *In Behavioral Decision Making*, edited by G. Wright, New York: Plenum Press

Index